Old and New Horizons of Sandplay Therapy

This thoughtful and comprehensive book sheds new light on Sandplay Therapy, a method founded in the 1960s by Dora Kalff. It is based on the psychology of C. G. Jung and Margaret Lowenfeld, with inspiration from eastern contemplative traditions. This method is effectively used for psychotherapy, psychological counselling and development of the personality with children and adults.

This book grew out of the collaboration of a supervision and research group with Italian therapists which regularly met for a period of over 10 years under the guidance of Martin Kalff. It focuses on how to understand in more depth the processes clients experience in Sandplay Therapy. An important feature of Sandplay is the possibility to create scenes in a box with sand. Worlds arise through the shaping of the sand and the use of miniatures, humans, animals, trees, etc. These creations manifest inner conflicts as well as untouched healing potential.

This book discusses a number of techniques based on mindfulness such as 'spontaneous embodiment', the use of colours, spontaneous poetry, 'entering into the dream', to understand the work done in a Sandplay process and dreams and presents examples of clinical cases. These techniques are not only valuable for supervision but can also be used in therapy to help clients reconnect with body and feelings.

Martin Kalff is a Sandplay Therapist and teacher of meditation. He is a teaching and founding member of the International and Swiss National Society of Sandplay Therapy (ISST/SGSST). He teaches Sandplay in Switzerland and different countries worldwide, with an emphasis on ERCS, the Experience Related Case Study and Supervision, which he developed.

Paolo Ferliga is a Jungian Psychotherapist, former Teacher of Philosophy and History at the High School Arnaldo in Brescia, as well as Educational Psychology at the University Bicocca in Milan. He has published several books in the field of analytical psychology. He founded Campo Maschile, a research-action group exploring male identity, and chairs dream-related and active imagination workshops in Italy.

"Old and New Horizons is a beautiful depiction of using mindfulness in Sandplay. The depth and intimacy of these cases is enriched by the mindful attention of both clients and therapists. There is much to benefit from and much to learn from this integrated approach."

Jack Kornfield, PhD, Teacher of Vipassana Meditation, writer, co-founder of Insight Meditation Society in Barre (Massachussets) and of Spirit Rock Meditation Center in Woodacre (California)

"Martin Kalff introduces a profound, fresh approach to case study deeply rooted in the wisdom of the body and a lifetime of meditation practice and international teaching. Readers will take an enchanting journey into Kalff's consultation room with his Italian colleagues that stimulates the brain, opens the heart, and wraps a warm blanket around the soul. His masterful weaving of depth psychology, neuroscience, and mindfulness techniques make this seminal work for sandplay therapists a useful resource for psychotherapists and supervisors across disciplines."

Lorraine Razzi Freedle, PhD, American Board of Pediatric Neuropsychology (ABPdN), President of Sandplay Therapists of America

"With thoroughness and sensitivity, Martin Kalff introduces new theories and perspectives impacting knowledge of Sandplay Therapy. His many years of experience as a therapist, meditation teacher, and consultant bring fresh viewpoints into focus. Examples from clinical sandplay sessions, as well as the work of his colleagues illustrate a deep convergence of Jungian depth psychology, meditation practices, mindfulness, and neural integration. Careful analysis of the somatic experiences of client and therapist, as a clinical dyad, invite a new lens in which to observe and appreciate emerging ideas in this unique therapy."

Judy D. Zappacosta, Marriage, Family, Child Therapist, Certified Teaching Member of International Society for Sandplay Therapy (ISST) and of Sandplay Therapists of America (STA)

Old and New Horizons of Sandplay Therapy

Mindfulness and Neural Integration

Martin Kalff Author
Paolo Ferliga Editor

Routledge
Taylor & Francis Group

LONDON AND NEW YORK

First published 2022
by Routledge
2 Park Square, Milton Park, Abingdon, Oxon OX14 4RN

and by Routledge
605 Third Avenue, New York, NY 10158

Routledge is an imprint of the Taylor & Francis Group, an informa business

British Library Cataloguing-in-Publication Data
A catalogue record for this book is available from the British Library

Library of Congress Cataloging-in-Publication Data
Names: Kalff, Martin, author. | Ferliga, Paolo, editor.
Title: Old and new horizons of sandplay therapy : mindfulness and neural integration / Martin Kalff ; edited by Paolo Ferliga ; contributions from L. Battini [and 10 others].
Description: Milton Park, Abingdon, Oxon ; New York, NY : Routledge, 2022. | Includes bibliographical references and index.
Identifiers: LCCN 2021016223 (print) | LCCN 2021016224 (ebook) |
Subjects: LCSH: Sandplay--Therapeutic use.
Classification: LCC RC489.S25 K35 2022 (print) | LCC RC489.S25 (ebook) | DDC 616.89/1653--dc23
LC record available at https://lccn.loc.gov/2021016223
LC ebook record available at https://lccn.loc.gov/2021016224

ISBN: 978-0-367-75673-4 (hbk)
ISBN: 978-0-367-75539-3 (pbk)
ISBN: 978-1-003-16350-3 (ebk)

DOI: 10.4324/9781003163503

Typeset in Times New Roman
by Taylor & Francis Books

Cover image: Mary Cassatt, 'Children Playing on the Beach', 1884, oil on canvas, Ailsa Mellon Bruce Collection, National Gallery of Art, Washington DC

To Dora Kalff
and to all of those who maintain and develop
the spirit of the Sandplay
in a changing world

Contents

Figures

Epigraph

To see a World in a Grain of Sand
And a Heaven in a Wild Flower
Hold Infinity in the palm of your hand.

William Blake

Acknowledgements

Figure 1.1 appears here courtesy of Oliver Wright and the Dr Margaret Lowenfeld Trust.

Figure 1.2 and Figure 2.1 are taken from *The Red Book* by C.G. Jung, edited by Sonu Shamdasani, translated by Mark Kyburz, John Peck, and Sonu Shamdasani. Copyright © 2009 by the Foundation of the Works of C. G. Jung Translation copyright (c) 2009 by Mark Kyburz, John Peck, and Sonu Shamdasani. Used by permission of W. W. Norton & Company, Inc.

Figure 2.9, the Zhi khro mandala, appears here courtesy of the Ethnographic Museum of the University of Zurich, IN21131, Martin Brauen, Berne, Switzerland.

Chapter 3 is an adapted excerpt from 'Experience Related Case Study: Like a Masked Ball' by Martin Kalff, in the *Journal of Sandplay Therapy*, 22(2) Walnut Creek, CA, 2013. It is included here with the permission of the *Journal*.

Introduction

Paolo Ferliga

This book was written to present the work of research and experimentation on Sandplay Therapy conducted by Dr. Martin Kalff and a group of Italian therapists[1] who have been collaborating with him over the last ten years meeting regularly in his home in Zollikon, by Lake Zurich.

In the 1970s Dora Kalff's inspired intuitions gave birth to Sandplay Therapy, which, in her son Martin's design, would develop in time into a fresh approach calling attention to the resonance that the scenes traced in the sand trigger in both the client's and the therapist's body. This design, put forth in November 2007 to the Zollikon Group by Martin Kalff, was met with interest and enthusiasm. In the following discussion, everyone contributed their own ideas as well as personal experience, thus supporting Kalff's design and providing encouragement to plan further research which is presented in full for the first time in this collection of essays.

Playing with sand is a primary experience for children – feeling the sand and kneading it with water is fun and, at the same time, fosters the development of the child's imagination and creativity. Dora Kalff built on this experience and turned it into a diagnostic and healing tool for children suffering from psychological disorders. Two bright blue sandboxes are set up in the therapist's practice, filled with, respectively, dry and moist sand as well as a whole miniature world, made of various items on display on shelves. While playing, the child can enact unconscious conflicts and come into contact with the profound energy of the psyche. The process of transformation thus brought about within the child can be observed by the therapist through the figures and symbols arranged in the sandbox. Soon this type of therapy was extended to adolescents and adults. Sandplay enables them to come in contact with the Self – the hub of psychic life – by regression to the preverbal stage of their psychic life, and to develop those creative and transformative capabilities that ease healing.

During her supervision meetings on clinical cases which entailed the use of Sandplay, Dora Kalff would recommend psychotherapists to always adopt a non-judgmental attitude and to try and develop their own ability to love. A curious and open approach, able to embrace images and symbols emerging from the sandbox without lapsing into judgment or one-sided interpretation. Such an attitude enables the therapist to experience a sense of freedom which is non-verbally communicated to clients, thus helping clients tap into its transformative power also within themselves. The ability to love – defined as the heartfelt wish that the client may finally be free from suffering – enables the therapist to see the patient as a person who can learn to acknowledge and come to terms with some negative and previously unacceptable traits of the Self.

Starting from these premises, Martin Kalff devised a new process which he tested with his clients and the supervision group in Zollikon. The novelty of his approach lies in shifting the attention from observing the scenes in the sandbox to the observation and recording of the bodily perceptions elicited by those sand images, both in their maker and in the observer. The act of listening to the bodily experience serves as the starting point from which to begin the quest for a deeper understanding of the images inhabiting the client's sand creations and dreams.

By laying the stress on bodily experiences, Kalff follows, from a theoretical point of view, the phenomenological research conducted by Edmund Husserl and Merleau-Ponty on the 'lived body' (*Leib*) as linked to the psyche, in contrast to the 'thing-body' (*Körper*) in its mere physicality. From a purely psychological perspective, his approach follows in the wake of Carl Gustav Jung's analytical psychology, which envisages an internal relationship in the subconscious between body and psyche, between instinct and archetypal images. Alongside 'active imagination', which for Jung is a means for transforming overwhelming emotions into images, Kalff proposes the practice of meditation as useful to call attention to bodily experiences. Accordingly, Jung's idea – expounded notably in his seminars on Nietzsche's *Zarathustra* – that the body should be given as much attention and respect as the mind, is therefore fittingly complemented by Kalff's proposal.

Kalff's approach radically differs from those that view the body and its instincts as the locus of ambivalence and lack of meaning, with meaning falling solely within the scope of consciousness. This approach has stemmed not only from a one-sided and simplistic interpretation of Plato's[2] thought, but it also represents the tendency of a part of contemporary psychology to focus solely on the mind while consigning the body to the realm of the non-psychic and of the mere tangible, excluding psychic states. This approach, though, perniciously severs the psyche from the body and reduces the body to a mere thing.

Yet, according to Kalff, it is precisely in the body's symbolic ambivalence and in its ability to respond un-univocally to the images arising from the unconscious that lies a privileged access route to the comprehension of psychic experience. Under his guidance, in the Zollikon Group we have found out that the different bodily responses the very same Sandplay scenes would elicit from each of us, provided us with new insights breaking unexplored paths and prompting unthought-of before solutions. Not only this. We have also become aware that the therapists's meditation practice and attention to their own body may contribute an impact on the psychological condition of the patient, as shown in some case studies presented in this collection. In Sandplay Therapy, in effect, by starting from the movement of the hands, client and therapist establish a dialogue primarily through body language rather than through verbal language. Thus, body language becomes the shared language of the analytical pair, and listening to it contributes to laying solid foundations for the transferential[3] relationship.

For the sake of its potential contributions to theoretical research, it is worth emphasising the key role Kalff assigns to the relationship between the process of individuation and neural integration, both equally fostered through Sandplay Therapy. Kalff shows how the use of sand may help establish connections with (often forgotten) early experiences, activate the right hemisphere of the brain, where creativity is located, and enhance vertical integration connecting body, limbic system (primarily involved in the regulation of emotions) and cerebral cortex (presiding over rational consciousness). It is the work on the body and with the body that simplifies the process of neural and psychic integration, indispensable to achieve a full personality development and, sometimes, interrupted or frozen by traumatic experiences or other forms of psychic distress.

While reviewing the levels of neural integration identified by neuropsychiatrist Dan Siegel, Kalff lingers over 'transpirational integration', meaning the experience of feeling part of a larger whole, of transcending one's physical identity. At this level, a new perceptual mode is activated and, in Dan Siegel's words, *the sacred* penetrates our every breath and our innermost essence[4]. This aspect of neural integration and the emphasis on the sacred is recalls Carl Gustav Jung's idea that the experience of Self, which is the hub of the individuation process, in consciousness acquires a 'numinous' character, almost divine. In a very personal take on Jung's *The Red Book*, Kalff expands on the parallels between the individuation process and recent theories on brain structure in neuroscience: the *individuation process*, the existential process of becoming oneself, is found to progress alongside the *process of neural integration* – two sides of the same coin.

Kalff's research also resonates with the Embodied Simulation Theory propounded notably by Vittorio Gallese subsequent to the team led by Giacomo Rizzolatti's discovery of the mirror neuron system.[5] The theory argues that the observation of actions or behaviours in others activates in the observer the same neural circuits that control the actions carried out by the performing subject, and may offer important clues for the understanding of the dynamics underlying both Sandplay Therapy and the relation between therapist and patient.

From a strictly methodological standpoint, Kalff reintroduces the practice of Mindfulness (awareness meditation) in the therapy for psychic and psychosomatic disorders, a practice developed in Western culture by Jon Kabat-Zinn, founder of the Mindfulness-Based Stress Reduction Center at Massachusetts University. This type of mindfulness practice teaches how to concentrate non-judgementally on the present moment and to find the inner space where awareness of one's own physical sensations and emotions arise. Kalff is a qualified meditation teacher, he has met with the Dalai Lama several times and worked alongside many Tibetan Lamas. He incorporates Buddhist teachings into his practice to spawn full awareness of one's mental states as well as empathy and compassion.

In keeping with the Buddhist respect for every living creature, compassion is not exclusive to humans, but is extended to animals, too. This is perhaps one of the most original aspects of Kalff's theoretical and therapeutical approach. Building on Jung's remarks about the inner animal – which often shows up in our dreams – and the key role it plays in our psychic life, Kalff connects it to the value we should attach to the life of the outer animal; that is, the animal actually living around us. Special attention should be paid to the animals showing up in the sandbox during Sandplay Therapy, to the relationship the patients have with them and, more generally, with nature. In this collection we offer a sample of one of Kalff's numerous public contributions on the issue of animal treatment and suffering, issued from his lifelong fondness for animals and from his belief that their wellbeing contributes to the psychological welfare of the individual as well as of the community.

Martin Kalff's essay ends on a case study showing the fruitful relationship connecting Sandplay work, dream analysis and bodily experience within therapy.

As mentioned at the beginning of the present introduction, Kalff's contribution is the first and most substantial part of this book, followed by contributions by a handful of the Italian therapists who have worked with him. In the second part of this volume, the reader will find some remarks, but also emotions and feelings, on the part of supervision group participants who have been trained as Sandplay therapists. The writing style of the volume therefore reflects the unique affective voice of each author, in the attempt to remain true to the body language that has inspired the entire research. The new method is analysed and presented focusing on the repercussions it has had on the participants of the group, thus contributing to their training as Sandplay therapists. The group's work is described as a ritual going through different phases and whose strength lies precisely in the recurrence of gestures and visits paid to the Zollikon house. Meditation sessions, movements, silences and words alternate with shared meals, enabling the reader to vicariously partake of the experiences behind our work.

In the third and last part of the book, some successful therapeutic experiences in which Kalff's method has been utilised are illustrated: a child suffering from elective mutism, a young woman with a troubled childhood, a girl with an experience of abuse, another girl displaying autistic traits, a woman trapped in her inner images, a deeply wounded man. Their stories are told alongside the pictures of some sandbox scenes and with the accounts of the resonances within the group and the subsequent impact on the therapeutic setting.

This volume is due for publication in the fourteenth anniversary of Dora Kalff's *Sandspiel Seine therapeutische Wirkung auf die Psyche* [6] and our hope is that it will contribute to draw attention to her teachings and to break fresh ground for theoretical research and clinical practice.

Notes

1 Zollikon Experience-Related Sandplay Study Group also referred to as Zollikon Group.
2 This interpretation is based on Socrates's words as reported by Plato in one of the *Dialogues*, 'Phaedro', aimed to prove the soul's immortality, where it is claimed that, in order to fully grasp the truth, we need to transcend our body. This interpretation is questionable, though, insofar as Plato's view of the psyche is more complex than this and as, in other dialogues, he complements instinctive aspects of the psyche with rational ones.
3 In psychoanalysis, 'transferential relationship', or simply 'transference', is the bond between patient and therapist characterised by subconscious processes, which, if properly analysed, may lead to healing.
4 D.J. Siegel, *The Mindful Brain: Reflection and Attunement in the Cultivation of Well-Being*, W.W. Norton & Company, New York-London, 2007.
5 The discovery of mirror neurons was made by a team led by Giacomo Rizzolatti at the University of Parma (Italy) towards the end of the 1980s. For further details, see G. Rizzolatti and C. Sinigaglia, *So quello che fai. Il cervello che agisce e i neuroni specchio* (Raffaello Cortina Editore, Milan, 2006) and G. Rizzolatti – C. Sinigaglia, *Specchi nel cervello. Come comprendiamo gli altri dall'interno* (Raffaello Cortina Editore, Milan, 2019). As for the Embodied Simulation Theory, see V. Gallese and M. Guerra, *Lo schermo empatico. Cinema e neuroscienze* (Raffaello Cortina Editore, Milan, 2015).
6 D.M. Kalff, *Sandspiel Seine therapeutische Wirkung auf die Psyche*, Rentsch Verlag, Erlenbach-Zürich, 1979, first English Edition: *Sandplay. A Psychotherapeutic Approach to the Psyche*, Temenos Press, Cloverdale, California, 2003.

Part I

A new perspective: The individuation process in Sandplay Therapy: Neural integration, resonances in soma and psyche

Chapter 1

Historical premises

Martin Kalff

Margaret Lowenfeld: body and preverbal thinking

In order to place the 'Experience-Related Case Studies'(ERCS)[1] into the theoretical and practical context of Sandplay Therapy, it is worthwhile to briefly review the main steps in the origins of Sandplay as, at present, many of its original elements find new meanings and applications.

Since its very beginning, Sandplay has encompassed bodily perceptions and experiences. Sand is offered to children to be touched, experienced, formed, shaped, explored, felt. However, any direct contact with sand may be easily avoided by placing the figures onto its surface without touching the sand itself.

The idea of using sand in therapy dates back to the 'World Technique' devised by Margaret Lowenfeld (1890–1973). Her approach may be rightfully viewed as one of three roots of Sandplay Therapy – the other two being Jungian psychology and Eastern contemplative traditions, which will be delved into in the following chapters. Dora Kalff (1904–1990) combined these three approaches within Sandplay Therapy. However – whereas the influence of both the Jungian approach and of Margaret Lowenfeld's work are distinctly recognisable – the Eastern contemplative traditions still remain somewhat concealed.

Dora Kalff had studied at the C.G. Jung Institute in Zürich (1949–1953).[2] Her talent in working with children had been noticed by her analyst Emma Jung as well as by C.G. Jung himself, who both suggested she should study Margaret Lowenfeld's World Technique in order to develop an analytical approach to this technique geared towards children. Accordingly, in 1955 Dora Kalff spent one year in London to study in depth this up-and-coming technique for children.[3]

Through the World Technique Margaret Lowenfeld created a powerful tool for the treatment of 'nervous and difficult' children at her clinic in London and, later on, also of adults.[4] The discovery and the use of 'playing' as a means of healing within therapy was a yet further contribution made by Lowenfeld. Her approach was based on the use of sand in a box measuring about 75x52cm, with a depth of 7cm (29.5x20.5x2.8 inches).[5] It may be noted

DOI: 10.4324/9781003163503-2

at this point that the dimensions of the box used later by Dora Kalff were 49x72x7cm (19.3x28.3x2.8 inches). In addition, there was a large collection of figures. Children were offered the chance to plunge their hands into the sand, play with it and shape landscapes, mountains, valleys, or whatever would spontaneously emerge, and then populate the emerging scene using figures of humans, animals, houses, cars, bridges, trees, etc.

Margaret Lowenfeld presented the children with the materials along with the explanation that "many things are more easily said through images and actions, rather than through words".[6] The exhortation to play is therefore based on an important insight concerning the limits of verbal expression (Figure 1.1).

Lowenfeld made an important distinction between what she called the 'primary' and the 'secondary' mental system. The 'primary' mental system (also referred to as 'protosystem') is described as "all mental processes between age zero and the age where cognitive processes occupy a normal field of the mental activities". The 'secondary' system designs "all thought that can be expressed in prose".[7] Furthermore, the primary system can be defined as:

> personal, idiosyncratic, massive and multidimensional, by its very nature, incommunicable to others in words. The development of the Primary

Figure 1.1 Margaret Lowenfeld, courtesy of the Dr Margaret Lowenfeld Trust

System goes hand in hand with the development of the Secondary System, which is reasonable, practical, governed by causality, shared with other people and, to a large extent, describable through language.[8]

Emotions are among the chief organising principles through which children experience the world according to the primary system. Lowenfeld explains: "things which made me feel bad" belong together, as do "things which made me feel warm", etc. She also discussed "emotionally-toned" clusters in terms of the building blocks of the primary system. Lowenfeld concluded by adding that the "contents of the primary system" cannot appear in the secondary system[9], which enables us to fully grasp the importance of her World Technique as a tool for the expression of the contents of the primary system.

At the same time, Margaret Lowenfeld discarded the terms 'unconscious' and 'conscious' introduced by Freud and Jung. Indeed, Lowenfeld believed that it was incorrect to name something as 'unconscious' just because it is not expressible through words. Moreover, Lowenfeld was mainly working with children whose consciousness was not yet fully developed.

Lowenfeld's argument appears to be valid and of great importance. Indeed, we often tend to identify 'being conscious' with the ability to express ourselves through language. If anything, it is necessary to pay more attention to those forms of consciousness which are not verbal, as those that arise during creative activity or through gazing at an image – be it through painting, working with clay or Sandplay. The perception of the image, its realisation intended as the external manifestation of an inner content, and the awareness of the sensations which are involved in this process, are a yet further way to develop awareness through a creative activity. These ways to develop awareness are closely related to what Erich Neumann defined as the 'matriarchal consciousness',[10] different from the 'patriarchal consciousness', which, by contrast, is connected to abstraction and distinguishing abilities. According to Neumann, matriarchal consciousness can be compared to the activity of contemplation. Neumann's comments on this matter are indeed enlightening, and correspond in many respects to what has emerged from our research and supervision group with regard to creative methods:

> Here understanding is not, as for patriarchal consciousness, an act of the intellect as a rapidly comprehending organ that perceives, work through, and organizes; rather it means 'conceiving'.... [T]he whole person is gripped and moved by the contents.... Matriarchal qualitative time is unique and singular as gravid, pregnant time in contrast to the quantitative time of patriarchal consciousness.... Hence, symbolically, matriarchal consciousness is usually not situated in the head, but rather in the heart. Here 'understanding' also means an act of feeling that comprehends. In contrast the process of thinking and abstraction typical of patriarchal consciousness is 'cold', since the 'cold blooded' objectivity demanded of it necessitates establishing distance that presupposes a 'cool head'.[11]

Neumann also discussed a perception accompanied by a process of mindfulness and attentiveness. He wrote:

> Typical for this observing consciousness is the act of contemplation where energies are guided towards a content, process, or midpoint while the ego establishes a participation with the emotionally coloured content and lets it impregnate and permeate. This differs from the extremely patriarchal consciousness that distances and abstracts itself from the content.[12]

The consciousness which arises during Sandplay seems to correspond to the 'matriarchal' one described by Neumann. As proposed by Estelle Weinrib, the author of *Images of the Self*, 'healing' occurs on this level. In her words: "Psychological healing ... is an emotional, non-rational phenomenon that takes place on the matriarchal level of awareness hypothesised by Erich Neumann".[13]

The understanding that developing awareness requires going through different chronological phases – including becoming emotionally aware of preverbal levels – does not necessarily entail the necessity to go as far as Lowenfeld in completely rejecting the terms 'conscious' and 'unconscious'. Accordingly, I propose to conceive of Sandplay as an approach capable of opening a window on both the *personal* and the *collective* unconscious, as hypothesised by C.G. Jung. The personal unconscious comprises forgotten, repressed and dissociated contents, which used to be conscious at some point in life. Jung's view of the *personal* unconscious corresponds to the Freudian definition of the unconscious, meaning that it is of a personal nature and contains what Jung referred to as 'feeling-toned complexes'. By contrast, the *collective* unconscious is not a personal acquisition and has never been conscious. Its contents are archaic imprints coming from a common human heritage, which Jung named 'archetypes'. Archetypes themselves represent the mind's tendencies, similarly to instincts, and they do not have a specific form. They are the bedrock of common cross-cultural motifs to be found in religion, mythology and fairy tales.[14] These motifs are based on fundamental notions regarding the feminine, the masculine, the figure of the mother and the father, wisdom, spirituality and experiences such as birth and death, etc. Accordingly, they make a cross-cultural psychic common ground even while making cultural differences more visible.

As creative activities ease the development of awareness, Sandplay – but also active imagination, dreams and the understanding of co-transference – can provide privileged access to the covert world of the collective unconscious, and may eventually guide its contents towards a more verbal or 'solar' level of consciousness.

Furthermore, Lowenfeld's distinction between the primary and secondary system – one being more emotionally toned and preverbal, and the other more language-related – could be seen as a harbinger to the distinction between 'implicit' and 'explicit' memory. Implicit memory, according to Bonnie Badenoch, is the only type of functioning memory during the first 12 to 18 months of our lives. Among others, implicit memory also encompasses behavioural impulses and affective experiences that are based on repeated experiences and become mostly unconscious mental models setting expectations about life. They are, as we may add, non-verbal in nature. Therefore, we may define them as psychic contents of non-verbal nature. In the brain, the central site of implicit memory is the amygdala, which plays an important role in creating meaning, and distinguishing what is dangerous from what is not. The amygdala develops early on in ontogeny and continues to be active throughout life.[15]

Explicit memory starts to function only once the hippocampus reaches its maturity and the middle prefrontal region is activated. One of the main functions of explicit memory is the memory of facts, then followed by autobiographical memory which enables each individual to tell the story of one's own life in words.

According to Peter Levine, implicit memory plays a key role in trauma. He has pointed out that: "Indeed, persistent maladaptive procedural and emotional memories form the core mechanism that underlie all traumas, as well as many problematic social and relationship issues".[16] This also highlights the limits of a therapy mainly based on a verbal approach. Levine continues:

> However, conscious, explicit memory is only the proverbial tip of a very deep and mighty iceberg. It barely hints at the submerged data of primal implicit experience that moves and motivates us in a way the conscious mind can only begin to imagine. But imagine we should, and understand we must, if we are to work effectively and wisely with trauma and its memory traces in both body and mind.[17]

This enables us to fully appreciate the effectiveness of Lowenfeld's method, where playing with sand and figures helps the client express the world of implicit memories and become aware of it.

Alongside Lowenfeld's findings, the ERCS attaches importance to preverbal thinking and implicit memories through Sandplay. Indeed, this provides greater awareness regarding how our own preverbal thinking and implicit memories influence the way we view Sandplay installations. This way, the purpose that Sandplay as a method of access to preverbal communication is meant to serve is fully achieved.

Observations on transference/countertransference/co-transference

Lowenfeld also expanded on transference. In her book, she explains that when she first started working with children, she was trying to devise a method enabling them to express their emotional and mental states "without the necessary intervention of an adult either by transference or interpretation ... my objective is to help children to produce something which will stand by itself and be independent of any theory as to its nature".[18] In other words, Lowenfeld recommended that the child's expressions should not be influenced by the therapist's transference or projections on the child. The child should also be shielded from the therapist's theory-based interpretation.

The statement can be understood as the expression of a concern about providing children with a space that may be free from manipulation and preconceived theories. This can be seen as a choice which demonstrates great respect for the child's autonomy. However, it is clear that her attempts to exclude transference do not correspond to the modern understanding of Sandplay and it is not possible.

Not providing verbal interpretations to the sand player is still current practice among Sandplay therapists – and this also with a view to protecting the game's spontaneous progression and its ensuing creative flow. With regard to transference, our understanding is different. For example, Dora Kalff often emphasised the role of 'relationship'. A key element in relationship is what she called the "free and protected space" that the therapist needs to ensure the client. Jungian analyst and Sandplay therapist Kay Bradway later introduced the term 'co-transference' with the aim of describing the simultaneous nature of the inter-feelings running between therapist and the client, which differs from the traditional concepts of transference/countertransference. Bradway believes that these feelings are determined by past and present, positive and negative, conscious and unconscious events between client and therapist.[19] Current Sandplay therapists largely agree on this understanding.

The analysis of the transference is also extendable to the figures used by the client. Indeed, some figures selected by the client may represent qualities ascribed to the therapist/counsellor, for example the use of a nurse or doctor in the representation of a car accident. Such a representation could indicate that the child, despite the crisis, is starting to benefit from the therapist's helping attitude. Sometimes, during the review[20] of such scenes, the clients themselves reveal that a specific figure was used for representing the therapist. In contrast with this view, Lowenfeld would say that the transference was directed to the green apron worn by the therapists of her Institute, who would take shifts in treating the same child. Furthermore, she is reported to have said that the transference was directed to the sandbox and not to the therapist.[21]

However, Margaret Lowenfeld beautifully described the interaction between the child and his/her representation:

> In the worlds the child is confronted by a piece of its own feeling, thinking, remembering – life set out by himself for his own study – there is an extraordinary force in this confrontation – the child having made the picture has to accept it as his own.[22]

According to this description, an important process takes place when the child experiences the 'world' he/she has made. The child is confronted and has to cope with a part of their own life, feeling, thinking, and remembering, which occur outside of themselves as a three-dimensional play, whereas they had previously been hiding inside.

This statement helps us understand that the sandbox and the 'world' (as Lowenfeld calls it) created inside of it, represent a third element that goes beyond the co-transference between the sand player and the therapist. The sandbox world is to be considered as a liminal space, which is neither the therapist's or the sand player's, where wounds and healing forces can be expressed in a symbolic way, held, accepted and witnessed by both the sand player and the therapist in a process which ultimately involves them both.

Accepting one's own sand creations and the feelings they evoke may pose a threat and be perceived as overwhelming by someone who has a weak Ego or momentarily has low defences. Accordingly, in such moments a reassuring relationship with the therapist is of paramount importance. However, at the same time, through the act of creation, the sand player can also experience their own autonomy. For this reason, implicit projections involved in the transference towards the therapist may be partially withdrawn and accepted as previously unknown aspects of oneself.

ERCS takes into account the complex nature of co-transference and provides the tools to become aware of how the therapist's own co-transference is triggered just by listening to the client's life story and then by looking at the scenes created in the sand.

Sandplay and the individuation process according to Carl Gustav Jung

While studying with Margaret Lowenfeld, Dora Kalff soon discovered that in some of the series of the children's worlds, the process of individuation as described by C.G. Jung was easily recognisable. Once back to Switzerland, Dora decided to explore this parallel in greater depth in her own clinical practice and, in agreement with Lowenfeld, she called her method 'Sandplay Therapy' to distinguish it from the 'World Technique'.

Jung defined the individuation process as follows:

> The meaning and purpose of the process is the realisation, in all its aspects, of the personality originally hidden away in the embryonic germ-plasm; the production and unfolding of the original, potential wholeness. The symbols used by the unconscious to this end are the same as those which mankind has always used to express wholeness, completeness and perfection: symbols, as a rule, of the quaternity and the circle. For this reason, I have termed this the individuation process.[23]

Jung refers to a human potential which has existed from the beginning, and which is present since birth as an embryonic form or a seed. Jung calls this potential 'wholeness', and the aim of the individuation process is to fulfil it. According to Jung, it is a lifelong task and it may not always prove possible to completely carry it out. However, there are moments in one's life where one can be touched by the individuation process. These moments help connect with the inner meaning of one's own psychic life and, especially during difficult times, find a new direction.

Besides 'wholeness' or 'totality', Jung also used the word 'Self' to describe this dimension. Jung distinguished between 'I' and 'Self': 'I' is conceived of as the core of conscious personality, whereas the Self is conceived of as subject of the whole psyche, which also includes its unconscious parts.[24] Therefore, the Self transcends the limited world of the Ego. It is noteworthy that Jung described the Self as a subject, which suggests its qualities are those of an agent. We believe that Jung saw in the Self its own hidden agent, responsible for the self-regulation of the psyche. Jung described the psyche's self-regulating system as follows:

> The psyche is a self-regulating system that maintains its equilibrium just as the body does. Every process that goes too far immediately and inevitably calls forth a compensation. Too little on one side results in too much on the other. Similarly, the relation between conscious and unconscious is compensatory. This is one of the best proven rules of dream interpretation. When we set out to interpret a dream, it is always helpful to ask: what conscious attitude does it compensate?[25]

Self-regulation is necessary to correct the one-sided attitudes typical of consciousness. According to Jung, dreams and fantasies bring up aspects of the unconscious psyche which have a compensatory relationship with the conscious attitude. For example, if one's view about oneself is too negative, dreams could indicate positive inner qualities. Paying attention to the contents of dreams and fantasies can help poise one's attitudes.

Jung's following statement suggests that the Self is the agent behind this process:

> But since everything living strives for wholeness, the inevitable one-sidedness of our conscious life is continually being corrected and compensated by the universal human being in us, whose goal is the ultimate integration of the conscious and unconscious, or better, the assimilation of the ego to a wider personality.[26]

What Jung calls 'the universal being in us' actually refers to the Self. Therefore, a fundamental function of the Self is also the hidden guidance it provides and which helps consciousness develop and process new insights coming from the inner or from the outer world.

In consequence, the Self is not only the source – present as a potential at the beginning of life – and the final goal – intended as the realisation of wholeness and of the individuation process – but it is also the subject that promotes this very individuation process. The study of given individual paths within Sandplay which were largely based on unconscious creations in the sand, often revealed an inner logic aiming at a more balanced and complete personality. These paths show the Self's activity as a self-regulating agent. In addition, a self-healing tendency characterises the Self, and it can be activated through playing, an activity which has the potential to bridge the gulf between the conscious and unconscious aspects of one's own personality.

Jung devised most of his theoretical concepts on the basis of his own experience, but also on his patients' dreams and fantasies. To convey the atmosphere experienced by Jung in recognising the Self as an inner guide, it might be helpful to quote an important dream of his:

> I found myself in a dirty, sooty city. It was night, and winter, and dark, and raining. I was in Liverpool. With a number of Swiss people – say, half a dozen – I walked through the dark streets.... The real city was actually up above ... we climbed up there. When we reached the plateau, we found a broad square dimly illuminated by street lights, into which many streets converged. The various districts of the city were arranged radially around the square. In the centre was a round pool, and in the middle of it a small island. While everything round about was obscured by rain, fog, smoke, and dimly lit darkness, the little island blazed with sunlight. On it stood a single tree, a magnolia, in a shower of reddish blossoms. It was as though the tree stood in the sunlight and was at the same time the source of light.... I was carried away by the beauty of the flowering tree and the sunlit island.[27]

Jung himself commented on the initial part of the dream, claiming that it represented his own feelings at that time, where everything was extremely "unpleasant, black and opaque". He then continued:

> But I had had a vision of unearthly beauty, and that was why I was able to live at all. Liverpool is the 'pool of life'. The 'liver' according to an old view, is the seat of life – that which 'makes to live'. The dream brought with it a sense of finality. I saw that there the goal had been revealed. One could not go beyond the centre. The center is the goal, and everything is directed towards that centre. Through this dream I understood that the self is the principle and archetype of orientation and meaning. Therein lies its healing function.[28]

However, he added that without such a vision he could have lost his inner sense of direction. The dream helped him reconnect with a sense of purpose and meaning to his life, especially after the painful parting with Freud.

Jung painted a mandala image which bears a complex relation to this dream. He called the painting *A Window Overlooking Eternity* (Figure 1.2). He then included it in the records of his personal inner journey and process of individuation in *The Red Book*. Instead of a magnolia tree, at its centre we can see a luminous rose or a jewel.[29]

The individuation process according to Dora Kalff

In her book *Sandplay. A Psychotherapeutic Approach to the Psyche*, Dora Kalff states her intention to illustrate how in her Sandplay cases the

Figure 1.2 A Window Overlooking Eternity, courtesy of W. W. Norton & Company, Inc.

individuation process can be witnessed. In her understanding of it, the contact with the sense of purpose or inner order – which she called 'manifestation of the Self' – was of primary importance.[30] Following Neumann, she maintained that the original phase is that of mother-child unity, where children fully depend on the mother as far as it concerns their needs, and where the mother stands for the Self in the eyes of the child. In this case the Self is a source of inner security and basic trust. We could say that this is the source of secure attachment.

As neuroscientist Louis Cozolino has pointed out, secure attachment is based on experiences such as

> the soothing touch, being held softly and securely, comforting warmth, the experience of homeostatic balance in regard to sleep, hunger, stimulation, repeated experiences of emotional transitions from states of distress to states of calm and a sustained positive emotional state.[31]

Researchers have related these experiences (among others) to increased "production of oxytoxins, prolactin, endorphins, and dopamine: the biochemistry of reward".[32] They are fundamental for the establishment of lifelong positive implicit memories which influence our style of relationships and trust in life. On the level of neuroscience, secure attachment resulting from a secure primal relationship represents the optimal balance of sympathetic and parasympathetic arousal.[33]

In the process of separation, the child increasingly experiences the Self as a quality in itself. The mother is being internalised. Erich Neumann has pointed out that, in this phase, an Ego-Self axis is established. The Ego can rest on the safe bedrock provided by the Self, issued from a positive primary relationship. It is also the source of a growing sense of autonomy.[34] Dora Kalff also maintained that in the second year of life and at beginning of the third, the Self manifests itself in symbols of wholeness. An important aim of therapy is therefore to re-establish access to this source of trust in children who either have never experienced it to its full extent or have lost it due to traumatic experiences.

> I want to designate the manifestation of the Self as the most important moment in the development of the personality. Psychotherapeutic work has proven that the ego can develop in a healthy manner only on the basis of a succesful manifestation of the Self, be that as a dream symbol or when represented in a sandtray.[35]

This is possible through the establishment of a "free and protected space" where the therapist, thanks to transference, "represents the protector, the space, freedom and, at the same time, the boundaries".[36]

Some remarks on the third root of Sandplay

Soon after C.G. Jung's death in 1961, Dora Kalff had a dream where Jung pointed to a heap of rice on her table and said: "You have to explore the Far East in greater depth than I have done".[37]

This dream is remindful of the ceremony of the Mandala Offering, where handfuls of rice are offered with a ceremonial purpose. It is the symbolic offering of the whole universe to the Buddha and to one's own spiritual guide. A round metal plate is used and 37 handfuls of rice are carefully placed onto it while being kept together by three concentric metal rings, the second ring being smaller than the first, and the third even smaller than the second. The 37 heaps represent the central mountain in a delimited world, surrounded by four main and four secondary continents. Various treasures associated to those continents and to ancient Indian rulers are also placed on the metal plate. Two handfuls of rice are placed on top to represent the sun and moon.

Jung himself had studied with keen interest traditional Asian texts, and had detected to his astonishment many parallels with his own understanding of the individuation process. This finding had helped him understand the universal and archetypal nature of this process. Key concepts used by Jung, such as the 'Self' and 'mandala', were inspired by Eastern ideas, the notion of Atman, and mandalas as conceived of in Hinduism and Buddhism.

In an interview, Jung was asked to characterise his method "without regard to how others would misunderstand or misuse it. Suppose that you could state it in a way that would fit your own truest feelings of it". He replied: "Ach" and continued, "It would be too funny. It would be a Zen touch".[38] It is clear that Jung felt a strong connection with the East, however he also warned against a shallow adaptation to Eastern forms of practice.[39]

Dora Kalff had many contacts with Zen teachers, among whom was Daisetz Suzuki, whom she had met at an Eranos gathering[40], where scholars from different fields inspired by C.G. Jung would reunite. She also visited Daisetz Suzuki in Japan. She met up several times with H.H. the Dalai Lama and many other Tibetan Lamas, who would often visit the centre for meditation which was joint founded by my mother and myself. During those meetings, there was a spontaneous and profound mutual recognition of each other's value. For example, one of the Dalai Lama's tutors, who certainly chose his words carefully, said that he felt like he and Dora Kalff had prayed together in a previous life.

On one occasion, right after meeting a high-ranking Tibetan Buddhist master, Dora Kalff noticed a surprising change in the Sandplay scenes by a boy who, up to that point, had mostly depicted his inner conflicts through the representation of battles and wars. However, that time the boy represented an Asian temple with lions standing at its gates, and right in front of them he placed an elephant which he said to be praying. Inside the temple, he placed a small figure of a Tibetan saint with a sword and a sacred book. Of course, the boy could not have known that the sword and book were two symbols associated with this saint. Neither did he know about the meeting between his therapist and the Eastern monk. After creating more scenes of this kind in the sand, the symptoms which had brought him to therapy started to change. Thus, it appears that the meeting between his therapist and the monk indirectly influenced the boy's Sandplay process and helped him progress.

Dora Kalff discussed her perspective on Sandplay Therapy with many masters of Eastern traditions and found many common points with meditation practices. A Zen master recognised remarkable similarities between her approach to Sandplay and the Zen approach, as in both approaches the stress is laid not on the outside, but on the inside, in order to naturally manage to find one's own true nature, or Self. Also C.G. Jung's statement points in the same direction: "here we must follow nature as a guide, and what the doctor then does is less a question of treatment than of developing the creative possibilities latent in the patient himself".[41]

In many lectures, Dora Kalff would use the term 'original Self' to indicate the Self's manifestation during the Sandplay process. On the one hand, this term is aligned with Jung's idea that the Self is present since the beginning of life. On the other hand, it also refers to the expression 'original Self' or 'true nature' and other similar terms used in Zen Buddhism to indicate Buddha's nature, which is present in everyone since the origin, that is, the beginning of life.

In Zen Buddhism, a series of images are used for illustrating how an individual can get in touch with his original nature. They are known as the pictures of the *ox herding*. The story is about an ox herder who has lost his ox. Step by step, the images and the poems which describe them tell the story of how he finds his ox again.

The ox represents our true nature and the way it is found, tamed, and brought home indicates how one can get in touch with it. Zen master Ohtsu explains the symbol of the ox as follows: "With the ox, however, it is our own heart or original nature that is supposed to be shown. He points metaphorically to that which we call the original nature, Buddha nature or origin of truth".[42] Furthermore, he adds that the disciple who wants to reach that level, needs to completely get rid of language and words: "The pupil must be completely detached from all words, thought and speech. An appropriation occurs there in which the pupil assimilates his own heart, his own nature".[43]

Dora Kalff herself studied these images and also gave lectures comparing them to Sandplay. On a few occasions Dora Kalff also commented that, in her view, the Zen Buddhist notion of the 'original nature' was deeper than Jung's understanding of the Self. The 'original nature', according to her, manifests itself beyond the Shadow and helps transform it. During Dora Kalff's lecture *Beyond the Shadow*, she claimed:

> Once we have reached the basic Self where all energies are usually concentrated in harmony and get in contact with this original nature through

meditation. These are known as the 'Ox we experience it in a numinous way, we can also see that energies which have been dark and destructive can transform and be experienced in a constructive way'.

In her lecture, she then proceeded to show numerous very impressive examples of these transformative Self images.[44]

At this point, we can't go more in depth into the analysis of Zen Buddhism and the notion of the Self. Suffice it to note that both Buddhism and Jungian psychology share the idea of an original potential wholeness that can be developed. This shows the common archetypal basis underlying both notions, despite the differences in cultural backgrounds, specific approaches and aims. Personally, I also had the opportunity to show some images of the Self's expression through Sandplay to a well-known Tibetan Lama. After carefully studying the scenes, he commented: "These images are proof that the Buddha Nature is present everywhere".

A statement by Dora Kalff on the therapeutic attitude

In the informative and thought-provoking book *Sandplay: Past, Present & Future*, Rie R. Mitchell and Harriet S. Friedman quote Dora Kalff's introduction to the book *Studies of Sandplay Therapy in Japan*. [45] This quote encapsulates a concise and exhaustive summary of her attitude towards Sandplay Therapy and bridges the gulf between this and mindfulness practice.[46]

> One important aspect of this freedom is (for the therapist) to become void of judgmental thoughts and free to accept the patient as he [/she] is. This could also be described as a state of receptive openness. In this state one does not prematurely judge what is created through the play, be it negative or positive. The attitude should allow anything positive about to happen to have the force to break through and express itself. There is no need for the therapist to label it as positive as it is not the explanation that should be valued, but the experience the patient is having. Likewise, it would be a mistake to label something as negative, because we cannot know ahead of time what may come from darkness. The state of freedom the therapist is to aim at should be such that by his mere presence this freedom can be communicated also non-verbally to the patient. In such a situation the patient may slowly also discover within himself [/herself] the transformative power of freedom.

The above-described attitude corresponds the practice of mindfulness, where it is important to create an inner space and develop unbiased awareness of bodily sensations and feelings. Neuroscientist Dan Siegel, inspired by his own experience of retreats according to the Vipassana[47] tradition, describes the attitude of being mindful as being "curious, open, accepting and loving".[48] One is open and receptive to whatever may fall into the scope of awareness. During the practice of mindfulness, this attitude is first directed towards one's own state of mind. However, it is also helpful to develop the same mindful attitude towards others and, of course, towards the clients through practising Sandplay Therapy.

This attitude has also been emphasised in the seminars (which I attended) held by the Tibetan Lama and Dzogchen teacher Tsoknyi Rinpoche.[49] He coined for it the term 'Handshake Practice'. Rather than trying to eliminate or get rid of unpleasant and disturbing physical sensations and emotions, he recommended witnessing them without passing judgements. Eventually, our presence of mind and those emotions – which may also change during the process – become like two hands in the act of a handshake. Once accepted, negative emotions may finally undergo change. He explained that this acceptance also leads to a deeper acceptance of oneself and, finally, to a state of 'essential love', where one is able to embrace both positive and negative elements. This essential love or feeling at peace with oneself then becomes the basis for compassion toward others. Without love for ourselves, we cannot love others.

During a personal discussion on Jung's concept of the Self, Tsoknyi Rinpoche suggested it could correspond to what he calls 'essential love'. The quote from Dora Kalff reported in the opening of this section continues with a discussion of the quality of loving acceptance as an important part of therapy and resonates well with the emphasis on loving acceptance mentioned above:

> Besides an inner freedom[,] the therapist should also attempt to develop his own capacity to love. Love means in this context to sincerely wish that the patient may become free of his [/her] suffering. It is a quality which allows the therapist to see the patient non only as patient but as another human being. If the patient experiences that he is accepted in that way, it will also enable him to look with love at those sides within himself, which previously he found to be unacceptable and negative. In that way the capacity to love works as a shelter or protection for that which is still weak within the patient. It allows that to grow which otherwise might be repressed by a non-caring attitude. The love expresses itself also in taking serious[ly] what is done or said by the patient.

Sandplay, as Gita Morena and Lorraine Freedle point out in their well written introduction to the new English 2020 edition of Dora Kalff's classic on Sandplay, has by now a substantial evidence base for the effectiveness of treatment.[50]

The practice of mindfulness according to Jon Kabat-Zinn and its applicability to psychotherapy

Jon Kabat-Zinn has successfully implemented mindfulness practices for stress reduction in his 'Mindfulness-Based Stress Reduction' (MBSR) Program. He defines it as follows: "Mindfulness means paying attention in a particular way: on purpose, in the present moment, and non-judgementally. This kind of attention nurtures greater awareness, clarity, and acceptance of present-moment reality".[51] Inspired by his own experience with the Zen and Vipassana meditation, Kabat-Zinn is the founder of the Stress-Reduction Clinic headquartered at the University of Massachusetts. He started to use this method with people suffering from chronic pain. Patients learned to cope better with their pain, and their personal suffering also decreased accordingly. He has also found evidence that meditation practices have healing effects on anxiety disorders, stress-induced ailments, cardiovascular disease, psoriasis, and depression.[52] For this reason, the program has been introduced in many clinics all over the world, and, especially in the USA, it has entered the field of education as 'Mindfulness in Education'.[53]

Mindfulness has been increasingly used within numerous forms of psychotherapy; for example, in 'Dialectical Behavioural Therapy' (DBT) founded by Marsha Linehan – successfully treating patients diagnosed with a Borderline Personality Disorder – and in MBCT, 'Mindfulness-Based Cognitive Therapy' developed by Zindal Segal, Marc Williams and John Teasdale. Jeffrey Schwartz's four-step program for the treatment of obsessive disorders,[54] as well as Acceptance and Commitment Therapy (ACT) and Compassion-Focused Therapy (CFT) by Paul Gilbert have incorporated elements of mindfulness into their approaches.

Christopher Germer, Ronald Siegel and Paul Fulton have published the book-length study *Mindfulness in Psychotherapy*, in which various contributors discuss these approaches, as well as latest research and the implications of using mindfulness in therapy.[55]The book contains for example chapters on mindfulness applied to anxiety disorders, depression, and psychophysiological disturbances. Vera Kaltwasser points to a study by Lidia Zylowska demonstrating that in cases of ADS (Attention Deficit Syndrome) the lack of concentration and hyperactivity have been significantly modified though the use of mindfulness training.[56] Luise Reddemann, founder of PITT (Psychodynamic, Imaginative Trauma Therapy), is the editor of a collection of insightful articles on mindfulness used in the context of psychotherapy. She rightfully emphasises in one of her own contributions on patients with personality disorder and trauma the therapist's need to acquire at least a basic knowledge of the practice of mindfulness if they are to use it in therapy.[57]

The origin of mindfulness and Buddhism

The term 'mindfulness' originates from the Pali word *sati* which means 'to remember, to be present with full awareness'. It is a mental skill which, through practice, can lead to higher levels of concentration. In Buddhism this ability is used for acquiring a deeper insight into the nature of reality, in its impermanence and lack of a substantial Self.

The traditional source for mindfulness practices in Buddhism are to be found in a written record of one of Buddha's teachings called 'The Foundations of Mindfulness' (Pali: *Satipatthana sutta*). In this context the most basic form of mindfulness is the mindfulness on the act of breathing. Here it may be useful to quote from the original text:

> Here a Bhikkhu [a fully ordained monk], gone to the forest or to the root of a tree or to an empty hut, sits down; having folded his legs crosswise, sets his body erect, and, having established mindfulness in front of him, ever mindful he breathes in, and mindful he breathes out. Breathing in for long, he understands: 'I breathe in long' or breathing out long, he understands: 'I breathe out for long'. Breathing in short, he understands: 'I breathe in short', breathing out short, he understands 'I breathe out short'. He trains thus: 'I shall breathe in experiencing the whole body'; he trains thus: 'I shall breathe out experiencing the whole body'. He trains himself thus 'I shall breathe in tranquillizing the body formations'; he trains thus: 'I shall breathe out tranquillising the body formations'.[58]

As we may note here, the text emphasises awareness of the breath, free of the intention to make the breath long or short etc. The act of breathing is noticed as it unfolds naturally. At the end, we encounter the term 'body formation'. This term refers – according to a later clarification within the same text – to the process of in- and out-breathing itself. Through successful practice, breathing becomes more peaceful, as Bhikkhu Bodhi explains.[59]

The instructions then proceed to emphasise mindfulness of different body positions such as sitting, standing, lying down and walking. Accordingly, it becomes clear that mindfulness practices may not be carried out only while sitting, but in any position. For instance, walking meditation consists in becoming thoroughly aware of the process of walking, of the sensations associated with lifting the feet and setting them down.

The text then extends the process of mindfulness to basic feelings such as 'pleasant', 'unpleasant', 'neutral' and to emotions, including anger and desire. Many mind factors are considered as objects of meditation, such as the five factors which hinder mindfulness, namely sexual desire, ill will, sloth and torpor, restlessness and remorse, and also doubt.

Although the meditation process finds some variations according to the different methods, a common feature is that of becoming aware of the presence and/or absence of the abovementioned sensations and emotional factors. This also holds true for those factors which hinder mindfulness, as the simple awareness of those factors may decrease their impact.

Currently, the focus of MBSR and other approaches is on cognizance of whatever arises in the present moment, without judgements. From this, one may form the wrong impression that mindfulness alone – that is, without an ethical framework or additional instructions – has been thought to draw the whole path towards the overcoming of basic suffering. For example, the presence of the five hindrances is not desirable. They include mental attitudes like desire, ill will, sloth and torpor, as well as others. Including the meditation on these factors as part of the foundations of mindfulness involves a clear ethical dimension. In order to overcome these hindrances, it is true that a non-judgmental attitude plays a crucial role, as one should simply pay attention to their functioning. Simple awareness can foster change by helping realise the transience of the five hindrances and therefore decreasing the power of their effects. However, if this does not prove sufficient, other techniques can be resorted to instead, like in the case of sloth or torpor, where focusing on light and brightness may help, as well as face-washing with cold water or eating less.

The abovementioned instructions from the earliest texts on Buddhism, based on the Pali canon, are both the bedrock and the starting point of Buddhist Vipassana, or 'insight meditation'.[60] The origins are to be found in early Buddhism. The modern expression 'mindfulness meditation' mostly refers to this practice and to secular adaptations deriving from it, such as 'Mindfulness-Based Stress Reduction' which, however, also draws from other sources within the large spectrum of the Buddhist traditions.

Nonetheless, there are also other closely-related historical developments in the Buddhist tradition based on mindfulness. For example, the Mahayana tradition, prevalent in Tibetan Buddhism, provides special instructions on how to achieve a state of focused concentration, called 'Shamata meditation', or the meditation of mental calming.[61]

A great part of recent research on the effects of mindfulness meditation is based on Vipassana and MBSR.[62] The ambitious and comprehensive project named 'Shamata' launched by Alan Wallace, uses Shamata meditation on breathing as one of the key tools of the research, which also features other practices like open awareness and compassion meditation.[63] However, little attention has been given to the different practices' effects on subjects during therapy and to whether there were any significant differences at all.

In general, findings from research have pointed out that (among others) mindfulness has positive effects on emotion regulation, increases positive affect, minimises negative affect and ruminations, and decreases stress and anxiety.[64] The practice of mindfulness can also increase the ability to relate to others with greater clarity, attunement and compassion. Results have also shown the positive effects of mindfulness practice on the immune system, on the speed of recovery from illnesses, and in maintaining a good heart health.[65] Furthermore, it has been found that mindfulness increases our ability to be aware of nonverbal emotional signals from others and, therefore, of their inner life.[66] Bonnie Badenoch also refers to a study which shows that middle prefrontal cortex and the right anterior insula grow thicker as a result of mindfulness meditation.[67] This is highly significant, because this area, according to Dan Siegel and Badenoch, is central for integration of various neural areas, such as the cortex, the limbic system, the brain stem. It plays a fundamental role for various levels of neural integration which will be discussed in more detail in the following chapter.[68]

Notes

1 See Chapter 3, p. XX.
2 In R.R. Mitchell and H.S. Friedman, *Sandplay, Past, Present & Future*, Routledge, London, 1994. The study period at the Jung Institute refers to years between 1949 and 1956. The study in England refers to 1956. The dates mentioned above are in accordance with what was reported in Bruno Hofstetter's doctoral thesis, *Das Sandspiel von Frau Dora M. Kalff*, Zürich, 1998.
3 Mitchell and Friedman dated the study in England as 1956. However, Hofstetter dates it as 1955, which I believe to be more reliable.
4 M. Lowenfeld, *The World Technique*, George Allen & Unwin, London, 1979; Id, *Understanding Children's Sandplay: Lowenfeld's World Technique*, Margaret Lowenfeld Trust, London, 1993.
5 *Sandplay, Past, Present & Future*, p. 10.
6 M. Lowenfeld, *The World Technique*, p. 5.
7 Ibid., p. 16.
8 Ibid., p. 16.
9 Ibid., p. 24.
10 E. Neumann, *The Fear of the Feminine*, Princeton University Press, Princeton, 1994, with the article: 'The Moon and Matriarchal Consciousness'.
11 Ibid., pp. 95–97.
12 Ibid., p. 105.
13 E. Weinrib, *Images of the Self*, Sigo Press, Boston, 1983, p. 22.
14 For more details, see C.G. Jung, *The Archetypes and the Collective Unconscious*, vol. IX, part 1, *The Collected Works of C.G. Jung*, Bollingen Series (henceforth referred to as CW), translated by R.F.C. Hull, Princeton University Press, Princeton, 1969.
15 B. Badenoch, *Being a Brain-Wise Therapist, A Practical Guide to Interpersonal Neurobiology*, W.W. Norton and Company, New York-London, 2008, pp. 24–26.
16 P.A. Levine, *Trauma and Memory: Brain and Body in a Search for the Living Past. A Practical Guide for Understanding and Working with Traumatic Memory*, North Atlantic Books, Berkeley, CA, 2015, p. 38.
17 Ibid., Introduction, p. xxii.
18 M. Lowenfeld, *The World Technique*, p. 3.
19 K. Bradway, Transference and Countertransference in Sandplay Therapy, *Journal for Sandplay Therapy*, 1(1), Walnut Creek, CA, Autumn 1991.
20 At the end of the therapeutic treatment with Sandplay Therapy, clients are given a chance to view the photographs of all of their sand scenes.
21 Oral communication by Dora Kalff in her seminars.
22 M. Lowenfeld, The World Pictures of Children: A Method of Recording and Studying Them, *British Journal of Medical Psychology*, 18 (pt.1), pp. 87–88 (Presented to the Medical Section of the British Psychological Society, March, 1938), quoted in R.R. Mitchell and H.S. Friedman, *Sandplay: Past, Present and Future*, p. 16.
23 C.G. Jung, *Two Essays on Analytical Psychology*, CW VII, 1966, § 186.
24 C.G. Jung, *Psychological Types*, CW VI, 1971, § 706.
25 C.G. Jung, *The Practice of Psychotherapy*, CW XVI, 1966, § 330.
26 C.G. Jung, *The Structure and Dynamics of the Psyche*, CW VIII, 1969, § 557.

27 C.G. Jung, *Memories, Dreams and Reflections: An Autobiography*, edited by Aniela Jaffé, translated from German by Richard and Clara Winston, William Collings Paperback, London, 2019, p. 234–235. Shamdasani quotes a slightly different version from C.G. Jung's *Black Book* in *The Red Book. Liber Novus*, Edited and Introduced by Sonu Shamdasani, Philemon Series, W.W. Norton and Company, New York, 2009, p. 217.

28 C.G. Jung, *Memories*, p. 235 f.

29 From Jung's various comments, it is not quite clear whether he painted this mandala before the dream (and then it may have influenced the dream itself) or after it. Cf. C.G. Jung, *The Red Book*, p. 318, footnote 296.

30 D. Kalff, *Sandplay. A Psychotherapeutic Approach to the Psyche*, Analytical Psychology Press, Sandplay Editions, Oberlin, OH, 2020, p. 1 ff. (the previous edition was edited by Temenos Press, Cloverdale, 2003).

31 Summarised by Louis Cozolino in L. Cozolino, *The Neuroscience of Human Relationships: Attachment and the Developing Social Brain* (2006), W.W. Norton & Company, New York-London, 2014, p. 116.

32 Ibid., p. 117.

33 L. Cozolino, *The Neuroscience of Psychotherapy*, W.W. Norton & Company, New York-London, 2002, p. 209.

34 E. Neumann, *The Child*, translated by Ralph Manheim, Maresfield Library, Karnac Books, London, 1973, p. 47. See also M. Jacoby, *Individuation und Narzissmus. Psychologie des Selbst bei C.G. Jung und H. Kohut*, München, 1985, p. 60.

35 D. Kalff, *Sandplay. A Psychotherapeutic Approach to the Psyche*, p. 4.

36 Ibid., p. 7.

37 Personal communication to the author.

38 R. Moacanin, *Jung's Psychology and Tibetan Buddhism. Western and Eastern Path to the Heart. A Wisdom East-West Book*, Wisdom Publications, London, 1982, p. 48.

39 For more information about this, see M. Kalff, C.G. Jung's Encounter with the East, in *Psychological Perspectives*, C.G. Jung Institute of Los Angeles, 2000, n. 41 and M. Kalff, The Negation of Ego in Tibetan Buddhism and Jungian Psychology, *The Journal of Transpersonal Psychology*, 15(2), Palo Alto, 1983.

40 The Eranos Meetings ('Eranos' being the Greek word for 'potluck meal' where each of the guests contributes food to be shared) began in 1933 by the initiative of Olga Fröbe-Kapteyn and under the inspiration of Rudolf Otto. These yearly meetings were originally held in Ascona on the banks of Lake Maggiore, and brought together scholars from different fields: sinology, Islamic studies, Egyptology, Indology, chemistry, biology, astronomy, comparative mythology, mysticism, Zen Buddhism, literature, philosophy, political sciences, psychology.

41 C.G. Jung, *The Practice of Psychotherapy*, CW XVI, 1966, § 82.

42 *The Ox and his Herdsman. Commentary and Pointers by Master D.R. Otsu and Japanese Illustrations of the Fifteenth Century*. Translated by M.H. Trever, Hokuseido Press, Tokyo, 1969, p. 25. In the German original we have 'Anfängliches Selbst' [Original Self]' in place of 'Original Nature': *Der Ochs und sein Hirte, erläutert von Meister Daizohkutsu R. Ohtsu*, Neske Verlag, Pfullingen, 1958–1988, p. 55.

43 Ibid., p. 28.

44 D. Kalff, Beyond the Shadow, The Special Lecture on the Sixth International Congress of Sandplay Therapy in Japan, *Journal of Sandplay Therapy*, 16(1), Walnut Creek, CA, 2007.

45 D. Kalff, *Preface,* in H. Kawai and Y. Yamanaka (ed.), *Studies of Sandplay Therapy in Japan*, Seishin-Shoboh, Tokyo, 1982, pp. 227–229.

46 R.R. Mitchell and H. Friedman, *Sandplay: Past, Present & Future*, p. 61.

47 Vipassana, meaning 'to see things in depth, as they really are', is one of the oldest meditation techniques in India. It was rediscovered and taught more than 2500 years ago as an art of living, a way to get rid of any kind of suffering.

48 D. Siegel, *The Mindful Brain*, p. 15, p. 332. COAL is the acronym for 'Curious, Open, Accepting and Loving'.

49 Tsoknyi Rinpoche is the author of several books. For example, *Open Heart, Open Mind: Awakening the Power of Essence Love*, Harmony Books, New York, 2012. My summary is based on my notes of his seminars.

50 L. Freedle and G. Morena in *Foreword*, p. x, in Dora Kalff, *Sandplay, A Psychotherapeutic Approach to the Psyche*, Analytical Psychology Press, Sandplay editions, Oberlin, OH, 2020.
    An overview to Evidence Base in relation to Sandplay provides Christian Roesler in Sandplay Therapy: An Overview of Theory, Applications and Evidence Base, *The Arts in Psychotherapy*, Elsevier, Number 64, 2019, pp. 84–94.

51 J. Kabat-Zinn, *Wherever You Go, There You Are. Mindfulness Meditation in Everyday Life*, Hachette Books, New York, 1994, 2007, p. 4.

52 P. Lehrhaupt, L. Meibert, *Stress bewältigen mit Achtsamkeit*, Kösel, München, 2010, p. 17.

53 V. Kaltwasser, *Achtsamkeit in der Schule*, Beltz Verlag, Frankfurt, 2008, p. 58.

54 B. Badenoch, *Being a Brain-wise Therapist*, p. 176 ff.

55 C. Germer, R. Siegel, P. Fulton, *Mindfulness and Psychotherapy*, Guilford Press, New York-London, 2013.

56 V. Kaltwasser, *Achtsamkeit in der Schule*, p. 59.

57 L. Reddemann, *Kontexte von Achtsamkeit in der Psychotherapie*, Kohlhammer, Stuttgart, 2011, p. 105.

58 *The Middle Length Discourses of the Buddha. A new translation of Majjhima Nikaya*, translated from Pali by Bhikkhu Nyanamoli and Bhikkhu Bodhi, Wisdom Publication, Somerville (Massachusetts), 1995, p. 145 f. In Pali language *majjhima* is the second of the five nikayas (collections) of the Sutta Pitaka, the collection of discourses, attributed to the Buddha and a few of his chosen disciples, which contain all the fundamental teachings according to Theravada Buddhism. Excellent commentary by B. Analyao, *Satipatthana: The Direct Path to Realisation*, Windhorse Publications, Cambridge, 2003.

59 Ibid., Note 142, p. 1191.

60 Vipassana teacher Joseph Goldstein in Mindfulness, A Practical Guide to Awakening, *Sounds True*, Boulder, CO, 2013, analyses the *Satipatthana Sutta* making clear its relevance for Vipassana.

61 Described in B. Alan Wallace, *The Attention Revolution: Unlocking the Power of the Focused Mind*, Wisdom Publications, London, 2006.

62 D.M. Davis and J.A. Hayes, What are the Benefits of Mindfulness? A Practice Review of Psychotherapy-Related Research, in *Psychotherapy 2011* (American Psychological Association), 48(2), pp. 198–208.

63 See: www.sbinstitute.com/Shamatha-Project;www.shamata.org.

64 D.M. Davis and J.A. Hayes, What are the Benefits of Mindfulness? pp. 198–208.

65 B. Badenoch, *A Brain-Wise Therapist*, p. 176.

66 D. Siegel, *The Mindful Brain*, p. 6.

67 B. Badenoch, *A Brain-Wise Therapist*, p. 175. She refers to S.W. Lazar, C.E. Kerr, R.H. Wassermann, J.R. Gray, D.N. Greve, M.T. Treadway et al. in Meditation Experience is Associated with Increased Cortical Thickness, *Neuroreport*, November 28, 2005, 16(17), pp. 1893–1897.

68 Ibid., p. 271 and D. Siegel, *Mindsight, Transform your Brain with the New Science of Kindness*, Bantam Books, Oxford, 2010, pp. 21–22.

Chapter 2

Neural integration and individuation

Martin Kalff

A first look at neural integration, individuation and Sandplay

In this chapter I shall attempt to point out the connections between the concept of neural integration and the Jungian concept of individuation. Louis Cozolino has reviewed several psychotherapeutic approaches from the point of view of neural integration and has concluded that the primary focus of psychotherapy seems to be the integration of affect and cognition.[1] If we consider that Jung, for example, had in mind an improved integration of the four main functions – namely, thinking, feeling, intuition and sensation – we could view his aims as going beyond the integration of affect and cognition. However, such a view would entail finding correlates in the brain processes for intuition and sensation, according to Jung's definitions.

In her book *The Brainwise Therapist*, Bonnie Badenoch explores in great detail the relationship between therapy and neuroscience and devotes a whole chapter to Sandplay. She points out that the very use of the sand element – be it wet or dry – is instrumental to vertical integration connecting body, the limbic region, and the cortex in the right hemisphere of the brain. Touching the sand can help re-establish a connection with early implicit memories of wellbeing or of painful experiences. Wet sand, for example, may look sticky, coarse or fear-inspiring; dry sand, by contrast, may look uncontrollable, resisting, fearful etc. Using figures to create scenes in the sand helps activate the right hemisphere, and thus come up with stories based on implicit, unconscious themes. She also emphasises the therapist's duty to pay attention to emotions, unshaped thoughts, bodily sensations, conjured memories, etc. Through the Sandplay of the patient, the implicit memory of the therapist may also sometimes be triggered. She therefore rightfully warns against drawing ultimate conclusions about the play, as they may be tainted by our own subjective perception.[2]

In the meantime, after the publication of the present book in its original Italian version, Sandplay Therapist Lorraine Razzi Freedle published a noteworthy article in the *Journal of Sandplay Therapy* with a helpful table relating activities in Sandplay to brain regions. Here she relates such activities as

DOI: 10.4324/9781003163503-3

sensory play, massaging the sand, pounding, dumping, flooding, destroying it, as well as the use of reptiles, snakes, and monsters to the activity of the brainstem and diencephalon. Creative play, symbolic expression, attachment themes and use of animals are connected with the limbic system. Storytelling, reflections, abstract, spiritual themes and the use of human Sandplay figures are more related to the neocortex.[3]

Levels of neural integration and the role of mindfulness

Dan Siegel, a contemporary pioneer in the field of brain science, has identified nine types of neural integration: It is worthwhile to examine them in some more detail as follows.[4]

Integration of consciousness and mindfulness meditation practice

The integration of consciousness refers to a mental quality which allows to maintain calm within a state of chaos, and it can be enhanced through mindfulness meditation. In this regard, Siegel quotes one of his patients:

> From the hub of my mind, I can view all the chaos, fear, terror, threats, brushes with death, wishes, and plans for death, pain … but in the hub, I am not those states, I am only the knowledge of those states … finally making sense of it all.[5]

Siegel explains that the open and non-judgmental presence of the therapist may prove enough to support the integration of consciousness. It involves acceptance of whatever arises in one's own awareness. Siegel encourages patients to develop awareness of their own breath and to pursue this practice at home. Then, he suggests extending awareness beyond the breath to whatever arises into consciousness.[6] Imagining oneself at the centre of a wheel may help achieve this kind of mindfulness, as one can observe all the states of mind appearing on its circumference. In this sense, the centre of the wheel is a metaphor for the brain's prefrontal region.[7] A key role here is played by the development of an 'inner witness' which supports being present with, instead of identifying with one's own sensations and emotions.

Vertical integration: brain and emotions

After delving into the topic of the integration of consciousness, Dan Siegel has described the vertical integration which connects the body, the limbic system (primarily involved in the regulation of emotions), and the cortex (primarily involved in rational consciousness). The vertical integration corresponds to what Cozolino refers to as 'top-down integration', which "includes the ability of the cortex to process, inhibit and organise the reflexes, impulses, and emotions generated by the brainstem and limbic system".[8]

The middle prefrontal region represents the focal point of the vertical integration, as this region is found at the intersection of the brainstem and the limbic region.[9] Focusing on the body sensations, such as becoming aware of the sensations produced by one's own feet touching the ground, by hands resting on knees, or by practicing the 'body scan' – as with MBSR and other meditative approaches – is an effective method to develop vertical integration.[10]

The 'body scan practice' consists in forming awareness of and getting in touch with the 'felt sense' coming from different areas of the body, starting from the feet up to the head, or vice versa. The goal of this type of practice is to stay in touch with and to be present with every sensation arising in the body, beyond the simple enumeration of 'foot', 'knee', 'abdomen' etc. with the aim to grasp a direct experience of the physical sensation involved such as lightness, heaviness, tightness, warmth, cold, pulsations, vibrations etc.

Dan Siegel views this practice as a way to get in contact with emotions pervading the body. However, this practice is not devoid of drawbacks when applied to therapy. Siegel describes the case of a patient who reported a strong feeling of panic arising whenever she reached the area of the chest during meditation. In consequence, Siegel temporarily brought the body scan practice to a halt and introduced other types of self-exploration strategies, such as developing the awareness of the movement of her fingers: this allowed her to explore a safe inner space. After succeeding in reinforcing her trust in her own ability to 'reside' with her emotions, Siegel did return to the body scan and helped the patient observe the sensation of panic that had previously arisen – this time, from a safe distance and without feeling overwhelmed. A few images reported by the patient during a later session enabled Siegel to trace the panic experience back to her fear of her father and stepmother. This in turn led to another, profoundly healing, vision: the comforting memory of the only photograph of herself and her natural mother who had passed away when she was only a three-year-old.[11]

Luise Reddemann, who has written on this subject, recommends taking small steps in the exploration of the body with patients dealing with person-ality disorders and trauma. In such cases she suggests, for example, starting with the perception of the chair or the floor in contact with the body, or by evoking positive visual or auditive sensations, in order to underline that the body is capable of engendering joyful experiences. Thus, she guides the patient to call to mind positive experiences acquired through eyesight or the sense of hearing. After such a preliminary phase, the patient can be invited to shift their attention to the breath, noting for example the effortlessness of breathing, its ever-changing nature and so on. She also emphasises the value of 'pendulation' between positive and negative experiences and vice versa, which can be included at this or another point.[12]

'Pendulation' was first recommended by the eminent trauma specialist and founder of Somatic Experiencing, Peter Levine. His use of the term 'pendulation' is encompassing and includes an exploration of opposite sensations such as 'completely frozen' and 'less frozen', 'helpless' and 'powerful', feeling 'islands of safety' and 'feelings of badness' within oneself.[13]

Trauma may be viewed as an example of lack of vertical integration at a neuronal level. It is, as Peter Levine calls it, an 'experience of disembodiment', both when someone is overwhelmed by bodily sensations and when they shut down to avoid them. He effectively describes vertical integration or embodiment, by contrast, as "mind and body, thought and feeling, psyche and spirit, as held together, welded in an undifferentiated unity of experience".[14]

Horizontal integration: right and left hemisphere

Horizontal integration is sometimes also referred to as 'left-right' or 'bilateral integration'. It serves the purpose of optimising the cooperation between the left and right hemispheres of the brain, and can properly develop only when vertical integration is well-established.[15] It allows for the maximum integration between our cognitive and emotional experience.[16]

Dan Siegel points out that, in the earliest years of life, the right hemisphere is more developed than the left. At this stage, the brain can grasp and reproduce non-verbal signals which dominate the modes of communication typical of the early stages in human development, including facial expressions, tones of voice, gestures, body stances etc. The right hemisphere mostly works in a holistic way, as it deals with images, body perceptions, and emotions. The mode is type 'E': this *and* that can simultaneously be true. The left hemisphere is connected with rationality, linear and verbal communication, the drawing of lists, grading things – all activities which develop faster in the middle of the second year of life. The left hemisphere is more of an 'either/or' point of view, or 'O' mode: if this is right, then the other one is wrong.[17] A yet further important aspect of lateral integration is the capacity of wording feelings and emotions. Patients suffering from alexithymia (in which lateral integration is missing) are unable to experience and consciously describe their feelings, cannot recall dreams and have limited imagination. This has been related to deficits in functions usually identified within the right hemisphere.[18]

Siegel illustrates the therapeutic integration of the hemispheres through the astonishing case of a 92-year-old patient reported to him by the patient's son, who was concerned about his father's depressive state of mind. The patient had a history of a childhood lacking in emotional warmth, and his professional life had required high logical and intellectual skills. He had an excellent memory for details; however, he would recount stories from his own life as well as family life with the utmost detachment. Siegel put the patient under observation and concluded that this behaviour was a consequence of a predominance of the left hemisphere; the patient needed help in developing the characteristics typical of the right hemisphere. Siegel adopted several techniques including the body scan.[19] He asked the patient to identify facial expressions of anger, fear happiness, etc., and to imitate them using facial expressions. He was also asked to keep a journal to record images and emotions and describe experiences, then he was asked to watch TV with the sound off and to focus on the images only, etc. At the end of the therapy, the patient was finally able to access his emotions. The experience was so liberating for both him and his wife that she felt as if he had had a brain transplant. She was amazed by how well he was able to tune to other people's feelings and how happier he was than ever before. The patient felt his life had taken on a new meaning.[20] I find this case history particularly appealing, as it shows in detail the techniques used for sti-mulating the right hemisphere and demonstrate the improvement in the quality of life that a bilateral integration can ensure.

According to an interesting hypothesis advanced by Siegel, mindfulness stimulates bilateral integration by enhancing awareness of one's sensations and emotions of mind and by activating a more distant witnessing function of those states. Body scan and awareness of one's own breath depend on the functional ability of the right hemisphere to access the body directly. The presence of an inner witness with the ability to recognise and name the experiences undergone by an individual may be related to the way the left hemisphere functions.[21]

Jill B. Taylor's experience of the right hemisphere of the brain

Neuroscientist Jill B. Taylor has provided a first-hand account of a stroke she underwent. Her experience provides an insight into the world of the right hemisphere of the brain and, in an astonishing way, it also sheds light on cer-tain aspects of mindfulness practice.[22] She witnessed the unfolding effect of a brain haemorrhage which inundated the left hemisphere of her own brain with blood, thus progressively impairing its functioning. She lost her coordination and balance, experienced excruciating pain in the head, her right arm got paralysed, and was no more able to talk or to understand language. However, in time she also experienced silence and peace from the usual ongoing mental state experienced in a normal state. She felt enveloped by a sense of calm and glowing euphoria. All the memories of the past or dreams about the future had dissolved and she now felt a sense of complete wholeness with her body.

During brief intermissions of clarity of thought, she managed to get help. It took eight years to fully recover the functionality of the left hemisphere, during which she had to learn basic skills all over again, like the use of a fork, and slowly also language. During her long recovery from the stroke, she enjoyed a pervading timeless sense of inner calm and happiness, a feeling of being connected with everyone, which caused her to question the good of returning to the outside world. In the end, it was the prospect to recount the deep peace she experienced to the outside community which provided the motivation for her recovery.

In her study, Taylor argues that living intensely in the present moment is the key to the feeling of peace, and that it was the shutdown of the left hemisphere of her brain that enabled her to experience it. The right hemisphere provides the experience of a timeless 'here and now', something similar to eternity. The left hemisphere, on the other hand, organises experiences in a chronological sequence – past, present and future.[23]

Jill Taylor's account underlines many of the elements that characterise mindfulness. During the practice, there is a movement away from the ongoing inner commentary, away from thoughts about the past and the future, and concentration on the present moment aiming for awareness of one's own sensations. This is a gateway to inner peace and joy. From Jill Taylor we learn that it requires a shift to the right hemisphere of the brain. At this point, I like to quote Jill Taylor's own words as a powerful call to abide in the present moment, which is a central theme to mindfulness:

> To the right mind, no time exists other than the present moment, and each moment is vibrant with sensation. Life or death occurs in the present moment. The experience of joy happens in the present moment. Our perception and experience of connection with something that is greater than ourselves occurs in the present moment. To our right mind the moment of now is timeless and abundant.[24]

Jill Taylor's most surprising intuition is probably identifying compassion[25] as one of the typical qualities located in the right hemisphere, which also seems to govern the understanding of life as universal and one. She explains:

> The present moment is a time when everything and everyone are connected together as *one*. As a result, our right mind perceives each of us as equal members of the human family.... Our ability to be empathic, to walk in the shoes of another and feel their feelings, is a product of our right frontal cortex.[26]

As a way of conclusion, Taylor encourages people to access the qualities located in the right hemisphere and to integrate both circuits, left and right, the left providing the tools to communicate with the outer world. She highly prizes, among others, a slower approach to life, the importance of pausing and asking oneself: "How does it feel to be here and to be doing this?". Closing the eyes and intentionally paying attention to the temperature of the air, the feeling of one's clothes, the quality of the fabric, soft, scratchy, light or heavy, the feeling of one's own skin – tensing and releasing, and then relaxing the muscles. This way, a person can gradually access the world of sensations and limit the activity of a busy mind. Lastly, Taylor argues that the simplest way to access the peace located in the right hemisphere is through gratitude.[27]

Memory integration: integration of implicit memory and explicit memory

In addition to the three aforementioned forms of neural integration, Dan Siegel has also focused on the integration of memory, narrative integration, state integration, temporal integration and interpersonal integration. In order to fully understand what they are, it may be useful to summarise Siegel's and Badenoch's discussion of those forms.[28]

Briefly, 'integration of memory' has to do with the ability to recognise how past implicit memories and their feeling tone affect the perception of current events. In the book-length study *Mind your Brain*, Siegel reports the case of a young adult who experiences irrational fears about a new job that she has been offered. By exploring these feelings, and by achieving a more settled and relaxed state of mind, an image of herself falling from a bicycle as a child and the feeling of getting hurt eventually surfaced. This helped her understand that the present fears were rooted in a past experience which was emotionally affecting her perception of the present situation. Thus, implicit memory – which by nature is not connected to time – helped her overcome her fears by building a connection to explicit (or biographical) memory.

Narrative integration: talking about oneself with sentiment

This type of integration fosters the ability to recount our own life experiences in a felt way by attaching a meaning which goes beyond mere rationalisation. Such an ability to narrate one's own story can be an indicator of a secure attachment experienced by the narrator during childhood, or of their ability to achieve it in the present. Narrative integration uses the left hemisphere's ability to select and plot a time sequence to create a story. Including in one's own story both positive and negative experiences is important in order to attach meaning. To examine the quality of the narration, which is an indicator of the type of attachment, Siegel resorts to attachment interviews.[29]

State integration: accepting opposites

This type of integration has to do with acceptance and integration of conflicting inner states, such as the need for closeness and aloneness, autonomy and dependence, taking care of someone and the will to control that very same person. This type of conflict often manifests itself in the form of Obsessive-Compulsive Disorders (OCD), where in the course of the very same day carefree moments may coexist with moods mostly driven by fear and by the ensuing need to control it. Here, too, Siegel uses a mindfulness-based programme which includes starting a dialogue with the agent that controls the mind. Indeed, a lack of integration of states leads to chaos or to rigidity.

Temporal integration

This type of integration focuses on becoming aware of the impermanence of life, its uncertainty, its lack of stability and its resulting in death. Integration takes place when – after we have become aware of our own or other people's mortality – we purposefully embrace its meaning. Our attitude towards life will change as a consequence to it.

Interpersonal integration

Personal integration is built up through the abovementioned types of integration, whereas interpersonal integration is achieved through the ability of being in resonance with others. From a neuronal point of view, this type of activity is mediated by mirror neurons. 'Mirror neurons' is the name given to the process in which the same neurons responsible for the planning and performance of an action or a state of body and mind are also activated upon observing the analogous action performed by someone else or the equivalent state displayed by someone else.[30] Pain, emotions and bodily sensations displayed by someone else are, therefore, simultaneously, spontaneously and automatically felt in ourselves. Accordingly, mirror neurons are instrumental to the understanding of emotions and intentions of others, an ability which has been called 'Theory of Mind' (TOM).[31] The ability to mirror the Other's inner processes lies at the core of empathy and compassion. Moreover, it is at the basis of co-transference and also makes the theoretical foundation of ERCS, the method proposed in this book. It may be important to mention that this mirroring ability does not work well when someone is stressed or anxious.[32] It is also for this reason that reducing stress with the help of mindfulness and finding ways to create an inner sense of feeling secure play an important role both in therapy and in supervision. This furthers interpersonal integration and results in the "we/us" of wellbeing both on an individual and on a group level.

Transpirational integration, the self and individuation

After introducing the eight levels of neural integration, Siegel discusses the concept of 'transpirational integration'. This level is akin to Jung's concept of experience of the Self.

Transpirational integration inspires all the dimensions of a person's being with life. In *Minding Your Brain*, Siegel explains that the reason for which he uses the word 'transpirational' is because 'transpiration' refers to an experience in which the person feels part of a larger whole, by transcending the self as defined by physical boundaries. At this level, not only can one experience a connection with other human beings, but can also experience a pure or essential self which foreruns external adaptation or accommodation.

Moreover, it opens the mind to a different dimension of perception. He continues: "The sacred suffuses each breath. Our essence, each step the holy penetrates each breath, our essence, each step through this journey of life".[33] In the same text Siegel also acknowledges that there exists a convergence between contemplative and religious practices on the one hand and, on the other, the experience of happiness and mental health as the focus of secular studies, insofar as transpirational integration may be detected in both.[34]

Notably, the (at least, to me) unexpected emphasis on the 'holy' connects well with the fact that C.G. Jung noted that the experience of the Self – which, from the perspective of the more limited world of Ego Consciousness, is an experience of connection with a larger whole – has a 'numinous' quality. To quote Jung on the Self:

> Its phenomenology is exemplified in mandala symbolism, which portrays the self as a concentric structure, often in the form of a squaring of a circle. Co-ordinated with this are all kinds of secondary symbols, most of them expressing the nature of the opposites to be united. The structure is invariably felt as the representation of a central state or of a centre of the personality essentially different from the ego. It is of numinous nature, as it is clearly indicated by the mandalas themselves and by the symbols used (sun, star, light, fire, flower, precious stone, etc.).[35]

Jung then expands on the body-mind connection and on the importance that the experienced centre may also become "a spiritus rector of daily life". This perfectly corresponds to Siegel's view of the extent to which transpirational integration fully pervades life.

The language used here by Siegel and Jung is so similar as to have prompted me that indeed there may be a close connection between what Jung calls the 'individuation process' and Dan Siegel's concept of 'neural integration'. Among other commonalities, may I point out the similarity between Jung's idea of the union of opposites and what Siegel expresses in his 'neural integration of states'.

Jill Taylor also notes connections between her own experience and Jungian psychology. She discusses conflicting parts of personality and the need to reconcile them. Of course, engaging in this reconciliation also turned out to pave her way towards healing. As we have learnt, this involved the reconnection of the functioning of the right and left hemispheres of the brain. In this context, Taylor briefly touches on the typology developed by C.G. Jung and relates his view of the four functions to the right and left hemispheres; accordingly, she ascribes feeling and intuition to the right hemisphere, and thinking and sensation to the left.[36] This certainly makes a lot of sense.

As previously discussed, in the process of individuation one is confronted with the task of achieving a balance of the four functions, although of course it can never be fully attained, as especially the integration of the so called 'inferior function' is viewed by Jung as next to impossible.[37]

Neural integration and individuation in *The Red Book*

Jung came up with the germs of the individuation process through his exploration of his own mind recorded in *The Red Book*. [38] He felt compelled to open up to the world of dreams and inner images as a way to overcome a deep crisis which he was going through. This crisis followed the separation from Freud and was linked to his subsequent need to find his own path. In addition, there was also the threat to his marital life posed by the beginning of his liaison with Toni Wolf. On a collective level, it was also the time right before the outbreak of World War I, the news of which was broken on him by threatening visions. The earliest records of his journey he entered in the first of the *Black Books*, from which he would later copy many passages into *The Red Book*, a painstakingly crafted text inspired by the Middle Ages and to which he would also add some breath-taking illuminations and illustrations of his own making.

It is at the beginning of *The Red Book* that he described an inner passage from the 'spirit of this time' to the 'spirit of the depths', indicating the change of attitude which he needed to achieve in order to preserve his mental health. Here follow some of his characterisations of the two different attitudes:

> I have learnt that in addition to the spirit of this time there is still another spirit at work, namely that which rules the depths of everything contemporary. The spirit of this time would like to hear of use and value.... The spirit of the depths has subjugated all pride and arrogance.... He took away my belief in science, he robbed me of the joy of explaining and ordering things, and he let devotion to the ideals of this time die out in me.[39]

About the spirit of the depths, he then points out: "My speech is imperfect. Not because I want to shine with words, but out of the impossibility of finding those words I speak in images. With nothing else can I express the words from the depths".[40]

It was this passage towards images, dreams, and the letting go of the need to explain which enabled him to meet his soul not as an object of scientific study, but as a living and self-existing being. It was only in this way that he realised that he had lost his soul "whose wealth exists in images".[41] It is, in the light of our previous discussion of lateral integration, also a passage about the functioning of the right hemisphere, which presents itself as a non-rational realm beyond words, as a source of images. The world of logic, classification, words, explanations, had to be left behind in order to gain access to this other side, and for Jung to begin his own process of individuation. It led him step by step to the encounter and integration of conflicting parts within himself, manifesting as dream figures, a story of murder, meeting ancient figures such as Salome and Elias, a hermit, images of a devil or shadow, death and renewal of the image of god, a descent into hell, and an encounter with an inner guide – amongst others.

Figure 2.1 The Red Book

Jung here narrates this inner journey in a way which shows the depth of his feelings and the power of his physical reactions. For example, in describing a particularly horrific scene, he writes: "I break out in a profuse cold sweat … the horror paralyses me: what will happen?"[42]

The work of bilateral integration of the right and left hemisphere began for Jung by crafting a 'narration' of his (often) stormy inner life in the so-called *Black Books*, personal journals where he would jot his dreams and figments of imagination. The process continued through selecting and copying chosen passages from the black books in a painstakingly executed medieval font in

The Red Book, where Jung added hand-painted illustrations as well as comments and reflections to the narratives about inner experiences that had surged from his own depths. Later, through the development of a systematic psychological language in his academic publications – a language which often bears witness to his flair for living experiences first-hand in terms as 'shadow' and 'anima' – the bilateral integration reached a new level of completion. Jung had to open himself first to 'the spirit of the depths', thus 'limiting' (so to speak) the impact of the left hemisphere on the brain. Later on, he would increasingly connect the world of the 'the spirit of the depths' with the world of rational concepts. This served as a basis for building – along with the watchful observation of the healing processes of his patients – a complex psychological system to describe and communicate the universal nature of what first he had to experience himself.

Jung did not know, of course, the current form of mindfulness practices. Yet, it is known that he practiced some yoga.[43] Moreover, the very way in which he painted and wrote the font of *The Red Book* testifies to his own way of mindfully being present with what he was doing. His love for the simplicity of life in a very physical sense (which he would later practice by retreating periodically into the solitude of his tower in Bollingen, a primitive work of stonemasonry offering not much comfort and where he used to cook in a simple fireplace) offered ample opportunity for mindfulness.

Neural integration and individuation: the need to integrate the animal within

Our modern brain has preserved some evolutionary traces from our animal ancestry. With respect to this, it is worth mentioning the theory of the 'triune brain' expounded by Paul D. MacLean in the 1970s.[44] The theory attempts to account for some of the conflicts arising between our rational, structured, educated attitudes, and the deeper instinctual drives which clash with them. In Sandplay scenes made by children showing symptoms of ADHD[45] the conflicts may manifest for example through the use of the figures of dinosaurs invading a carefully constructed city and destroying much of it.

Some of our reactions, especially when we are faced with threat and danger, require speed and therefore bypass the more elaborate (yet slower) process of thinking related to the neocortex.

Cozolino summarises this theory thus:

> At the core is the reptilian brain, little has changed through evolutionary history and it is responsible for activation, arousal, homeostasis of the organism, and reproductive drives. The paleomammalian brain (or limbic system) – involved with learning, memory, and emotion – wraps around the reptilian brain. The highest layer, the neomammalian

brain – primarily the cerebral cortex and a large portion of the corpus callosum (the bands of nerve fibres connecting the left and right hemispheres) – is required for conscious thought and self-awareness.[46]

According to MacLean's theory, the reptilian brain coincides mostly with the brainstem. His theory is compatible with Darwin's evolutionary theory, as well as with observations regarding emotional expressions which are common among humans and animals alike.[47]

Cozolino argues that, from a contemporary point of view, the theory is probably oversimplistic, as it does not take into account the changes that the reptilian brain and paleomammalian one have gone through, but only considers the evolution of the neocortex. Moreover, Cozolino points out that there are no clear demarcations between layers, as MacLean suggests, insofar as regions such as the insula and the cingulate cortex belong to both the paleo- and the neomammalian cortices.[48]

There is no doubt, however, that the human brain shares many evolutionary traits with animals, for example the primitive subcortical fight-or-flight response circuit in common with reptilian ancestors, which enables immediate response to a sudden threat. More details about this are provided by Peter Levine in his contribution to the work on trauma which is also largely based on ethological observations, that is, the study of animal behaviours. In his bestselling book *Waking the Tiger*, he claims that:

> No matter how highly evolved humans become in terms of our abilities to reason, feel, plan, build, synthesize, analyse, experience, and create, there is no substitute for the subtle, instinctual healing forces we share with our primitive past.[49]

In outlining Porges' polyvagal theory of emotion, Peter Levine points to three evolutionary levels[50] which are relevant to the understanding of trauma and its workings. The most primitive reaction upon confrontation with threat, when escape is not possible, is an 'immobilisation', or 'freeze' response, for which the unmyelinated vagus nerve is responsible.

The same reaction is observed in animals when they fail to escape a threat, like an impala falling to the ground when attacked by a cheetah. From the outside, the impala looks dead and makes no visible movement. This is an altered state of consciousness during which no pain is experienced, which offers the possibility of coming back to life and escaping in a split second when the cheetah is off guard. Levine argues that humans share with animals this primitive reaction to threat.

However, it may be observed that when animals get out of immobilisation, a tremor goes through the entire body – this allows them to discharge the pent-up adrenaline-driven reactions, which were triggered before escaping or attacking. In humans who experienced freezing in life-threatening situations, there is the similar need to discharge the energy through tremor and/or other physical reactions, such as anger-driven physical movements of self-defence. If such discharge does not take place or is suppressed, the person may remain frozen emotionally and physically throughout much of their life. Levine concludes that, since trauma and its effects abide within the body, work on trauma needs to take place on the physical and preverbal level, as the speechless terror of trauma cannot be broken through by words alone.

The origin of immobilisation is to be found in early fish species and dates back to about 500 million years ago. The following step in evolution led to the development of the sympathetic nervous system, which originated in reptiles about 300 million years ago. This system is relevant for the response of mobilization, and is active during flight-or-fight responses. When mammals appeared about 80 million years ago, a new development occurred in terms of attachment system. It is referred to as the 'smart vagus' or 'social engagement system', and consists of the myelinated branch of the vagal system which exerts an inhibitory, modulating and calming effect on the arousal of the sympathetic system. Most importantly, it enables the communication of emotions via facial expressions and vocalisation. In a threatening situation, the first response is communicating one's own emotions to others by looking at them, making eye contact, and by making sounds. This is, for example, the only way in which babies can try and get help. If this level of reaction does not elicit the expected response, one resorts to the more primitive strategies issued from earlier stages of evolution.[51]

Accordingly, although the triune brain model needs revision and modification, it is helpful inasmuch as it makes us aware of the important inheritance our brain shares with reptiles and mammals. Therefore, as noted by a neuroscientist, in the work with clients we have to be prepared to simultaneously treat a human, a horse, and a crocodile.[52] The following image (Figure 2.2) may provide a visual equivalent to this situation.

Carl Gustav Jung about the inner animal

In *The Red Book* we find Jung's interesting clarion call to live "one's own animal side". The author describes an inner vision of dead parts of himself which had to be left behind, but also of masses of dead people in human history, victims of force and power, including unredeemed victims of the persecutions of Christians. They caused unrest and seem rebellious. Jung commented: "They forgot only one thing, they did not live their animal side". Then, he paints a somewhat idealised picture of animals:

> Consider animals: how just they are, how well behaved, how they keep to the time honoured, how loyal they are to the land that bears them, how they hold to the accustomed routes, how they care for their young, how they go together to pasture, and how they draw one another to the spring ... there is not one that tries to enforce its will on those of its own kind.[53]

Figure 2.2 Representation of the triune brain in a Sandplay scene

The dead rise back from the collective unconscious mind as unredeemed aspects of the past. The dead introduce themselves as Anabaptists[54] on their way to Jerusalem in search of safety. The deeper Jung delves into the unconscious through the process of 'active imagination', the more these figures – which are part of Swiss religious history – actually emerge.

The Anabaptist movement was suffocated by the Evangelical Church, and many religious leaders were killed. In 1982, and again in 2004, the Evangelical Church pleaded guilty and apologised for their gruesome misdeeds against Anabaptists. The fact that Jung's father was an Evangelical pastor bears some relevance here.[55] It may be argued that the terrible vision of his son Carl Gustav could be interpreted as the rise of a collective shadow of the Church itself, shadow elements probably inherited from his father. Jung describes the dead as victims of power, radical souls without any hope, riotous and unredeemed. In responding to this vision, he felt he could have benefited from the modest and social nature of animals.[56]

Jung's further comments point in that direction:

> He who never lives his animal must treat his brother like an animal. Abase yourself and live your animal so that you will treat your brother correctly. You will thus redeem all those roaming dead who strive to feed on the living.[57]

The animal side we don't embody and live is projected onto our own fellow humans, who then appear to reflect the unknown shape of our own neglected parts. Many expressions we use to insult others – such as 'dirty pig', 'mad dog', or 'chicken' – are symptoms of these projections.

There also seems to be something missing from the lives of those who do not live their animal side, as they appear dead, deprived of the inner compass provided by instinct and animal wisdom. Thus, Jung's 'individuation' process and the journey described in *The Red Book* issue a clarion call to live one's own inner animal, and to integrate the animal side into one's life. Jung showed the importance of heeding the animal through the discussion of the case of an elderly woman whose belief in God was put to the test by the horrors of war. In her dream the patient was singing a hymn which expressed her belief in Christ and contained the words "Whose blood and righteousness shall be my festal dress and jewellery". While she was singing, she saw a bull madly running around in front of her window. Subsequent to taking a jump, the animal got one of its legs broken. She felt pity for the bull's agony and thought someone should kill him.

Jung observes that, in her dream, the woman had tried to appease her doubts by singing a praise to Christ. This stirred a conflicting animal element within her which, according to Jung, was an aspect that had been repressed by Christianity. He also points out that in Mithraism the bull was the focus of mythology, as opposed to the lamb in Christianity. He then comments: "But when the animal in us is split off by being repressed, it may easily burst out in full force, quite unregulated and uncontrolled". Jung argues that the dream is an attempt on the part of the unconscious to reconcile Christian ideas with their opposite, the animal instinct. The attention is shifted towards compassion for the suffering animal within. According to Jung, the tendency that surfaced in the dream has an intrinsic value, and he adds: "The Christian love of our neighbour can extend to the animal too, *the animal in us*, and can surround with love all that a rigidly anthropomorphic view of the world has cruelly repressed".

Repression, according to Jung, makes the animal beastly, and he believed that it is because of such a repression that Christianity has spilt so much blood through the wars it has waged. Thus, he highly valued the establishment of a healthy relationship with one's own inner animal, and continued:

> If every individual had a better relationship to the animal within him, he [/she] would be also set a higher value on life. Life would be the absolute, the supreme moral principle, and he would react instinctively against any institution or organisation that had the power to destroy life on a large scale.[58]

The animal in Sandplay

Living one's own inner animal is a point of paramount importance which also finds expression in Sandplay. When looking again at a Sandplay scene, one should pay attention to whether the scene contains humans or animals. If both elements are present, another question should arise as to whether there is harmony between humans and animals or – as with Jung's example – there is conflict. The conflict between humans and animals can be expressed in manifold ways. Animals may be shot, hunted, slaughtered, confined in small spaces, they may attack humans, and so on.

A ten-year-old boy with anger-management issues (primarily directed against other fellow pupils and his own parents) built several sand scenes in which animals rebelled against the abuse on the part of technology, which was seen as a threat to both them and their environment (Figure 2.3). In one scene, humans build pathways deep into a virgin forest, destroying great part of it on their way. The boy shows animals attacking trucks, jeeps, baggers, and even houses. A rhino spears an excavator with its horn, buffaloes surround a jeep, a lioness knocks a truck over, elephants overthrows a building, tigers tears down a street and stops a truck from passing, and so on. A mighty phoenix bird, sided with the animals, perches on a small hill on the far-left side and surveys the whole scene.

The boy's anger was conveyed by images corresponding to sad occurrences in the present world, which are certainly also a source of anger for those who care about animal life, the environment and other related issues, such as climate change. Every day we get to witness to what extent greed may destroy rainforests – our planet's breathing apparatus – thus depriving animals as orangutans of their habitat and threatening them with extinction.

Figure 2.3 The rebellion of the instinct

Detail: a lioness knocks a truck over

In another sand scene, the boy depicts a group of humans chasing zebras, buffaloes and elephants to butcher them. The animals are freed by another group of humans who approach the scene in a tank. This hails the beginning of a cooperation between man and animals, were it not for the conflict about the right of man to kill animals for food, which the boy (who was vegetarian) strongly questioned.

Only in one of the last scenes does peace come about for the animals, when, far from any human activity, they settle down in an oasis in the desert. Conceivably, this corresponds to the boy's decreased vulnerability to the behaviour of others, and therefore a lesser proclivity to fight back.

Out of balance: our relationship with outer animals

The summary of the Sandplay process provided above does not only clearly show the inner conflict underlying impulse control, but also exposes the more generalised and dangerous conflict the human race is waging against animal life.

Animals have currently been reduced to mere means of production. They are victims to unprecedented levels of cruelty as they go through a process of being reared and slaughtered on a scale which was unheard of during Jung's lifetime. The sheer numbers are staggering: 60 billion land animals and 1,000 billion marine animals killed every year for consumption.[59] Profit, and not their well-being, determines the treatment of those animals. Their living conditions are dire: for example, a typical battery-farm a chicken lives in 0.043 square meters of space. This is less than European A4-sized sheet of paper.[60] As many as 50,000 chickens are housed in the same coop. Under these conditions, they cannot stretch their wings, move around, or scratch the ground; accordingly, they become aggressive and peck at each other. Instead of allocating them more room, their beaks are trimmed.[61]

Regular use of antibiotics is needed for bare survival. In the USA, 80% of antibiotics produced are employed on animals. The overuse of antibiotics is responsible for antibiotic resistance (MRSA).[62] This increasingly represents a problem, as patients with MRSA need to be confined to isolation wards and treated exclusively with reserve antibiotics, as first-line drugs are no longer effective. Every other poultry package in Germany has been found infected with MRSA-resistant germs.[63] These substances are found in rivers, in the soil and in drinking water.[64] This is just one example of the extent to which animal mistreatment at the hands of humans impacts our own health. In industrial rearing conditions, animals are not even permitted to reach maturity naturally, but are genetically and hormonally conditioned to grow faster and produce more while dooming them to suffering and illness for the sake of profit.

Despite being unlawful, the system fails to prevent chickens from being boiled alive and cows from being slaughtered while still conscious and without anaesthetic. This applies to an estimated amount of 39.6 million chickens per year in the European Union, according to a report published by *Compassion in World Farming Trust*. [65] A butchery employee testified: "I have seen thousands and thousands of cows undergo the slaughter process alive".[66] The employees in charge of preventing this from happening do not have enough time to monitor the fast-moving, automated process of butchery and cannot stop the machines as it would lower productivity.[67] One employee of Tyson Food reports:

> So, you have what is known as a 'killer', whose job is to catch those birds so that they are not scalded alive in the tank. They come at you 182–186 per minute. There is blood everywhere … on your face, your neck, your arms, all over your apron. You are covered in it. You can't catch them all, but you try. Every time you miss one you 'hear' the awful squawk it's making when you see it flopping around in the scalder, thumping against its sides. Damn, another 'redbird'. You know that for every one you see suffer like this, there have been as many as 10 you did not see.… You shut down all emotions eventually.[68]

Nowadays literature, movies and television reports are available to bear witness to the many forms of torture inflicted on animals for mass production. A further issue is the loss of biodiversity, with the extinction of entire species due to the impact of human activity.

Besides the issue of pain inflicted on animals, a second crucial issue is the impact of meat production on climate change and world hunger.[69] By way of example, the production of one pound of beef produces 50 times the amount of gases compared to the production of 1kg of wheat, contributing to the worsening of the greenhouse effect. All in all, meat production is said to contribute to global warming more than the transport sector, which is estimated at 13%.[70] A great part of agricultural production is not used for human consumption, but as animal fodder. Growing soya for animal consumption requires massive deforestation of rainforests. In the United States, 70% of cereals produced and 80% of drinking water is used for intensive animal breeding[71] – this requires 775 million tons of wheat and corn every year, which could feed about 1.4 billion starving people.[72]

All of this provides reason enough to reduce or stop altogether the consumption of meat, or at least ensure it comes from producers who attach importance to animals' well-being. The hope is that if more knowledge about the current abuse of animals becomes available and wide-spread, measures will then be taken to reduce it. However, at present the impact of information remains limited and the problem persists.

In the discussion of the patient's dream, Jung points out that our anthropocentric vision of the world needs to be questioned. The movement for animal protection has been called 'speciesism' and has been defined by Peter Singer as "a prejudice or attitude of bias in favour of the interests of members of one's own species and against those of members of other species".[73] It amounts to a collective, self-centred attitude, which justifies the abuse of animals in the service of the so-called 'interest' of humanity and its greed. This attitude has been defended since antiquity – philosophers such as Aristoteles, and theologians such as Saint Augustin thought that animals existed in order to serve humans.[74] Saint Thomas of Aquinas maintains that "love of one's neighbour" does not include animals.[75]

The belief that animals do not feel pain and do not have feelings is often used as a justification for cruelty against them. Descartes – whose dictum "cogito ergo sum" is a manifesto of rationality – claimed that "animals are nothing but simple machines, automata. They feel neither pleasure nor pain nor anything else at all".[76] In the light of modern knowledge, this has been proven to be false. Animals are known to feel compassion and display altruistic behaviours.[77] Could it be that the lack of empathy and inability to feel is being projected onto animals by those who deny feelings in animals?

Our relationship with animals seems out of balance and may also be seen as an indicator of a collective psychic health problem or, at least, as a dangerous one-sided attitude. In the terms of Jungian psychology, it is a manifestation of the Shadow. If one approaches issues expressing a shadow quality, one usually meets denial and resistance. The issue of the suffering of animals in industrial meat production is an example of that. We also have reason to believe that the lack of access to one's own inner animal determines a lack of concern for outer animals.

Balancing the triune brain: some hopeful dreams on the relationship with animals

The development of a positive relationship with one's own inner animal may be achieved alongside an increase of inner balance as well as of self-confidence. This can be illustrated by a meditation experience and subsequent dreams reported by a client who had come to work on a variety of issues touching upon her relationship with the masculine and negative effects of a previous illness. She was already well advanced in the awareness of her inner processes and, incidentally, had animal protection close to her heart. At some point, I guided for her a meditation on the inner animal, a practice which I have developed. In this kind of meditation, after a moment of silence you are invited to allow an animal to appear unpromptedly. This is the inner animal, and it expresses an instinctive part of the meditator. You examine how the animal feels and you also open to the emotions and physical sensations it evokes. In the next step, you determine what the animal needs in order to feel contented, and then you imagine offering whatever it needs. In the end, you experience the contentment of the animal again in your felt sense and emotion. Here follows the description of what she experienced:

> I saw the horse in a narrow stable box. The reddish-brown horse obviously did not feel well – I had the impression he felt completely constrained. He was vigorously banging his hooves against the wooden walls of the stable. Wooden slivers and splinters were fluttering around. While keeping a steady eye on the horse, I opened the box, and addressed the horse with a soothing voice until he turned his head towards me and was able to see me. With enticing words and a carrot in my hand, I calmly stood next to the opened box. Now the horse had noticed the opened lock-up, and was coming towards me. I managed to get a hold of the horse's reins and led him to a wide pasture. Here I set him free. I didn't have to impart any instructions anymore! The noble, elegant animal neighed, dashed full of lust and energy, boisterously took leaps, resumed running again, slowed down, galloped and started cantering – and came towards me! He stood before me, and I didn't say or even think anything, nor gave it any instruction. The animal's joy, liveliness, power, and the drive towards freedom was communicated to me so I could really feel it. Now I was able to caress and stroke the horse, look into his eyes, now gentle, mysterious and yet familiar.... He turned towards me. I got completely lost in those soft, deep eyes, until also this experience dissolved softly.

I have quoted her description in full as it brims with life and conveys well the intimacy of the experience which follows the release of the inner animal from its restraints. This meditative experience was followed by a dream in which she visited a horse stable. One of them stretched out its head towards her. She was able to feel its unbounded joy and expectation to be petted. The spark of the scintillating joy of the horse fully came to her and the horse, brimming with confidence, laid its head onto her chest. She in turn put her arms around the horse. She would later say it was as if she and the horse had always known each other, and felt mutual devotion and trust. The joy of this encounter lingered on the whole day. In the dream it was said that the horse was male, a gelding.[78] She felt that it had to do with her relationship with the masculine which had begun healing.

In another dream she had to clean windows or mirrors in a woman's house. This woman was living with a big, gorgeous venomous snake. As she engaged in the task of cleaning, she had no problem with the snake in spite of its closeness to her. The snake was aware of her presence, and even looked in her direction. Its expression was benevolent, peaceful. Later, the snake's owner moved it further away, so that she was able to speed up her work, but the dreamer could still see it.

She was aware of the possible sexual meaning of the snake. The closeness with that aspect of the snake brought her to another healing step in terms of her relationship with men. Both the horse and the snake appearing in the dreams reminded me of the vertical integration of the brain, the need to work with 'a human being, a horse and reptile' at the same time. Through the meditative elements in our therapeutic work, she also got more closely in touch with the world of physical sensations and emotions – a likewise important basis for neuronal integration.

Meditating with the outer animals, meditating on the inner animals: a film

For some years I had the opportunity to teach meditation courses in an alpine retreat centre on Mount Rigi, Switzerland: the name of the retreat is Stiftung Felsentor, and it also has a section devoted to the protection of animals. A few rescued animals that have been restored to freedom have found shelter there, and in the day time they are allowed to roam freely. Among them are sheep, goats, pigs, and also chickens, ducks and geese. They are devotedly taken care of by Franciscan nuns and Zen expert Sister Theresia. One day the idea dawned on me to give the groups of visiting meditators the opportunity to sit in silence with those animals, outside or sometimes even inside the stables. The encounters with those animals had a special feeling about them, as the participants had already achieved a much higher awareness through meditation. Alongside some accounts of the witnessing of various amazing abilities of such animals as cows, turtles, and eels, this experience enabled many meditators to realise on a deeper level that animals are sentient, feeling beings deserving our respect and fair treatment. I once had the opportunity to shoot a short film with the help of a fine director which illustrates this work with a twofold focus on both the inner and the outer animal.[79]

Mandala as a symbol of neural integration

To come back to Jung's individuation process, it may prove useful to examine a selection of images painted by one of his analysands – images he understood to illustrate well the individuation process.[80] Jung provides rich and insightful understanding of the images, which I recommend studying directly in his text. My goal is only to call attention to the unfolding animal symbolism in those pictures – a symbolism which I view as an expression of the neural integration of the brain encompassing all the evolutionary levels, namely the reptile, the mammal and the human.

Suffice it to mention that these pictures have been painted by a 55-year-old American woman in search of her roots in Europe in connection with her own mother's origins in a moment of her life when she felt stuck in her development. Jung mentions a "positive father complex" and an ensuing difficult relationship with the mother.[81]

In the first painting she expressed her feeling stuck through a scene inspired by an unprompted inner image (Figure 2.4). The lower part of her body was stuck between some rocks by the sea. She felt imprisoned and helpless. Then Jung appeared dressed like a sorcerer from the Middle Ages. This sorcerer touched the rocks with his magic wand, whereupon the rock crumbled down and she was finally able to step out and break free.

Figure 2.4 Stuck and helpless

The image depicts the lower part of her body – the sphere of the instinctual processes triggered by the womb and sexuality – as if frozen and stuck. It is an image which is close to the experience of those who, under the impact of trauma, remained 'frozen' or 'paralysed'. Jung does not provide enough information about her for us to understand whether in one way or another she had gone through traumatic experiences marked by helplessness. He does mention, however, a difficult life and a major surgical operation. We can sense from the image that the vertical integration providing access to the whole sphere of the body may have been stuck as well. The liberating healing force appears to be activated through her encounter with and transference on Jung. His appearance in her imagination as a sorcerer from the Middle Ages nicely reflects Jung's keen interest in alchemy and inner closeness with the Middle Ages, which we have already discussed with regard to the fonts used in *The Red Book*. The image does not express the woman's liberation yet, although – as Jung notes in his commentary – the rounded stones suggest the shape of eggs and thus point in the direction of new seeds of life in contrast to the piercing, sharp stones that the woman embraces.

In the second image (Figure 2.5), Jung's patient portrays a lightning bolt setting a rounded object with a reddish core in stark contrast to the surrounding rocky landscape. Could it be the representation of a breast? The painter herself came to the understanding that the round object was a fitting symbol standing for human individuality. The act of liberation is here

Figure 2.5 New life seeds

expressed, as Jung notes, not any more in terms of a human encounter, but of an impersonal one occurring within nature. The sphere, as Jung observes, is a symbol of a mandala in embryo, and, as such, a universal symbol of wholeness. The red colour inside it points towards a beginning of an emotional growth which starts to thaw a frozen self-image.

It is in the third image (Figure 2.6) that animal symbolism shows up for the first time. A sphere moves through outer space and on the left, also in outer space, a snake appears. In this image a black winged snake penetrates into the core of a circle resembling a plant as well as a stylised womb. The painter was aware of the sexual connotation of this image representing fertilisation. This was the start of a whole series of mandala images, dreams and inner transformations that accompanied it. It also led to the development of the ability on the part of the analysand to feel despondency about her own lack of offspring.

In the above image (Figure 2.7), we see a wonderful, light-radiating mandala, with a blue 'soul flower' in the centre; the sphere is divided into an upper part with rainbow-coloured half circles and a lower part with snakes moving on brown, earth-coloured lower half circles. In the lower part also the head of a ram is portrayed between two crows. A few signs from the I Ching[82] are also included, incorporating influences from the East into the circle. The polarity of the snake and the bird is a recurrent pattern in mythology, and it often shows up in Sandplay images. They may well represent (among others)

Figure 2.6 Fertilisation

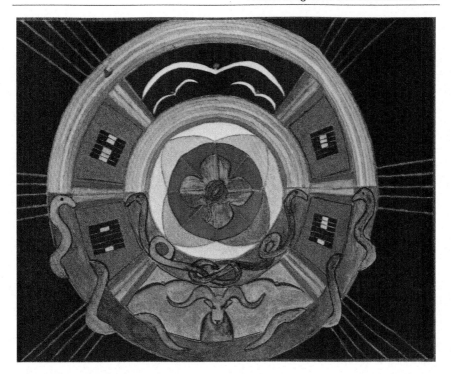

Figure 2.7 Completing the opposites

the mental ability to detach and observe, on the one hand (a quality ascribed to the prefrontal cortex), and, on the other hand, the impulsive and reflex world pertaining to the limbic and reptilian systems of the brain. The mandala also features the ram, an animal belonging to the mammalian realm. It indicates the task of integrating both body and mind. In his elaborate commentary on it, Jung also expands on the opposites of the three white birds as symbolic of the spirit and divine trinity contrasted by a lower trinity made by the two black crows and the ram, expressing a lower trinity that represents shadow aspects of Christian spirituality.

In the nineteenth picture (Figure 2.8) several different levels appear to converge within the circle: we see the human level represented by a man with birds in the upper circle, men riding a horse and an elephant in the left and right circles, as well as a man with snakes in the lower circle. Then the animal realm is represented by the bird, the horse, the elephant and the snake. As Jung's client was progressing in her individuation process, the image possibly also suggests the integration of functions of the neocortex, the limbic system, and the reptilian brain, or neuronal circuits pertaining to those evolutionary levels in the brain. These four medallions are also in the colours often attributed to the four Jungian functions – namely, yellow for intuition, red for feeling, blue for thinking and green for sensation –

Figure 2.8 Neural integration

which could also be seen as an indication of the client's advanced individuation process.[83] Thus, these mandalas point both to the individuation process and to the progressing neural integration of the brain. This bolsters the hypothesis that the mandala may be viewed as a symbol of neural integration.

The symbolic value of Buddhist mandalas

In this section, I'll turn to Buddhist mandalas. Understanding their deeper nature will help us see how not only can they be viewed as symbols pointing to a deep level of individuation, but also of neural integration. C.G. Jung did not fail to notice that the mandalas he himself or his clients had spontaneously painted (often based on dreams or on the process of active imagination) shared a common archetypal ground with the mandalas from the Far East, notably of the Buddhist lore and the Hindu one. As a matter of fact, the term 'mandala' – which he used for these circular structures – had itself been borrowed from Asian culture.

In Buddhism mandalas mainly occurred in the late phase of Buddhism, which is known as Tantric Buddhism. Tantric Buddhism, in turn, is part of Mahayana Buddhism (Figure 2.9). An important feature of a mandala[84] is a central palace as the dwelling of the Buddha. This concept had already arisen in the pre-Tantric Samdhinirmocana Sutra, where we find the following passage:

Figure 2.9 The mandala palace

The Bhagavan [title of the Buddha] was dwelling in an immeasurable palace arrayed with the supreme brilliance of the seven precious substances, emanating great rays of light that suffused innumerable universes ... an unimpeded mandala ... arisen from the root of supreme virtue that transcends the world. It was characterized by perfect knowledge, the knowledge of one who has mastery.[85]

The description is surprisingly similar to the abode of wisdom described in the alchemical text *Aurora Consurgens*, published, translated and commented by Marie Louise von Franz. There we find that whoever enters this palace is filled with bliss and stands face to face with the Sun and the Moon. The walls of that abode are of pure gold, and the gates scintillate with pearls and jewels. Various forms of virtue are said to lie at its foundation.[86]

The development of a transcendent abode of the Buddha in Tantric Buddhism includes the idea that this appears on top of mount Meru, the central mountain of the universe, surrounded by various circles of protection (sometimes circles of fire) which cannot be penetrated. It is not of a physical nature, but a manifestation of the wisdom of the Buddha in the form of light and energy.

Mandalas constructed with sand or in paintings represent a bidimensional plan of the mandala which has to be imagined in three dimensions. The centre is occupied by a square structure representing the palace with four T-shaped entrance doors. They are placed on a crossed *vajra*, a type of thunderbolt, partially visible on the four sides outside the walls. These walls are surrounded by various protection circles, including cemeteries and walls of fire surrounding the ones occupied by fierce forms of the Buddha. They are used in initiation rites, where disciples are introduced to the mandala, as well as the Buddha residents.

The Buddha forms in the mandala are referred to as 'deities'. The initiation rite empowers disciples to engage in a regular practice of 'deity yoga' involving visualisation of the mandala and its deities. In deity yoga, one connects with their own inner potential to become awakened by imagining the state of awakening itself represented by the enlightened world of the mandala. The mandala can be understood as a symbol of the Self and the practice consists in imagining all the potentials of wholeness to be fully realised.

In Tantric Buddhism we find a great number of peaceful manifestations of the Buddha in a subtle form known as 'body of delight' (Sanskrit: *Sambhogakaya*). They include both masculine or feminine forms such as the Buddha of compassion, Avalokiteshvara, or the feminine Buddha, Tara. However, we also encounter Buddhas in wrathful appearance. Some tantric forms of the Buddha are also shown in erotic union, symbolic of the union of wisdom and compassion. This wealth of different forms is said to arise according to the disciples' varying dispositions and needs. If we study some of the mandalas in Tantric Buddhism in detail, such as, for instance, the *Chakrasamvara Mandala*, it becomes evident that the mandala and the specific forms of Buddha deities, dwelling there are the result of a transformation of basic negative mental dispositions such as ignorance, anger and passion into a state of liberation or awakening. Chakrasamvara has four heads, 12 arms and is in union with his consort Vajrayogini with one head and two arms. Their feet press down a masculine figure and a feminine one who represent pre-Buddhist deities. This is a very different image from the traditional representation of the Buddha as a monk in the position of meditation: even if Chakrasamvara and the consort overthrew the pre-Buddhist deities, they manifest in a similar form as those deities. It is explained that, in the process of taming the pre-Buddhist deities, the Buddhas took the same external form as those deities. From the Buddhist standpoint, the pre-Buddhist deities symbolise mental disturbances or shadow elements which need to be overcome, such as anger and desire. However, in their appearance the Buddhist deities, they maintain aspects of this 'shadow' they have overcome, purified from their destructive qualities and preserving some of its fundamental energy.[87]

Liberation is a state beyond suffering which is caused by disturbing mental afflictions. Buddha's manifestations in wrathful forms are indicative of a state where the disturbing mental factors are completely appeased, but the energy inherent in them has remained. This purified energy, separated from its destructive potential, can be redirected and used for energetic compassionate action. This process of transformation of basic negative emotions shows close parallels to the idea of transformation of the shadow C.G. Jung has put forth and, as mentioned above, as Dora Kalff and others have observed in the Sandplay process.[88]

In Sandplay, in effect, patients may first express their disturbing emotions (such as anger, restlessness, despondency, fear) through animals which they view as horrible, like bugs and snakes, or through depicting violent conflicts and catastrophes or chaotic situations. We can regard these first Sandplay scenes as expressions of undesired inner states, shadow aspects of the individual. In a later phase, similar elements may show up again, but arranged in a circular mandala-like pattern along with other figures representing psychical positive and unthreatening aspects; these are sometimes placed around a valuable centrepiece, such as a jewel or a personality. Violent conflicts are transformed into purposeful battles, and chaos gives way to more organised structures. In Sandplay, these images express the Self, which is capable of setting free and of complementing aspects previously arousing fear and worry in the psyche.

From a neurological perspective, it may be rightfully assumed that a complex level of neural integration proves necessary to reach these goals. It has to be understood as some type of transformative synthesis of subcortical impulses and higher mental and spiritual levels. Tantric Buddhism – which has conserved the practice of mindfulness in terms of the capacity to focus without distraction on the visualisation of the mandala and its deities, along with its new emphasis on images which is not to be found to that extent in early Buddhism – must have provided a fertile basis for such neural integration.

In light of our previous discussion of the integration of animal qualities, it might be interesting to note that some of the Buddha forms described in Tantric Buddhism feature animal heads such as the lion-headed female Buddha of the Dakini[89] type and the fierce, buffalo-headed Yamantaka. They occupy the central place in their respective mandala abodes. Tantric texts provide a great variety of accounts for the way specific Buddha forms came into existence. These accounts focus on the taming of those forces, often represented by pre-Buddhist deities, who need to be transformed and liberated to be awakened. One of the accounts of the origins of Yamantaka, the form of a Buddha with the head of a buffalo, may be used as a way of example, as it sheds an interesting light on some aspects of neural integration.[90]

It can be summed up as follows: a yogi who had already greatly developed his own mental qualities was meditating in isolation in a mountain cave. In his deep meditation he transcended into states beyond the ordinary physical world. As he was meditating in this way, a group of cattle rustlers brought a stolen water buffalo into the cave, killed it and started to eat its meat. Then, they finally saw the meditating yogi. As they feared to have a witness to their misdeeds, they cut off his head. When the yogi returned from his travels into other realms and discovered that he had no head anymore, he fell into a state of panic and anger. In the dark he found only the head of the buffalo and placed it onto his body in place of his head. He was overcome with blind rage and vengeance and, using his powers, not only did he slaughter the thieves, but, as his anger escalated, he killed many others, and became a veritable lord of death. In order to stop his raging destruction, followers of the Buddha made offerings and prayers to the Wisdom Buddha Manjushri. Manjushri saw no other way to subdue the raging yogi than to manifest in a similar wrathful form, the form of the buffalo-headed Yamantaka, a name which translates as 'The One Who Puts an End to Death'. On top of the buffalo-headed Yamantaka, he placed his own peaceful face as Manjushri. This way, he managed to fully subdue the raging buffalo-headed yogi and obliged him to become a protector of the Buddha's teachings under the name 'King of the Dharma' (Sanskrit: *Dharmaraja*).

The description of the yogi's meditative experience contains a dissociative element which may be held responsible for causing an inclination toward falling prey to split-off emotions such as anger. Subsequent to undergoing the traumatic violence at the hands of the rustlers, the rage and defence needed for survival gushed forth. The buffalo-headed yogi is symbolic of a state of being completely overcome by instinctual drives and of loss of balance as it can occur in traumatised individuals. They can be "flooded with intrusive emotions like terror, rage and shame", as Peter Levine observes.[91] The head of the Wisdom Buddha on top of the buffalo head of Yamantaka may in turn be understood as the supervisory presence of the impulse-inhibiting aspect of the middle prefrontal cortex. This is instrumental in the taming of the raw energy of rage and helps restore the psychic balance.

Through his own work with traumatised patients, Peter Levine discovered that allowing healing animal instincts to surface can lay the groundwork for spiritual experiences. This is the case when the compressed survival energy can safely be released through a gradual process of 'titration' and 'pendulation', key concepts in Somatic Experiencing. Titration essentially refers to the release of energies in very small amounts, and pendulation designates swinging back and forth like a pendulum between positive and reassuring sensations and more distressing ones. The application of these measures requires mindfulness. This leads to a safe and gradual discharge through physiological reactions such as trembling and shaking. These are, as previously mentioned, the spontaneous reactions observed also in animals coming out of immobilisation.

Following this gradual and controlled discharge, Levine's clients have often not only restored the equilibrium between the sympathetic and parasympathetic nervous system, but have also experienced such states as ecstatic joy, exquisite clarity, an all-embracing sense of oneness, peace and wholeness – all indicators of a deeply spiritual experience. Accordingly, Levine concludes that: "A surprising and unexpected tenet emerged: that spiritual experience is welded with our most primitive animal instincts".[92] This may also well be the case with the ancestral message conveyed by the fierce and animal-headed Buddhas who represent the wisdom needed to safely overcome and redirect blind rage.

This helps us better understand mandala symbolism in terms of neural integration moving vertically, and horizontal integration, up to transpirational integration. Thus, probing into the complex background of Eastern mandala symbolism can further contribute to bolstering the hypothesis of the mandala as a symbol of both neural integration and of individuation.

Notes

1 L. Cozolino, *The Neuroscience of Psychotherapy*, p. 61.
2 B. Badenoch, *Being a Brain-Wise Therapist*, 221 ff.
3 L. Freedle Razzi, Making Connections: Sandplay Therapy and the Neurosequential Model of Therapeutics, *Journal of Sandplay Therapy*, 28(1), Walnut Creek, California, 2019.
4 D. Siegel lists nine forms in *The Mindful Brain*, p. 292 ff., and in D. Siegel, *Mindsight*, p.71 ff.; B. Badenoch, *Being a Brain-Wise Therapist*, p. 33 ff.
5 D. Siegel, *The Mindful Brain*, p. 296. Another clinical example in D. Siegel, *Mindsight*, p. 178 ff.
6 D. Siegel, *The Mindful Brain*, p. 295 ff.
7 D. Siegel, *Mindsight*, p. 181.
8 L. Cozolino, *The Neuroscience of Psychotherapy*, p. 29.
9 B. Badenoch, *Being a Brain-Wise Therapist*, p. 34
10 D. Siegel, *The Mindful Brain*, p. 297 ff.
11 Ibid., p. 298 ff. D. Siegel, *Mindsight*, p. 132 ff.
12 L. Reddemann (editor), *Kontexte von Achtsamkeit in der Psychotherapie*, Stuttgart, 2011, pp. 107–112.
13 P.A. Levine, *An Unspoken Voice, How the Body Releases Trauma and Restores Goodness*, North Atlantic Books, Berkeley, California, 2010, p. 78 ff.
14 Ibid., pp. 279 and 282.
15 B. Badenoch, *Being a Brain-Wise Therapist*, p. 35.
16 L. Cozolino, *The Neuroscience of Psychotherapy*, p. 115.
17 D. Siegel, *Mindsight*, p. 106 ff., cfr. L. Cozolino, *The Neuroscience of Human Relationship*, p. 63 and the chapter on laterality in L. Cozolino, *The Neuroscience of Psychotherapy*, p. 105 ff.
18 These ailments are mostly due to deficient functions located in the right hemisphere. Cf. L. Cozolino, *The Neuroscience of Psychotherapy*, p.121, and *The Neuroscience of Human Relationships*, p. 69 ff.
19 Body scan is a mindful practice consisting in systematically paying attention and forming awareness of different body areas with a view to authentically 'feeling' and lingering on each of them.
20 D. Siegel, *Mindsight*, pp. 102–116.
21 D. Siegel, *The Mindful Brain*, p. 304.
22 J.B. Taylor, *My Stroke of Insight*, Hodder, London, 2009. My summary is based on this book (author's note).
23 Ibid., pp. 30–31.
24 Ibid., p. 30.
25 Ibid., pp. 134, 139, 170, 171.
26 Ibid., pp. 30–31.
27 Ibid., pp. 159–174.
28 D. Siegel, *The Mindful Brain*, p. 292–320; D. Siegel, *Mindsight*, pp. 71–76; B. Badenoch, *Being a Brain-Wise Therapist*, pp. 33–41.
29 Adult Attachment Interviews (AAI) are semi-structured interviews in which participants are asked to describe and evaluate attachment relationships in their own childhood following the model devised by John Bowlby.
30 J. Bauer, *Warum ich fühle, was du fühlst. Intuitive Kommunikation und das Geheimnis der Spiegelneurone*, Wilhelm Hayne Verlag, München, 2006, p. 23.
31 Ibid., p. 50.
32 Ibid., p. 34.
33 D. Siegel, *The Mindful Brain*, p. 320.
34 Ibid.

35 C.G. Jung, *Mysterium Coniunctionis*, CW XIV, 1970, § 776, p. 544.

36 J.B. Taylor, *My Stroke of Insight*, p. 134.

37 C.G. Jung, *Psychological Types*, CW VI, 1971, § 763, p. 450.

38 As Sonu Shamdasani explains in his foreword to the *The Red Book*, in 1913 Jung began this experiment on himself, a confrontation with the unconscious. Throughout this experiment, which ended in 1930, he devised a psychological self-exploration later named 'active imagination'. Jung would initially jot down his fantasies in the so-called *Black Books*, then he reworked them, added a few considerations, rewrote it in Gothic and Uncial fonts, and illustrated and illuminated this red leather-bound volume – hence, the name *The Red Book* – sporting the title *Liber Novus*.

39 C.G. Jung, *The Red Book*, p. 229.

40 Ibid., p. 230.

41 Ibid., p. 232.

42 Ibid., p. 288.

43 In his autobiography, Jung reveals that he would sometimes practice yoga in order to the master strong emotions overcoming him. Once calm was restored, he would allow images and the new-found internal voices to re-emerge and express themselves. The practice was intended to stimulate active imagination, whose objective is different from that of mindfulness, but we can find some parallels insofar as both are useful to clear the mind from thoughts and delve more in depth into the inner self. C.G. Jung, *Memories,* p. 212.

44 P. MacLean, *The Triune Brain in Evolution: Role of Paleocerebral Functions*, Plenum, New York, 1990.

45 ADHD is the acronym for Attention Deficit/Hyperactivity Disorder, and it refers to an evolutionary condition affecting the self-control system characterised by lack of focus and attention, as well as hyperactivity. The neurobiological and/or environmental genesis of the disorder is, and has been, subject of dispute within the scientific community.

46 L. Cozolino, *The Neuroscience of Psychotherapy*, p. 8.

47 C. Darwin, *The Expression of the Emotions in Man and Animals*, John Murry, London, 1872.

48 L. Cozolino, *The Neuroscience of Human Relationships*, p. 17.

49 P.A. Levine and A. Frederick, *Waking the Tiger – Healing Trauma*, North Atlantic Books, Berkeley, CA, 1997.

50 S.W. Porges is a researcher at the Kinsey Institute, Indiana University, and studies the interaction between psychology, neuroscience and evolutionary biology. Porges's development of the polyvagal theory sheds light on how the autonomic nervous system (ANS) controls reactions and behaviours of individuals who have suffered a range of traumatic experiences, such as sexual abuse, bullying, and traumas of the reproductive system which were diagnosed and treated. At present, Porges is developing the Kinsey Institute Sexual Trauma Research Consortium to help people overcome the effects of trauma. The polyvagal emotion theory developed by Porges posits that, in humans, the general state of the nervous system and the behaviours and emotions connected to it, rest on three fundamental sub-systems of neuronal energy. The most primitive of the three systems, is around five hundred million years old, and is shared with the very earliest fish species. The functions of this system are immobilisation, metabolic conservation, block, and it solely affects internal organs. The second system – more advanced in evolution and possibly dating back to the era of reptilians (three hundred million years ago) – shows the emergence of a global system of physiological activation corresponding to the sympathetic nervous system. Its function involves mobilisation and

escalation of the action (as with a fight-or-flight response) and it reaches the limbs. The third system, the most recent, dates back to eighty million years ago and can only be observed in mammals: it is a sub-system of the parasympathetic nervous system which in turn regulates the mammalian (or intelligent) vagus nerve, neuroanatomically connected to cranial nerves responsible for facial expressions and vocalization. In primates, it mediates complex social behaviours, attachment, and emotional intelligence.

51 P.A. Levine, *In an Unspoken Voice*, p. 97 ff.; L. Cozolino, *The Neuroscience of Human Relationships*, p. 85 ff.

52 Hampden-Turner quoted in L. Cozolino, The Neuroscience of Psychotherapy, p. 9.

53 C.G. Jung, *The Red Book*, p. 296.

54 Anabaptists would only baptise adults and they believed in the separation of Church and State. They had been present in Zollikon, and a person whose house I now inhabit, on Hinterzünen Street, belonged to the movement.

55 On relation between Carl Gustav Jung and his father Paul Achilles, see Paolo Ferliga, *Il segno del padre. Nel destino dei figli e della comunità*, Moretti & Vitali, Bergamo, 2nd Ed. 2011.

56 In this context, animals should be considered as the social engagement system and, therefore, should be related to the 'paleo-mammalian brain'.

57 C.G. Jung, *The Red Book*, p. 296.

58 C.G. Jung, *The Role of the Unconscious in Civilization in Transition*, CW X, 1970, § 30–33, pp. 20–22.

59 M. Ricard, *A Plea for the Animals*, translated by Sherab Chödzin Khon, Shambhala, Boulder, CO, 2016, p. 55 (original version: M. Ricard, *Plaidoyer pour les Animaux*, Allary Edition, Paris, 2014, p. 69).

60 J.S. Foer, *Tiere Essen*, Kiepenheuer & Witsch, Köln, 2010, p. 97, English Ed. J.S. Foer, *Eating Animals*, Little Brown and Company, New York, 2009.

61 A.F. Goetschel, *Tiere Klagen an*, Fischer Tagebuch, Frankfurt am Main, 2013, p.78.

62 M. Ricard, *A Plea for the Animals*, p. 66f.; J.S. Foer, *Tiere essen*, p. 163; A. F. Goetschel, *Tiere klagen an*, pp. 72–74.

63 *Der Agrarwahnsinn*, 3 SAT TV, 13 September 2012.

64 M. Ricard, *A Plea for Animals*, p. 67.

65 Ibid., p. 83.

66 Ibid., p. 82.

67 A.F. Goetschel, *Tiere klagen an*, pp. 83–84.

68 M. Ricard, *A Plea for Animals*, p. 84.

69 A thought-provoking and alarming study on the huge impact on climate change at the hands of the industrial production of meat is Dr. Moses Seenarine, *Meat Climate Change, the 2nd leading Cause of Global Warming*, Xpyr Press, Los Angeles, CA, 2016.

70 M. Ricard, *A Plea for Animals*, p. 61.

71 Ibid., p. 60.

72 Ibid., p. 58.

73 Wikipedia, *Speciesism*. P. Singer, *Animal Liberation* (1975), Harper & Co., New York, 2009, p. 8.

74 M. Ricard, *A Plea for Animals*, pp. 12–14.

75 Ibid., p. 14. Aquinas, *Summa Theologica*, II-II, q, 25, a.3, quoted by Larue, *Le végetarisme et ses ennemis*, pp. 104–105.

76 Ibid., p. 15.

77 M. Ricard, *Altruism, The Science and Psychology of Kindness*, Atlantic Books, London, 2015, Chapter 17, *Altruistic Behaviour Among Animals*, Marc Bekoff, Jessica

Pierce, *Vom Mitgefühl der Tiere*, Animal Learn Verlag, Bernau, 2008 (*Wild Justice. The Moral Life of Animals*, University of Chicago Press, Chicago, IL, 2009).

78 A gelding is a male foal that has been castrated as – in some horse breeders opinion – this makes the horse tamer and less prone to distraction than a stallion, and accordingly more suitable for such horse races as steeplechase.

79 *MediTiere!* Movie director Erika Eichenberger. Movie web in different languages: English: https://youtu.be/gwBAFzRvrR4; German original: https://youtu.be/dFWnf-KSIEM

80 C.G. Jung, A Study in the Process of Individuation, in *The Archetypes and the Collective Unconscious*, CW IX, 1969, § 525–626, pp. 290–354.

81 Ibid., § 525, p. 291.

82 *I Ching*, or *The Classic of Changes*, is deemed as the earliest Chinese classic, dating back to even before the establishment of the Chinese empire. Regarded by Confucius as a source of wisdom, it is popularly viewed as a divination text and it is utilised by scholars for delving into its mathematical, philosophical and physical principles. It lists several methods of divination ranging from tortoise shells to the tossing of three coins.

83 Jung's theory on personality traits (see *Psychological Types*) is grounded in the first place in the distinction between introvert and extravert. In the second place, Jung identifies four basic distinguishing psychic functions: sensation, intuition, thinking, and feeling. Each of these functions enables us to adapt to the world and to life. Thinking rests upon logical processes, feeling on value judgements, sensation perceives facts, and intuition senses the possibilities those facts may open up.

84 The Sanskrit word 'mandala' loosely translates as 'circle'. Jung couldn't help noticing that both he and his patients would spontaneously paint (often inspired by dreams or active imagination) images sharing a common archetypal ground with Asian mandalas, notably Buddhist and Hindu ones. The word 'mandala', used for naming these circular patterns, comes itself from Asia.

85 *Wisdom of the Buddha, The Samdhinirmocana Mahayana Sutra*, Dharma publishing, Berkeley, 1995, p. 5.

86 M.-L. von Franz, editor, *The Fifth Parable of the Treasure-House which Wisdom Built upon a Rock* in *Aurora Consurgens: A Document Attributed to Thomas Aquinas on the Problem of Opposites in Alchemy*, Inner City Books, Toronto, 2000, Chapter X, pp. 101–119.

87 See M. Kalff, *Selected Chapters from the Abhidhanottara Tantra: The Union of Female and Male Deities*, Columbia University, Ph.D. 1979. Available through University Microfilms International.

88 *The Process of Individuation* in C.G. Jung (conceived and edited by), *Man and his Symbols*, Doubleday & Company Inc., Garden City, New York, 1964, pp. 158 ff.

89 In Tibetan Buddhism, Dakini or Khandroma is a female Buddha. It translates as 'skygoer', 'sky dweller' or 'sky dancer'.

90 J. Landaw and A. Weber, *Images of Enlightenment, Tibetan Art in Practice*, Snow Lion Publications, Ithaka, 1993, 2006, p. 124 ff.

91 P.A. Levine, *In an Unspoken Voice*, p. 263.

92 Ibid., p. 348.

Chapter 3

A new supervision and therapeutic method

Martin Kalff

A new starting point

After about 20 years of work with Sandplay, which I utilise to further self-awareness and ease the individuation process, there has been a shift in my understanding of this work. On an external level, it started with the dissolution of an Italian supervision group I had accompanied for several years at my home in Zollikon. I noted an increasing lack of interest manifesting in irregular attendance and even tension among the participants. I decided to start with a new group including some of the participants from the former group. I felt it was time for a new emphasis in the review of cases, the scenes created by the clients in the sand, their paintings and dream images. As a result, the current group consisting of Italian therapists came into being: The Zollikon Experience-Related Study Group. By now it has come to conceive of itself as a group of supervision and research focused on a new approach towards a new understanding of Sandplay Therapy. On the occasion of the 22nd ISST Congress on Sandplay in Venice, I gave an overview of this approach and called it 'Experience-Related Case Study' (ERCS).[1]

The new emphasis of ERCS has aimed to include more direct awareness of the physical sensations and feelings participants would undergo while reviewing case material. Earlier, I had had the opportunity to attend many supervision seminars as well as case presentations all over the world and, eventually, as a teaching member, I had also taught this type of seminar myself. Much gain and insight could come from this type of exchange taking place prevalently on a verbal level. In all of this, of course, the experience and personality of the leader of the seminars proves crucial. Indeed, many of the seminars and case presentations with Sandplay images have become a transformative experience for the participants themselves.

Dora Kalff used to note that participating in a case presentation where there was a good approach to the solution of the problems would lead the participants through the same type of process, thus helping them establish a connection with their own positive potential. For this reason, when she presented her cases in a calm and sympathetic way, frequently many participants were deeply touched by

DOI: 10.4324/9781003163503-4

the process and felt deep inspiration. By observing and discussing the Sandplay creations, something got transformed within them. Notably, some of the Japanese teachers – who would frequently comment very little on the symbolic meaning of the images they presented – were able to create a space to become well-aware of the pain as well as the wonder and silence in some of the work they shared. Prof. Kawai, one of the founding members of the Japanese Society for Sandplay, was able to effectively convey the idea that the whole process in the sandbox or any striking elements of it are the result of the transference or the relationship between therapist and client.

In addition, in some of the seminars I attended, Prof. Kawai spoke of the difference between a 'strong transference' and 'deep transference'. A strong transference would be based on feelings of anger or strong attraction, whereas a deep transference he describes as an emerging relationship between the *Hara* of one person and the *Hara* of the other. *Hara* refers to the centre of gravity located below the navel. In martial arts it is also referred to as the "place from which the 'Sea of Qi'" can be reached and influenced.[2] *Qi* refers to vital energies which – as I had the chance to experience with my Aikido teachers – in the practice of martial arts is more basic and powerful than just the physical force based on the muscles. In his work on *Hara*, Dürckheim paraphrases it as the original centre in the human being, beyond the relativity of the ego, where the opposites have been united.[3] It could well be compared to the idea of 'wholeness' in the Psychology of C.G. Jung. According to Kawai, this 'deep transference' is a stage that needs to be reached to ensure the healing and improvement of his patients, and by listening to his presentations, it was possible to vicariously experience that stage.

Likewise, many of the case presentations and supervision groups I attended have proved helpful. They have helped build trust in the transforming power at work in many of the case studies. At the same time, the capability of the teachers to embody the qualities necessary to ease such processes could be experienced through their explanations and the quality of their presence.

Other experiences – albeit valuable – have also led me to understand that the emphasis on verbal exchanges could also bring along a certain competitiveness among the participants or the collective exclusion of some points of view which did not seem to fit into the direction that the discussion was taking. At its worst, I have learnt that some of the difficulties experienced by the clients could affect the mood of the groups in a negative way and give rise to ill-concealed aggressions, judgmental attitudes, and loss of empathy for some of the clients.

In making a new start, I intended to preserve what I felt valuable since the beginning, but at the same time to create more opportunities for the participants to share more than ideas. The aim was to access also the (often) unconscious sensations and emotions behind the ideas and concepts. The underpinning is that sensations and emotions come first, are mostly unconscious, and yet determine to a large extent the way we think and the way we express ourselves.

To achieve this, I decided to draw more fully on my experience of meditation, which at that time already included more than 30 years of practice. The project was to use those aspects which are not related to the practice of a particular religion to present some of the essential points in a secular way. Encouragement for such a step came – among others – from the successful adaptation of the practice of mindfulness into a therapeutic or clinical setting by Jon Kabat-Zinn.[4] I started to use moments of mindfulness to help participants to become more aware of what happens inside. 'Mindfulness' or 'being present with' can be seen as a fundamental aspect in any type of meditation. The use of colours and other creative media had already played an important role in workshops for psychologists and the general public I had proposed on major topics of Jungian Psychology and Buddhist studies. It was a way to convey knowledge different from my experience with university studies, which I perceived as one-sided and left-brain oriented.

I therefore drew on my previous teaching experiences and my own practice in order to help the participants in case study groups and supervision sessions to access co-transference sensations and feelings which arise from exposure to the presentation of the clinical history, the description of the relationship between therapist and client, and, of course, the Sandplay scenes.

Bodily sensations and feelings spontaneously arise, and it is natural to accept that other individuals may have different responses than oneself. There is no right or wrong in emotion-driven responses. We can more easily acknowledge that there exists a variety of possible responses in different people. If, however, we shift to the level of concepts, we are much more tempted to see some ideas as right and others as wrong. This can easily result in competition. On the other hand, sharing with the group our primary responses helps each participant acknowledge the relativity of their own response and open up to different ways to look at a given content, thus overcoming a state of single-mindedness. On this basis, there comes a time for reflection and analysis such as connecting biographical elements with the pathology, and reviewing family structures and social factors by cross-fertilising insights from a number of branches. Among them, it is worth mentioning at least Analytical Psychology, the world of symbolic meanings, or other approaches such as Stan Grof's Transpersonal Psychology, Dan Siegel's theory and practice of Mindsight or Peter Levin's Somatic Experiencing, aspects of neuroscience, and Systems Theory – to mention just a few. This final step I would call 'experience-informed reflection', a reflection which lays open its sensory and emotional basis and is informed by it.

Bringing this approach into a group was an enriching experience. The response of the new group was such that it sparked off a shared enthusiastic exploration and exchange based on the new inputs. This increasingly led to the idea that the group of therapists was not just a supervision group, but also a research group. The group became fertile ground for attentive consideration and discussion of the impact of the awareness of sensory and emotional dimensions for the understanding of Sandplay scenes, dream images, active imaginations and other aspects of the work with clients.

The activity of the group has helped to fine-tune the initially promising tools, and in time has inspired me to add new elements to both method and reflection. The new openness of exchange also created a stronger coherence among the participants, if not a veritable emotional bond, a sense for many to experience the group as a refuge when confronted with difficulties in the therapeutic work.

The importance of mindfulness and perception of body sensations

Moments of mindfulness significantly help move away from an outlook that is too conceptual, opinionated, based on interpretative stereotypes or based on automatic, impulsive responses to scenes and situations.[5] I usually encourage supervision group participants or individuals coming for an individual supervision session to pay attention first to the bodily sensations which occur in the present moment. These sensations include warmth, coldness, heaviness, lightness, tension, heart beating, sweating, headaches, pain, fluidity, fleeting sensations like tingling, etc. The participants are invited to acknowledge these sensations without judgment or internal commentary. It is an opportunity "to drop into the body", an expression which I borrow from the Tibetan Lama Tsognyi Rinpoche (oral teachings, 2012), or to 'inhabit the body' in a relaxed way. If thoughts arise, the recommendation is not to follow them, not to get lost in them, and to gently return to the awareness of sensations. Eyes may be open or closed.

Then, it may also prove helpful to pay attention to the sensations elicited in the whole body by the act of breathing. It may be likewise helpful to keep an upright body position, a position which allows the free flow of energies in the body. Should feelings arise, such as sadness, anger, boredom, restlessness, it is good to acknowledge their presence and to avoid branding them as 'good' or 'bad', but to accept them, and explore them with a sense of curiosity. One can wonder: "How do I know that there is anger, how does this state of mind express itself through physical reactions?" and then delve more in depth.

Certainly, there can be variations to this introductory phase; the main point, however, is to connect with both one's own body and one's own inner self in the present moment. Then, after three or more minutes of this type of 'proprioception', participants are invited to focus on a given Sandplay scene or a description of a therapeutic situation. It makes an opportunity to take a fresh look at it, and the invitation is to pay attention to any new bodily sensations or feelings which are aroused at that moment. A member of the group describes the benefit of this practice as follows: "[Having a moment of mindfulness] helps me not to immediately attach an interpretive label to the image and enables the image as a whole to maintain a life of its own" (quote from a questionnaire administered to the participants). After experiencing the Sandplay scenes or a therapeutic situation this openly, the members of the group share, first, bodily sensations and feelings, and then other types of reflections.

At first, I noticed that people have a hard time distinguishing thoughts from feelings. The need to distinguish thoughts from feelings is something that Marshall Rosenberg – the founder of 'Nonviolent Communication' – strongly emphasised. For example, the statement, 'I feel that this person has a personality disorder', does not express a feeling, but an opinion. Expressions of feelings, he mentions, are for example feeling "inspired, alive, quiet, content, fearful, lonely, irritated, restless etc.".[6]

By sharing comments and focusing on sensations and feelings, other types of reflections may be achieved, notably based on psychological meta-theories such as Jungian categories, information about the meaning of given symbols, specific pathologies that may be at play, etc. In my experience, the moments of sharing bodily sensations and feelings have a strong impact on the group. Listening to the descriptions of first-hand experiences – such as feeling choked, elated, sad, tense, blocked, heavy, or pain in given areas of the body – helps make contact with the human being often hiding behind the professional persona. This may make an important step towards creating a 'free and protected space' for the clients or the supervision group work. To quote a participant:

> Working in this way, I have understood many things about myself in relation to the clients, but also in relation to the Other in general. It is as if it proved necessary to cast aside one's own truth to establish an authentic relationship and to meet the Other's truth.
>
> (Based on a questionnaire administered to participants)

As already encapsulated in this statement, it is tantamount to listening to the experience-based sharing of others, which helps develop awareness of the relativity of one's own experience. This is crucial, for example, when a complex has been stumbled upon, as it happens in counter-transference. It may help set oneself free from it, not only on a rational level of but also on an emotional one.

This is illustrated by the following quote:

> In order to bridle and process the deep anger I was experiencing while lucidly looking at a scene, I felt a need to confront myself with the other members' experiences, as mine own showed a tendency to hold fast to my unquestioned beliefs. Only the possibility to shift my perception to a place (in the scene) toward which others had directed it, helped me sense that the vortex, which had been created in my belly, started to gradually dissolve and couldn't keep me prisoner anymore and lost its gripping power of control.
>
> (Based on a questionnaire administered to participants)

This experience illustrates well how awareness manifests on the body level and how, through the sharing with others, it can be transformed.

Such insights are more difficult to achieve as long as one doesn't manage to transcend the conceptual level, as one is more likely to remain unaware of the presence of fixations on both the physical and the emotional level. This can easily translate into an adamant clinging to one's own opinions. To quote another therapist from the group on a similar point:

> The opening of our 'system' to other ways of experiencing and becoming aware of different sensibilities, helps understand the relativity of our own experiences, especially when they have been overly polarized on positive or negative aspects.
>
> (Based on a questionnaire administered to participants)

Allowing oneself to experience a scene or situation based on moments of mindfulness tends to increase the ability to empathise with the client.

The experiential factor also helps understand in a deeper and more unmediated way one's own counter-transference/co-transference triggered by the client's creations in the sand. As in the actual therapy session, one may become aware of the patterns which condition our subjective responses or projections: in such cases, some moments of introspection may prove very useful to determine the origins of one's own subjective responses in the light of one's own biography. In the end, this helps reduce our own projections onto the clients.

These workings have been effectively described by another participant:

> It appears that the counter-transference, which is brought about through experience, helps not to respond in a symmetric or compensatory way, and not to take out one's own negative feelings on the Other. Therefore, the practice of mindfulness results in a newly-acquired ability to objectify our experiences and needs, thus disburdening our client from our own 'projections' and unrealistic expectations.
>
> (Based on a questionnaire administered to participants)

Such awareness can prove crucial for the therapists presenting their work, because this awareness may mark the beginning of a change in attitude and response during the actual therapy session and help overcome blocks which may emerge in it.

As an example of this process, may I mention the experience of a participant working with a six-year-old child with elective mutism.[7] She reported to the group feeling disoriented in front of the child's silence. Using mindfulness and the other ERCS techniques actually helped her better understand M.'s silence and his images found more emotional resonance in herself. As a result of that understanding, she reports: "I started to speak less with M., to fill less his silence with my words, to be able to stay more at ease in his silence, instead of rushing, urging, or trying to elicit words from him". This and other insights helped him in his Sandplay process, through which he managed to represent the trauma behind the silence. In the end, he started to talk in the course of a therapy session. In that moment, the therapist realised that – rather than praising him for those words – the best response would be to embrace him in silence.

Additional methods built on mindfulness

There are a number of techniques which can help become conscious of personal emotional patterns in responding to client materials. All of these techniques stem from the preliminary bringing to awareness of sensations and emotions. The first I call 'spontaneous embodiment'. First, a scene or therapy situation is presented in all the necessary detail. The members of the group are then invited to stand up and are asked to inhabit their bodies in silence while heeding their breath. Then, they look at the scene or internally review the information on the session they have received. They later close their eyes again, listen attentively to themselves for a while, guarding against any physical drive to move – for example, their fingers – while gently rocking their body backward and forward. Eventually, when they are ready, they are invited to swing their body in any direction they may wish with larger movements to spontaneously express whatever may have been stirred inside them. After a few minutes one has been experiencing these oscillations, they rest for a while and are present to witness the 'echo' of the movement while it manifests in vitality, as well as in feeling exhaustion, tension, pain, sadness etc. affecting specific parts of the body. Again, these experiences are shared in the group and then reflected upon.

A variation of this is doing this self-exploration exercise in pairs. One takes turns in initiating a movement which is simultaneously mirrored by the partner who repeats the movement. This helps feel a deep resonance with whatever experience is expressed by the partner.

We have sometimes noticed that participants – while responding to the client's inner blocks showing through a Sandplay scenes – remained themselves blocked and unable to move, thus showing that the pain and difficulty of the client, their 'frozen' state, is felt very deeply. Sometimes, exploring such a situation even more in depth enables to tap into inner resources arising from deep inside the body, and ushering a liberation of the movement and an ability to express in a fluent way feelings through spontaneous body movement. Using the body as an additional resource results in a more felt participation and a deeper empathy with the client's inner world. There is the possibility – which calls for still more systematic observation – that through the body we can even 'touch' emotions which the patient has not even become aware of yet. This has been brought up by a participant:

Our body becomes a vessel resonating with the emotions the patient is not yet able to identify him/herself, and this opens up the possibility that he or she may become more able to process them.

(Based on a questionnaire administered to participants)

This makes sense to me, because, if in our work we stumble upon some hidden emotions in the client, also as a group, this will nonverbally flow back into the relationship with the client and facilitate new levels of integration.

In a similar way colours or even sounds – possibly, from drums – can be used for translating the contents of a Sandplay scene. Another effective strategy may be asking the members of the group to write a short poem in response to a moment in the Sandplay process or even a sequence of several Sandplay installations. In addition, if dreams are part of the process to be analysed, I use the technique of 'entering into the dream'. After an initial moment of mindfulness, one enters the dream image, relives it, imagines the dream scene as vividly as possible, and this way they achieve a 'felt meaning' of the dream. This can also be used while working with a client in Sandplay Therapy. This technique should be used with caution if, for example, negative elements in the dream are too powerful or if the client is in a state of hyper- or hypo-arousal. In such cases, the client may be oriented first towards a positive feeling or only parts of the dream may be selected to be felt or one may remain on a more analytical or verbal level.

In special cases – provided that there is enough time or the Sandplay image is particularly difficult to interpret – valuable results have been achieved through engaging in a simplified 'dramatization' of elements in a Sandplay scene. For this reason, each group member is asked to choose a figure of the Sandplay scene being discussed. Then, they reproduce in the room the same arrangement as the central figures in the Sandplay scene itself. After a moment of mindfulness, the participants slipping into the role of an individual figures pay attention to the emotions and body sensations of the figure they are meant to represent. Then, they are given the chance to make a statement to others with words or with simple gestures that represent what they think, feel, and intend to do. Again, afterwards there can be an exchange and reflection about the dramatization of the scene that has been performed.

Dramatization may also be used when attempting to better understand significant interactions between therapist and client. Here, after a moment of mindfulness, two participants enact a situation which happened between therapist and client as the others are watching. This can prove especially useful to figure out the interactions in a therapy with a child, where sessions are expected to entail more physical movement in the room.

Of course, it is not possible to work or play with each Sandplay image in a patient's process to the same extent, and it is up to the group leader to set the right analysis pace by moving quickly through some points and pausing longer on others. Lingering on some specific moments in the process enormously eases the achievement of the 'felt understanding' of follow-up review.

This approach opens a space for intensive and deep participation in the case-studies we are working on. As Jung mentioned, interpreting and understanding the clients' fantasies is less important for a therapist than experiencing them directly. I would add that this approach also enables us to help clients do the same.[8]

Concerning the issue of the importance to become aware of body sensations and emotions for supervision and in the context of therapy for both therapist and patient I recommend the book by Marian Dunlea, Body Dreaming in the Treatment of Developmental Trauma[9]. In particular, the method of "orienting" the author is suggesting, appears helpful to ensure in her words that both "Therapist and client may work in a productive state of homeostasis" It can be used, for example, as a preparation before the session for the therapist and during the session when difficult dreams or topics occur which might be too unsettling if approached in a direct way.[10] It could certainly also be used for a supervision group in the beginning or while working with difficult issues.

Like a masked ball

This process can be illustrated through the following analogy: when we wear a mask and its matching disguise, to some extent we start to become the character represented by that mask, and to move away from our ordinary consciousness towards the world represented by the mask. We will also dance and move in keeping with the personality attached to the mask, as well as laugh, shout and talk accordingly. Then, once we drop the mask, we return to our ordinary self which has been enriched and vitalised by this experience. I believe that this is what happens also in experience-related supervision: we step out of our ordinary selves, make room for a deeper participation in the worlds we are studying even with gestures and movements so as to become to some extent of what we perceive, even though we don't identify with it. We are able to return to ourselves, to our own inner centre, but at the same time we understand in a deeper way the outer world.

Experience-related case study also has implications useful for Sandplay Therapy. It encourages the therapist to engage in mindfulness practice – be it through MBSR, *Vipassana, Shamata* or the practice of yoga or *Qi Gong* – in order to become a mindful therapist. ERCS prepares the therapist to become more aware of their bodily sensations, emotions and the co-transference expressed on that level during therapy sessions.

Mindfulness can also in many ways be introduced into sessions, for example by encouraging clients who have just created a scene to pause and focus on bodily sensations and feelings evoked by the Sandplay activity. Not everybody is capable of doing this, but also this approach may help show to what extent somebody is capable of relating to their own feelings. This approach could also be used at the beginning of a session. In my experience, it helps clients develop more presence and focus on their own issues.[11] This said, great attention has to be paid in order to find out whether, for example, the person has enough ego-strength or resilience, as concentration can also arouse fears. There are also risks in introducing to mindfulness clients who are very dissociated from their own feelings. In general, however, a variety of approaches have been developed in current psychotherapeutic practice to put to use the benefits of mindfulness with a number of clinical disturbances,[12] thus this aspect could certainly also be explored for Sandplay.

Notes

1   M. Kalff, Experience-Related Case Study: Like a Masked Ball, in *Journal of Sandplay Therapy*, 22(2), Walnut Creek, CA, 2013. From this contribution the paragraphs 4.2, 4.3 and 4.4 of the present study have been quoted, reworked, and expanded.
2   Wikipedia on *Hara*.
3   K.G. Dürckheim, *Hara, die Erdmitte des Menschen*, Otto Wilhelm Barth Verlag, München, 1956, p. 14.
4   Compare Jon Kabat-Zinn's first book *Full Catastrophe Living: Using Wisdom of Your Body and Mind to Face Stress, Pain, and Illness*, Delta, Worcester, 1991.
5   This chapter is an adapted excerpt from Experience Related Case Study: Like a Masked Ball, by the author, in the *Journal of Sandplay Therapy*, reported here with the permission of the *Journal*.
6   M.B. Rosenberg, *Nonviolent Communication. A Language of Life*, 3rd edition, Puddle Dancer Press, Encinitas, 2015, p. 43–46.
7   See the contribution by Chiara Bottari published in the present volume.
8   C.G. Jung, *Two Essays on Analytical Psychology*, CW VII, 1966, § 342, pp. 212–213.
9   M. Dunlea, *Body Dreaming in the Treatment of Developmental Trauma*, Routledge, London and New York, 2019. It was published after the publication of the Italian original version of the current text.
10   Ibid. p. 7.
11   Daniel Siegel offers convincing and detailed examples of how mindfulness and the technique of the body scan – alongside other related techniques – can be applied to therapy in his book *Mindsight*.
12   C. Germer, R. Siegel and P. Fulton, *Mindfulness and Psychotherapy*, Guilford Press, New York, 2013, Section III, Chapters 8–13.

Chapter 4

A process of healing

Neural integration and individuation in Sandplay

Martin Kalff

May I express my gratitude to the patient whose healing process I will detail in this chapter for granting me permission to share with our readers selected images, related emotions, reported physical sensations and aspects of the story of a woman in her early forties. The following presentation endeavours to protect the anonymity of this client by focusing on her inner processes rather than on her personal details. The selected moments of this process are meant to shed new light on the workings of the psyche across different levels of neural integration and individuation when it is provided with a space to play and with the encouragement to experience to the utmost sensations and emotions connected with it. For an enhanced understanding of this process I have resorted to my notes from a review of the Sandplay scenes with the client's help; such a review was carried out after the completion of the therapeutic program. Any references to the review will be specified in next sections.

Background

The ostensible motivation for the client to embark on therapy had been the question: "How can I successfully meet irksome and numerous job-related demands even while preserving my humanity?" In the course of our work – which extended over a period of three years – a further motivation emerged, which can be paraphrased as follows: "How to build trust and develop capability to love in spite of a background of childhood abuse?" Important elements of her history include a life-threatening situation at birth including a C-section performed on her mother 14 days before her expected birth. In addition, her mother had developed MS after her birth, thus experiencing excruciating pain that impaired her walking ability. In consequence, she had to entrust relatives with her baby for one and a half years.

On top of that, the person she had been told to be her father later turned out not to be her biological father. Her mother only admitted that he wasn't her father on her deathbed. The explanation she then offered was that the client's stepfather was sterile. With the blessing of her husband, the mother had then conceived both my client and a son; their father was a man with

DOI: 10.4324/9781003163503-5

whom she had had a relationship solely in order to have children of her own. This fact was kept secret from the children, and they were made to believe that the stepfather was their biological father. The mother would later interpret her own illness as a punishment by God for her misdeed.

The biological father was known to her as an 'uncle'. When she was 32 years old, she told him that she knew him to be her biological father; this occurred shortly before his death. He had frequently come to visit her and her brother during her childhood, and she had always liked him. The stepfather, by contrast, sexually abused her in her younger days – which accounts for her feelings of disgust for him. Once she had reached adulthood, she confronted him about it. He made no reply to this accusation, but she got the impression that he had understood.

My client told me that the stepfather had developed an anxiety neurosis when she was 8 years' old and, in consequence, he was bedridden most of the time. Her mother had then been working in the family business and had been in charge of everything in spite of her illness. She would later die from cancer when my client was 25.

From a very early age she had been expected to help at her parents' shop and had been mainly in charge of cleaning. Because of the great amount of work the shop required, there had been no holidays for her. There had been other episodes of sexual transgression by people involved in the parental business. Her mother, frequently ill, had not been there to protect her.

Despite her difficult beginnings – marked by anxiety and narrowness of horizons – my client had managed to build for herself a successful professional life. However, her job was extremely demanding and she had trouble coping with some of its most stressful aspects. At some point, she even experienced a mental shutdown during a presentation in front of a large group – this, among other factors, motivated her to engage in Sandplay Therapy. Our work lasted three years. As she had to commute from a distant location for our therapy sessions and was highly motivated to process the emotional material provided by these sessions through drawing and reflecting at home, there frequently were long hiatuses between our sessions, sometimes of one or even two months.

An initial dream image

In her first session, she talked about various challenges in her work, provided biographical details and also brought up several short dream images. One of them was: "A herd of elephants is marching across a field with delicate plants, none of which are damaged by the elephants". I was particularly impressed with this image, which established a contact with the world of her own inner animal. The image combined the power and weight of the largest land animal with the delicate aspect of plants, yet the plants emerge miraculously unscathed from the elephants' march. A union of opposites has taken place in this dream, the large and the delicate. I interpreted the mystery of the image as a sign of hope. As I was listening to her, I was able to feel her power. She was in distress, but this had not broken her. At the same time, she was capable of describing her state of mind and emotions with subtlety.

The elephants live in herds led by a matriarch and have the ability to march long distances through desertic lands, with their leader sensing from a distance of many miles the water source that can quench their thirst. On a symbolical level, elephants have long been connected with wisdom. Had there always been deep inside of her a similarly latent sense of direction? I felt quite at ease in our mutual exchange, a certain flow which in this case came into being from the beginning of our therapy sessions. I suggested she should draw this as well as other dream images. She became so absorbed in this drawing task that this helped engender in her a sense of being alive, as she herself reported. In the second session more sharing of her past and present stress followed, along with tears.

The first Sandplay: a sense of trust

Then, at the third session, she was ready to engage in Sandplay. She experienced how her hands would reach deep into the sand, how something inside of her burst open at that. Afterwards, she became keenly aware of how the hands were raised. This first interaction with the sand aroused a feeling which deeply moved her. While discussing it, she admitted to feeling amazed by the overwhelming power of her own emotion, which was easy to witness and was felt by me as well.

The image was made of three figures drawn on a stretch of dry sand with a somewhat triangular elevation in the middle and soft flowing lines along its sides (Figure 4.1). At its centre lay a sitting Buddha in red robes. On the left there was the wooden figure of a little rabbit and on the right a reclining Chinese figure which she picked out in order to represent an old woman resting.

The image was a simple one, but meaningful to her. The woman is very tired, but she can rest – which also means she is able to fully surrender. By contrast, this is something her mother had never been able to do. She was moved to tears by this moment of letting go. She said that she felt trust. The reassuring presence of the Buddha in equipoise enabled her to feel so, she said. On top of that, even though the rabbit (a wooden one in her Sandplay scene) is an apprehensive animal, it can reveal its presence fearlessly while also feeling protected. Creating this Sandplay scene stirred within her the memory of a dream she had had three days earlier.

There was an obituary notice of the passing of the Dalai Lama. On the notice there were little images of wooden Buddha figures, which she connected with the wooden rabbit in her play. To her the Dalai Lama represented love and wisdom, a hope for the world itself. During the analysis of the dream I offered the idea that if, in her dream, the outer Dalai Lama passes away, the inner Dalai Lama should be nurtured. She very much agreed on this suggestion. When, at the end of the Sandplay process, we reviewed this scene and the related dream, she reported that the more she learnt to concentrate on the inner meaning, the easier it was for her to open up also to the outer aspect of

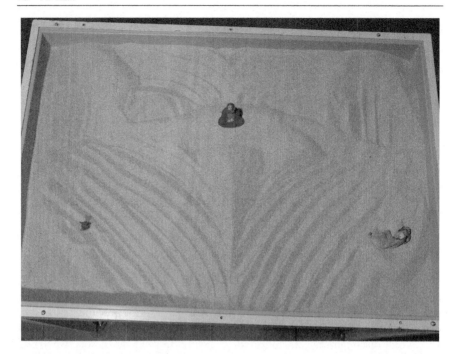

Figure 4.1 Self-reliance

Detail: resting Chinese Woman

the impermanence of life. This reminds me of Dan Siegel's discussion of the concept of temporal integration, the neural network in the brain which underpins acceptance of one's mortality and the impermanence of life.

In my understanding of it, the Sandplay conveyed an important message of trust, a trust in her inner workings, but also trust in our rapport. She said that with me she felt a space which made deep experiences possible. I saw – and I still see – this as a mutual process, as her trust and openness also made me feel open towards her. Trust is a valuable gift which makes play and – through play, neural integration – possible. She was able to discuss some events in her life which caused her to realise (among other things) to what extent childhood experiences may lead to re-enactments, in painful circumstances, of a time in her professional life where her trust had been abused and taken advantage of. She also recalled the times when she had to step into the cellar and kill rats with a stick. Once a rat climbed up inside her trousers – a feeling of disgust mixed with memories of abuse, which would sometimes also take place in the cellar.

Mother-child union on the animal level

Given the amount of negative memories burdening my client, I was glad to witness the surfacing of a positive one in the course of the following Sandplay session. It was the memory of a moment of peace, a time when she had sat alone near some beautiful birch trees at sunset. It was the Sandplay process that apparently conjured up this memory, as while telling it she was placing the small figure of a monkey holding a monkey cub as if they were peacefully sitting under some palm tree at the centre of the scene (Figure 4.1). She told me that – while arranging the figures – she experienced an unspeakable sense of quietude. The only urge she felt was that of silently resting her hands on the sides of the central shape moulded in the sand.

The appearance of a mother-child image on the animal level may be seen as the beginning of an important healing process taking place on the instinctual level. It is also the beginning of a healing of her negative relationship to the mother, or 'negative mother complex', as Jungian psychology calls it. In quite a number of Sandplay creations by individuals characterised by a negative experience of the primary relationship, I have noticed that symbols of the mother-child union often occur on the animal level first. This indicates a nonverbal level connected to the limbic system, or the level of the neomammalian brain.

In the corners of her Sandplay, my client had placed two Egyptian figures representing the god Horus in the shape of a falcon. She may not have known that Horus had been a major deity in the early Egyptian mythology, a solar god of light considered to be a protector of children. His quality of protector of children indeed fits the positive memory of childhood which the work in the sand had evoked. In our review at the end of the process, she commented that the sun had always been important to her, and that she had always perceived it as a protection.

She carefully placed also a shell with a seagull sitting on it, as well as a sea star in the blue space representing water. Also in this case associations which came to

Figure 4.2 Quiet and protection

Detail: monkey mother and cub

her at the time of the final review were striking. She then associated the seagull in the shell with a "flying pearl", as she called it. As is commonly known, a pearl is born of a secretion of the shell to protect itself from a foreign body. On the shell my client had applied a reddish spot which she saw as a blood stain, in turn symbolically related to the wound inflicted on the shell by the penetration of the foreign body. The precious quality of the pearl, then, originates from pain. Likewise, in her own life something precious had been born of a wound, as she realised more clearly through the work with Sandplay.

While musing on the story of *Jonathan Livingston Seagull*, she felt that Jonathan – like herself – had to embark unaccompanied on a difficult journey without ever giving up before finally succeeding. During the same session she also recalled a productive meeting with her boss at work. After this break-through, she continued to produce drawings inspired by her dreams and to bring them to the following therapy sessions.

Facing death and darkness

Then, in a later session she described a new dream:

> I was washing my hair. Then, I became suddenly aware that it was time to drink a deadly poison. I knew that – after drinking it – it would take from half an hour to two hours until death came.

She felt that probably much of her ego identification still had to die. In addition, she also dreamt that two of her female friends had passed away, one shortly after the other.

With regard to the former dream, I asked what she would do in the short time left before her death. Her answer surprised me. She said she would 'visualise'. Although she did not expand on what she meant exactly by 'visualisation', it dawned upon me to ask her whether she wished to 'visualise' right there and then. I felt that, in general, confronting someone with their last moment before death could trigger unwished-for fears, yet – based on the trust between us – I thought that she could make it through this experience emotionally unscathed.

I did propose a brief mindfulness meditation by focusing relaxedly on her breath. Then, I invited her to enter her dream, to imagine the moment of drinking the poison and the last one and half hour before dying. During her meditation, I was witness to a strong emotion on her part, conveyed both by the expression on her face and by some tears rolling down her face. As she was moving according to her 'visualisation', she also described the experience in progress. This enabled me to encourage her to focus on some specific details and to be present with them as her inner images and feelings were building up.

At first, she experienced a deep sense of nescience accompanied by darkness. The darkness then dispelled and she saw water, then a pond with lotus flowers. She proceeded further into the scene and saw the tiny filigree-like roots of the lotuses. Then, even further down, a new darkness was lurking. Suddenly, as she touched its deepest point, light rose. She saw and felt it in her feet, then it rose slowly up the body. At this point, I suggested she should fully open up to this experience and sense it through her body. She felt how progressively the whole body got filled with light and how it emanated outwardly. She was then able to accept what was happening as it was per se. I recommended she should stay a while and only eventually return to the sensation of breathing, then slowly come back to the actual world and open her eyes.

She spoke of a strong sensation in the breast. It was a strong experience for her to the point that she meant to recall it and linger on it also at home to draw it with coloured crayons. She showed me the drawing during the following session. I felt moved by how she had faced and embraced her own darkness. It had brought therapy to a turning point and, from the darkness of nescience, light finally emerged. I thought that it was important that the image she used for describing it was a tangible light which would move up the body from the feet. This helped her not to dissociate herself from her own body. Her encounter with death and with her dreams about death could also be seen as an early manifestation of what Dan Siegel, in his model of neural integration, has called 'integration of impermanence'.

Mother-child union on an archetypal level

In the following session she spoke about the passing of her cat. She had been helped in that moment of death and loss by an ex-partner. She told me that when the cat was put to sleep at the veterinary practice, she saw a rainbow outside the window. This synchronicity between the cat's death and the appearance of the rainbow just at that moment had given her a sense of comfort.

There later were further dreams revolving around death. At work she had a strong negative reaction to a person who – as she at some point realised – had a showy behaviour similar to her stepfather's. She then became aware of the need to separate her projections onto him from the reality of him.

After this, she approached the sand. Through silently digging into the sand, she experienced its depth, as if it may go further and further down. Below, she felt movement. Then, she created the following scene (Figure 4.3).

A neatly outlined shape emerged from the sand. Facing herself in the middle of the sandbox, she placed the image of the Egyptian goddess Isis holding her child Horus. Left and right, closer to herself, she placed two elephants. In the middle of an opening in the sand showing the blue background, she placed a coral branch. While shaping this simple scene, she experienced a deep sense of homecoming. The tears she shed made the emotional strength of this experience tangible. It was like a homecoming after many years, a strong sense of bliss. She was able to feel its depth also in her body. In the review of the image after having

Figure 4.3 Homecoming

completed the whole Sandplay work, she felt as if there the birth of a child had occurred on a divine level. The Mother figure was also there and it all felt like coming home on a spiritual level.

The goddess Isis can be seen as an archetypal mother on a transpersonal level: moving away from the mother-child union on the animal level represented in the previous creations in the sand, she now found an expression of that union on a spiritual level. The strong emotion connected with this image suggested further healing of the desertion she had to go through at the hands of her actual mother. In situations where actual parents failed to build basic trust, I have often observed that an archetypal or even divine level may be activated.

In the history of religion, the ancient representations of Isis with child would later inspire the images of the Madonna with child in Christianity. Regarding the two elephants, my client referred to the observation in nature and pointed out that they retreat alone when they are about to die. She connected this to her memories about the times when, as a child, she frequently had to retreat into speechlessness.

Again, in the review of her Sandplay process with me three years later, the image of the coral in its fragility reminded her of deep sorrow. To me, the shape in the sand was remindful of the shape of the body of an elephant – only the part with the legs and central part of the body – like a reassuring space provided by the wisdom of the elephants which had heralded themselves in the dream she had mentioned in the first session.

Detail: Isis with Horus child

Grappling with rage

In the following session, she reported an incident at work during which she had voiced her anger about a difficult situation in the team. She had strongly felt the energy of this anger but had also connected clarity with it. As a result of her intervention, new insights had been achieved by the team. We discussed the possibility of focusing on anger as a fertile source of introspection by paying attention to how it manifested and how it may also be processed. The following scene was inspired by this exchange on anger (Figure 4.4).

In the stirred-up wet sand in the middle far side in front of her, she placed a Katsina figure with a huge headdress. Katsina figures have been used in Hopi tradition since ancestral times to represent protecting spirits. The figure she used most likely represents what the Hopi call 'a butterfly female dancer' used in annual dances.

Figure 4.4 Fear and anger

Detail: Pomba Gira

Just below the Katsina figure, she placed a green angry mask from Bali with protruding eyes, huge fangs and its tongue sticking out. Right opposite the demon's mask and the large Katsina figure was a fierce half naked red female spirit from the Afro-Brazilian Umbanda religion, known as 'Pomba Gira'. Within that tradition she personifies female sexuality, beauty and desire. She is paid great respect because of her being notoriously wrathful. In this Sandplay image, she was under attack by two black bulls.

The figures used in this Sandplay session proved a means for her to express fearful and angry states of mind. Stirring up the sand was perceived by her as progressing towards pain. She said that this pain was so strong that it could turn into passion.

In the large Katsina figure she saw a force capable of cutting through all fetters: sheer destruction, yet also eye-opening illumination. The headdress she saw as a labyrinth. On the one hand, she felt as if one could get lost in it. On the other hand, she felt as if it could lead to the highest level of realisation. It was impossible to see what was behind the labyrinth, one could only have an intuition about it. It also aroused fear.

The red woman – whom my client perceived as a primordial woman – fearlessly showed her flaming, naked body. She was able to stand up to the energies radiating from the Katsina figure. She was threatened by two bulls. To her, as a pair, they represented both male and female force. In the history of symbols, bulls represent vital force and masculine power; their brutal force arouses fear. Many rites have ancestrally served the purpose of overcoming or even sacrificing the bull. The red lady was able to confront them and incorporate the force and power driving them. Thanks to this force, the red heroine can confront the demon opposite her. She sensed an incredible power radiating from the red figure, a passion. She exclaimed: "Now, today, if I encountered a monster outside of here, I would be able to stand up against it". "It is as if it may bestow lust for life, not to exclude anything", she also said. "Not to exclude anything" in my understanding refers to a sense of embracing the fullness of life. She was aware of the need to handle this energy very warily.

In a later discussion, while reviewing this image, she connected it with her stepfather's panic attacks that she had witnessed as a child. For example, he would scream, bang furiously against the door with a manic expression on his face. "In such a situation", she said, "I wanted help, my mother wanted help, but there was no help". As a consequence, this session proved useful to begin to get out of a deep sense of helplessness and make contact with the raw forces of survival and power in her.

A dream of transition to a new land

In the following session she shared two important dreams immediately after her latest Sandplay session:

Together with U and HJ in a car (two ex-partners). We drove towards a cliff. Beyond the cliff lay a new land. I drove off the cliff. The car flew like an airplane, I saw everything from above and then I landed in some unknown brand-new land. I left the car as a woman, they as two ravens. In the new land there was a huge river. I thought: "I am unable to cross it". The two birds spread their wings on the ground while overlapping them to enable me to lie down on them. Then they carried me across the river to the opposite bank. There was a feeling of melancholy and sadness.

It was a liminal dream. First, she drives off a cliff, then the ex-partners are transformed into ravens carrying her across a huge river and leaving behind familiar grounds. The unknown land felt like a volcanic island without human life. In those empty plains she was left all by herself. I suggested she should enter that dream in order to better feel its contents. Having done that, she said that being by herself had felt good. She also spoke about her longing for a close affective relationship, similar to the one she had been able to live with the two ex-partners in the dream. The dream may point to the need to leave behind the old relationships and to prepare for something new. It appears, however, that the past relationships had left a positive imprint, represented by the two ravens helping the transition. She now felt comfortable being alone. Sadness was due to the fact of having to leave the past behind in order to prepare for an unknown future.

I was impressed with the transformation of the companions into ravens, helpful inner animals representing subcortical levels which were activated within herself. As an archetype, the raven has been seen (among others) as a bird connected with death. This would perfectly match her previous dreams of death – death, though, seen as a point of transition leading to transformation. In several religions (including in the Hebrew version of the Old Testament) ravens have played the role of messengers of God. This role is perfectly aligned with my patient's dream about being carried by the wings of two ravens, as if carried by a mysterious transcendent force. This image also reminds of the legend of hermit Saint Meinrad, a Benedictine monk who had chosen to live in solitude to serve God in the isolation of a dark forest. Legend has it that he lived with two tame ravens which he had rescued from sure death. They would frolic around the saint's hermitage. Later, the two ravens became also the emblem of the monastery of Einsiedeln, built around the chapel originally constructed on the site of the hermitage.

Could it possibly be that, in dreams, ravens bode the achievement of a new spiritual dimension in solitude? On a later occasion, as she was radically questioning herself, I reminded her of the dream and pointed out that she was not anymore in that realm of doubt, but that she was already on her way to a brand-new land. This moved her deeply, and she immediately felt to be in that brand-new d, thus fully experiencing that new reality. She expressed gratitude for being able to feel it; I, too, felt moved by her intense response.

A dream about overcoming petrification

The second dream she shared during that session was the following:

> I am standing before a huge rock. I am looking for something. A white-haired woman says: "Watch out, this is the devil's rock". I look up to the rock. It comes to life. I see the head of a horse, it neighs or snorts, the stallion sets himself free, jumps down. I stand next to a fence and the stallion joins me.

The rock which comes to life and turns into a horse shows that her inner petrification or trauma-induced paralysis has already begun to loosen its grip (Figure 4.5).

Figure 4.5 The client's drawing of the horse

Peter Levine refers to the myth of snake-haired Medusa – who can turn everybody daring to look at her into stone – to illustrate the paralysing effect of trauma. As the myth has it, goddess Athena instructed Perseus not to look at Medusa; rather, he was to use his shield as a mirror in order to see only her reflection. Thanks to Athena's piece of advice, he was able to strike his deadly blow at Medusa without looking directly at her and thus risking petrification. Once beheaded, out of her neck sprang the winged horse Pegasus, which Levine interprets as a symbol of the body and instinctual knowledge. According to Levine, the myth also shows the importance of not confronting trauma directly. He explains:

> If we make the mistake of confronting trauma head on, Medusa will, true to her nature, turn us to stone.... When it comes to trauma, I believe that the 'equivalent' of Perseus's reflecting shield is how the physical body responds to trauma and how the 'living body' personifies resilience and feelings of goodness.[1]

The dream revolves around the devil's rock, which makes a strong indicator of the sinister quality of the inner paralysis the client carried in herself due to an unfortunate sequence of traumatic events in her life. Fortunately, there is a wise old woman warning the dreamer as she is looking for something of which she is barely cognizant. This points to an inner wisdom and knowledge which the dreamer is tapping into and which comes to help her. According to Jungian psychology, the old woman in the dream could be seen as a manifestation of the archetype of the old wise woman, an important guide for the Self.

The horse that succeeds in setting himself free and, in the end, stands close to the dreamer, is also noteworthy. I see in the horse my client's ability to relate to her body and emotions as vital and liberating forces, as with the previously mentioned Sandplay sessions. It is an experience of the "living body", as Levine has called it. Accordingly, it is not surprising that such a dream should immediately follow the previous, intense session.

The dream also seems to be somehow connected to the fact that many girls going through puberty develop a strong interest in horses. Pictures of horses would then be hung all over their bedroom, and they may also show a keen interest in horse-riding. The vitality and power of the horse perfectly symbolises the newly awakened energies that, at that age, also result in a keen interest in the other sex. My client had recently gone through troubled times, and therefore the horse dream may also point to a restoration of the instinctual part in herself that she had felt had been threatened by the outer circumstances in which she had found herself.

Sandplay scene with Torii and the golden feather

In the following session she worked again with the sand (Figure 4.6). She felt a strong emotion while feeling the sand in her fingers, as if she was falling

Figure 4.6 Heat and purification (bridge, Torii fire, golden feather and two small katsina figures)

into the void. This sensation was so overwhelming as to dwarf anything else. She raised her hands and moved them above the sand. While she was experiencing the void, they started to shake. Then the shaking transitioned to a gesture as if she was sowing seeds. She appeared to be deeply moved by this, and her movements were very slow.

She then felt the urge to use something very fine and small: in my collection she found a small golden feather. In it she saw something utterly new to her. She took two very small Katsina figures and placed them so that they seemed to be looking at the feather. She said one was male and the other female. Unlike the previously used large Katsina figure, they did not arouse fear. Next to the feather she also placed a fire to purify it. A Torii gate opens to that scene.

A Torii is a vermillion-coloured wooden or stone gate serving as the entrance to a shrine of the Shinto religion where spirits, gods, and deities are paid tribute to. A Tori marks the boundary between the secular outside world and the sacred world of the shrine. In the context provided by this Sandplay creation, it is worth noting that the Japanese characters used for Torii are those of 'bird' and 'to be'. Thus, many interpret a Torii as a sacred bird gate to mean a place which is easy for birds to reach. In a number of cultures, birds are seen as messengers between gods and humans. These associations of the Torii with birds were not known to my client upon placing the golden feather close to the Torii, but it beautifully complemented the meaning of the Torii itself. A bridge over a river, drawn by a line traced with her finger, would lead to this special place.

The shaking she experienced during that session was something that used to happen to her upon feeling exposed or having to deal with people she regarded as challengingly intellectual or intimidating, or for example when taking the floor while proposing a toast.

Speaking about this conjured up many painful experiences from her childhood. For example, once she had to draw a sun at school. The rays of the sun she had drawn turned out to be very shaky. The school teacher said that the drawing was very ugly and pulled her by the hair. In the following session, she also shared a disturbing and very early memory involving her stepfather. She had learnt to walk when she was about 8 months' old. "I see hands stretching out as if to help me. Then they are suddenly withdrawn, I hear laughter and I fall down". In the light of these memories, in all likelihood the tremor she experienced while engaging in the Sandplay session was due to a long history of insecurity being instilled in her. She found it liberating that – at some point during the Sandplay process – this tremor changed into a sowing gesture.

She also felt stirred by the symbol of the golden feather she had used. It is the object both the female and the male Katsina figures were looking at. In her view, it stood for the wish for an untainted relationship between male and female, very likely a spiritual dimension connecting them. The fire placed nearby provided warmth but also purification in view of the establishment of this spiritual bond. The passage over the bridge to this sacred space fittingly marked by the Torii brings to mind the previous journey to an unexplored land on the ravens' wings. The scene can be seen as a further important step taken towards a purification and enlightenment of the shadow cast on sexuality and relationship by the wounds of the abuse she had experienced.

A new beginning with Eros while coming to terms with disappointment

She had met a man. For the sake of convenience, we shall henceforth refer to him as 'B'. He was separating from his partner. Subsequent to this encounter, a positive period had followed, she had felt well and content with her personal and professional life. It was a resurrection-like experience. As this new relationship was strengthening, they would have meaningful exchanges on their life stories, and she would feel understood. He contributed to a sense of clarity and supported the dawning feelings of compassion she felt for her elderly stepfather whom she had got in touch with again. Later on, she shared with me a dream where an ill person resembling her stepfather broke into a motherly realm. She could see him only through a window glass, yet experienced a feeling of compassion for that aggressor.

In a budding relationship, both parties become aware of a sense of mutual love and sympathy. In this case, my client particularly prized a practical sense

of spirituality he embodied in her view. To me it felt as if the dream of landing in a new land carried by the ravens had started to manifest itself in this
relationship. However, after a few months, driven by a sense of loyalty to his
former partner, he decided to go back to her. Leaving aside a few sessions we
had had before this incident, I shall briefly discuss the session that had followed his decision to break up with my client.

While describing this painful moment, she connected it to the situation
when her mother had remained paralysed and had had no other choice but to
give her away right after her birth. At home she was able to take the baby she
had been at that time into her arms in her imagination. Touching the sand
summoned tears and sorrow connected to that situation (Figure 4.7). Working
with her eyes closed, she first noticed how the sand crumbled down in her
hands. Then a round shape arose from the sand. She held her hands around
the shape, and allowed them to rest there. She experienced a soothing feeling
just by leaving her hands there. As she opened her eyes, she finally took heed
of the shape: it reminded her of a mother's breasts.

Touching the sand clearly enabled her to reconnect with the comforting
feeling of a mother's breasts which she had been denied in the earliest stages
of her life, and her dormant sorrow for its loss had been activated by the
sense of abandonment she was presently feeling.

This experience helped her recall a dream. In the dream she had vomited.
The vomit, however, had turned into clay and she had managed to shape a

Figure 4.7 Finding a mother's breasts

vessel from it. She felt the dream to have been a dream of purification. After the session, it inspired her to work with clay at home. The following session she reported to have made a round shape topped by some sort of a round head. It looked like a primitive image of a person. With her hands, she removed from the body of that shape 13 small balls. She called them '13 Balls of Sorrow'. In the hollow left in the body of the clay a niche for light had been carved as if it had been a lantern. Thenceforth she felt very good again and she took to practicing yoga every morning.

I was struck by the extent to which she had managed to find again her inner stability thanks to her work with sand and clay. Removing the balls of sorrow from the body of the clay figure was tantamount to the act of getting rid of disturbing feelings through vomiting in the dream. Liberating herself this way had brought of a new light shining in herself. Achieving this not only through a mental process of imagination, but also through the sense of touch, had certainly helped anchor her experience in the realm of the body, thus activating the right hemisphere of the brain, and granting access to the sensory experience of bodily sensations. Eventually, this would change again as she developed back pains. They were connected to the sensation of having always carried a burden.

Burden and relief

Her feelings for 'B' seemed to rekindle for a moment when he made up his mind to file for divorce. However, he was only ready for a friendship with her, and no more. This proved a further disappointment for my client after raising her hopes, and she felt that it was too heavy to bear. Then, she approached the sand and moved her hands in it (Figure 4.8). She heaped a lot of sand on top of her hands. Then, she suddenly realised: "I have been carrying the whole world on my back. It is too much". Then, her fingers started to move, freeing her hands from the heaps of sand. With tears in her eyes, she remained in front of the sand, her hands deep in it. Her whole body, she said, had felt relieved. She then experienced deep relaxation, a letting-go.

Dream of an invasion of bulls

Despite the momentary relief experienced thanks to the sandbox, later the sense of feeling overstrained by the relationship with 'B' came back. The reason was that he had got closer to the partner he was divorcing. The rage she experienced subsequent to this was mainly turned against 'B''s partner, on account of her wish to have 'B' for herself. The feelings of rage manifested in a dream:

> An invasion of black bulls and women took place. There also were knights on black steeds. The scene was taking place somewhere in Spain, but the setting also had something unreal about it, it also felt like a Fata

Figure 4.8 Letting go

Morgana. The bulls were shining in the sunlight. The leader of the country was not at all prepared for the invasion, he and the people of the country had been distracted by a murder. While witnessing this scene I wondered whether the people still had a chance to escape.

She perceived the invasion as connected with the sense of 'too much'. Spain meant to her 'warmth' and 'heart'. The leader of the country reminded her of a kind person, but incapable of realising what was happening. It all appeared as if it was a Fata Morgana, and yet it eventually turned out to be a very actual threat. It was as if the bulls of the fourth Sandplay had come to life. In the earlier Sandplay session, the powerful red woman had been able to stand up against two aggressive bulls. This time, though, the dream emphasised more the overwhelming feelings of anger and jealousy. There were black knights, probably challenging the bulls, but not very effectively.

The rage she was experiencing in the actual situation felt overwhelming and extreme. It sprang also from a feminine force, as the dream (besides the bulls) also featured women. Could this be the anger of the woman in her who had suffered abuse during her childhood? Positive emotions connected with the heart and warmth, as well as the rekindled love for 'B', were under threat. The growing anger was certainly fuelled by manifold earlier losses, abuse and disappointment. She had grappled with her own anger by writing about it at home. A variety of earlier difficulties experienced in her childhood eventually came back.

The dream was a clarion call to get prepared for, alert to, and aware of her anger churning within, thus avoiding the risk of getting distracted like the leader of the country in the dream – perhaps, an aspect of her ego. However, the dream also pointed out that the leader of the country and the people were distracted. Maybe she had been too lost in her own feelings of disappointment. Thus, her life energies necessary to successfully grapple with the situation had been metaphorically murdered.

A golden umbilical cord

In the later session she discussed again her feelings of anger and sadness. However, she recalled that with 'B' there, she had first experienced trust and she felt grateful for that. She worked the sand with closed eyes. From the movement of her hands, the shape of a body spontaneously rose. She felt it to be the body of a baby. There was a moment of fear, of emptiness. Yet, there was also the awareness of the sand, of the body. She was able to reconnect with the feeling that something was there. Then, she had a vision of something like a golden umbilical cord. With her hands she carved a small opening into the body in the sand. The umbilical cord came spiralling down from above. In her own body she experienced a feeling of peace in the area between her breasts and navel. All around was water.

In the review at the end of her Sandplay process, while looking at the scene in the sand, she felt that the body had a quality of nakedness, vulnerability, but also authenticity. The umbilical cord nourished, and the nourishment it offered came from an altogether different dimension.

A delicate feminine

In the following session we talked about and worked on the images summoned by a phone call with 'B'. His emotional honesty had attracted her again to him and she had suffered because of the impossibility to be with him. In the sand, while moving her hands to shape it, she experienced a letting-go, a feeling halfway between sorrow and wellbeing. Then, something extremely delicate and lovely shaped up. The female figure that had appeared at the centre of the sandbox corresponded to real bodily sensations such as warmth, roundness, softness. She was moved to tears. The roses around this figure represented a calm safety. The main figure herself held a pink rose, serendipitously attuned to the motif of white and red roses. On top of the gate-like shape she placed two seagulls as well as another white bird which was sitting.

It appears that this image brought her into contact with a softer feminine side, quite different from the image of the wrathful red woman she had met in an earlier Sandplay session. In terms of relationship, the issue was whether she should let go and patiently wait until her love was proven right, or should rekindle her feelings for one of the ex-partners who had appeared in the form of a raven in an earlier dream.

Figure 4.9 A new womanhood

Dream of the wildlife park

During the following session she reported that 'B' had texted her: "In case it was of any interest to you, I'd like you to know that my wife has left me". On her own part, she felt that she had finally recovered much of the energy which she had lavished upon him. She realised that she had been too attached to him. She then brought up a dream that revealed a meaningful step taken towards making peace with her inner animal side. The dream went as follows:

> She was with a girlfriend in a clay pit (a place where she used to play as child). Farther up, she saw a bus coming from the left. It travelled along the edge of the pit. She feared it could fall into the pit. The bus disappeared into a forest. They walked into the forest and reached a small creek. It was reddish in colour, as there was a lot of red dirt. The bus had pulled over on the banks of the creek. She found herself in a wildlife park. There were children and wild animals. The children were hiding among the trees. They took a look around in order to assess whether it was a dangerous place. A poisonous hedgehog then arrived, immediately followed by a dog. She remained unperturbed. Small-sized tigers and panthers would hiss, but they would not harm her. On the right-hand side of the park zebras were lying on the ground. Then, a fully-grown adult lioness drew closer to her, yet it did not harm her. In a corner of the forest some gazelles were doing their morning gymnastics, they were in a

Detail: a woman in a position of meditation

position similar to that of humans sitting and begging. They looked very elegant. It was an old lady who was driving the bus. She was the owner of the park. My client did not know that there existed such a park so close to herself. The lady asked my client and her girlfriend to sign their names on a guest book. She was crooked, with grey hair. My client had the impression that the elderly lady was happy.

My client mentioned that, as a child, she had used to love playing in the clay pit. It was the forest of her childhood. There were some dangerous spots – once a child had had an accident there and had died. Therefore, she was not allowed to go there by herself. At home she had painted the dream and she wondered whether the 'witch' had over-tamed the animals in the park. However, in the dream they were completely free. The guest book was important precisely to safeguard them. She felt that being able to hiss like the tigers and panthers did could be important in her professional environment.

The dream showed a new important step in getting in touch with her inner animal. Thanks to the dream, she discovered that close to the place she was acquainted with – that is, close to her conscious personality – there existed a park inhabited by animals. Access to this part in herself was granted by her ability to play like a child. From her story it is quite clear that there was almost no occasion to play as a child, as she had to work. Playing in the sand – and notably the use of clay, in all likelihood – helped reconnect with the rare and almost forgotten opportunities she had had to play in the clay pit.

Making contact with unconscious parts of our psyche is frequently associated with fear and danger, as one has to leave behind the accustomed 'safety net' offered by consciousness. Moreover, as with this client's story, deep traumatic memories are stored in the unconscious and the fear to trigger them is also a part of the process of approaching latent emotions. Thus, access needs to be controlled so as to achieve this process without emotional harm. For this reason, the presence in the dream of a guest book is reassuring: it prevents the dreamer from wandering into the emotional world represented by the animals. Respect for the inner forces, represented among others by the lion, is therefore crucial.

Likewise, the presence of the old woman – the dreamer called her 'a witch' – who owns the place and seems to be in control of the animals, is important. The old lady also seems to be able to connect with the everyday world, as she comes and goes to this concealed place by coach. The dreamer perceives her as a happy person. Accordingly, we can assume that, if she is to be seen as a witch, she is a good one. The figure of the old lady reminds of the Lady of the Beasts, an ancestral figure prominent in Minoan, Greek, Cretan and near Eastern mythology described (among others) by Erich Neumann in his work on the great mother.[2] Examples of this archetypal figure are Aphrodite, Artemis, Diana and various unnamed goddesses such as representation of the goddess on a mountain in Crete, portrayed in the act of taming two lions. Neumann states that

> Whereas the male god in myth like the male hero, usually appears in opposition to the animals he fights and defeats, the Great Goddess, as Lady of the Beasts, dominates them but seldom fights them. Between her and the animal world there is no hostility or antagonism, although she deals with wild as well as gentle and tame beasts.[3]

In my client's dream, along with animals, there are also children, who are curious to see whether the dreamer shows signs of fear. Obviously, it takes some courage is to meet the poisonous hedgehog, the dog, the lion, small-sized tigers, etc., and the dreamer passes the test. It seems that a positive aspect of her own inner child proves helpful when approaching the emotions represented by the animals, including the ability to hiss if one needs to mark one's own territory. The fact that there are a variety of animals in this dream shows that – depending on the needs at hand – different attitudes may become more readily available, including the possibility to hide away like the hedgehog or, if needed, to react with the fierce attitude of the lion.

The gazelles busy doing their morning gymnastics are maybe a reference to her own daily yoga practice, taking place in the morning as an excellent and elegant means to develop focused awareness of inner bodily sensations, similarly to the practice of mindfulness. Her question about whether the owner of the park was overly controlling of the animals may be rather a projection of her own inherited tendency to overcontrol herself at work. The drawback to this overcontrol – as we have discussed with regard to this client at the beginning of this section – are too many emotions breaking through and causing a breakdown when she had to deliver a speech under too much inner pressure before a large audience.

In the dream – as she herself noticed – the animals enjoyed freedom within the limits of the park. Thus, the dream did not appear to indicate overcontrol. For her, of course, it was of paramount importance to achieve a middle ground in dealing with such feelings as the rage she experienced in the ups and downs of her latest relationship alongside the old wounds of desertion from her childhood. Overall, the dream made her aware of an enhanced ability to make contact with the non-rational world of the subcortical level in a new way under the protection of the image of a positive inner wise old woman, a mistress of animals.

Breaking free from a treadwheel

Again, on the topic of the inner animal, she brought up the following dream:

> I was observing a beaver. It was attempting to do a back flip on a bicycle. It fell again, and again, and hit its head hard on the floor. It hurt to see this. It tried again and again. I knew that, as long as it didn't succeed, its soul would not find peace. This made me sad.

She said that she had been able to observe how she herself had been doing this at work. She felt she should be less in the 'doing' mode and learn to let go. In her opinion there was too much ego involved, too much rationality at play. Therefore, proving herself an achiever all her life had always drained a lot of energy. The dream pointed to the metaphorical treadwheel she had been stuck in all of her life. It revealed a different perspective from the previous dream, which had pointed to the possibility of giving her animal side more space and freedom. It pointed to the restlessness which would ensue if she allowed herself to be too driven by her work, as she had internalised since childhood.

She spoke about an upcoming event where she was expected to address a large group of people. She wondered how she could better prepare for the task, thus avoiding another public breakdown. In a moment of silence, she allowed a fantasy to come up. She imagined that she would play a piece of music dear to

her and then build a bridge to connect the music to the topic of the presentation. Actually, she later managed to do exactly that, and it went very well.
Through the music, she found a way to activate the right hemisphere of the
brain and connect it with the more logic-oriented left hemisphere.

Finding an inner source of peace

In this period, she resumed dating 'B'. She felt finally 'seen', noticed, paid
attention to. The essential moments came about less through words than through
silence. In this type of encounter trust was able to develop. She experienced it to
be healing for her own masculine part. The way she described the encounter gave
me the impression that again the subcortical level of nonverbal communication
was able to be activated. Perhaps this quality was also part of the gift the dream
of the animals conveyed. She felt that 'B' had contributed in his own way to her
carving a quiet niche for herself in her own life. Also, in a later session she
claimed that the relationship with 'B' was flourishing again.

I shall leave out of the present study the analysis of another Sandplay session
which enabled her to feel an increased inner strength and stability in that period.
However, about two months later, a further painful standstill occurred – this time
resulting in what appeared to be a final separation. Sadness invaded her – and it
was related also to the feeling that she had been deprived of her own childhood.
In the course of our discussion I suggested a visualisation of these losses. Her
visualisation took place as follows:

> I find myself in a dark, deep cave. There, I see a white light and a pearl. It is
> a completely pure light, it has never been in contact with any other light. It is
> a very soft glow. It is very beautiful because all around it is so dark. It is a
> light in an absolute darkness. It is like a feeling of an original ground. It is
> like a place beyond all wounds, where there is something completely safe.

This image bore a striking similarity to the time when she had visualised the
moment before death. It was terser, though, and had a very essential quality.
It conveyed the belief that deep under any loss (including that of childhood)
there exists a "place beyond all wounds". About two months and two sessions
later, she had a short, yet numinous dream, which came about as if it had
been a further elaboration of this insight.

Dream: (beginning dropped).

> Some refugees are supposed to arrive in the forest where I am. I'm drawing
> closer to a tree. Entangled in its roots there is a being of incredible beauty,
> made of mother of pearl and gold.

She gave a description of this amazing being and during the session I
sketched it (Figure 4.10).

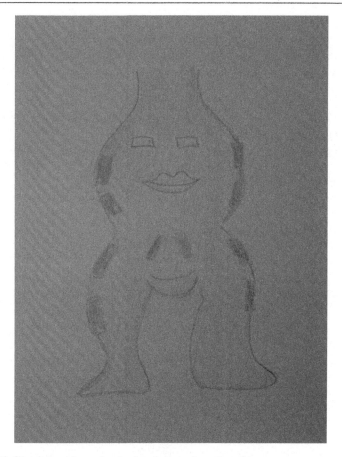

Figure 4.10 Sketch based on client's description of earth goddess

She commented that the being under the roots, a goddess, was of an incredible beauty. She had a male sexual organ, a kind of testicle. It was so striking in its mother-of-pearl and golden beauty that she wondered: "All of these losses – have they been necessary, in order to be given the chance to meet this goddess?"

There exist images of ancient epicene mother goddesses or idols, such as a hermaphrodite idol from the bronze age found in Yugoslavia.[4] They belong to the most archaic level of the mother goddess, where male and female qualities merged. This symbolical hermaphroditism may also be viewed as an expression of the union of feminine and masculine qualities indicating the wholeness of that being carrying the numinous quality of the Self. The dream goddess is connected to the roots and to Mother Earth. Gold and mother of pearl indicate the great value of this luminous being, the value of the Self as a great healing force.

The pearl born out of suffering had already shown up in the Sandplay featuring the shell and the seagull sitting on it, perceived by the client as a 'flying pearl'. The motive of the pearl had also turned up in the visualisation session, which in all likelihood from there also accessed the dream. When symbolic elements repeatedly occur with minor variations across different media like Sandplay sessions, fantasies and dreams (each representing a different window on the unconscious), their recurrence is an indicator of the significance of the underlying motif.

She said that thinking of that goddess and talking about her during the session 'provided a space'. She also said that one could not say much about her – hence, her urge to portray her, to shape her image. She already had some ideas about how to shape her out of clay.

Achieving this level of awareness beyond words could make an example of what Dan Siegel calls 'transpirational integration', or 'experiencing the Self' according to Jungian psychology.

Healing the split between body and mind

Two months later, among other topics, she mentioned that she had to find a caretaker for her stepfather, whom she had recently visited. In this visit she had been accompanied by 'B', who, after taking some time for himself, had found his way back to her one more time – this time, for good. Trust was finally built. She made a simple Sandplay scene featuring a well and a white double snake protecting a treasure (Figure 4.11).

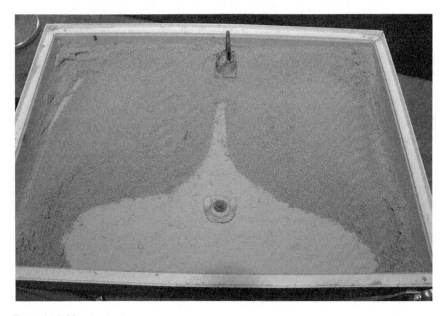

Figure 4.11 Naming instinct

Detail: the double snake

The well reminded her of a therapy art session where she had been asked to imagine pulling something out of a well. This was supposed to be a strong indicator of her psychological patterns. There was a beheaded person in the well, all caked in blood. She had to pull the head out of the well. The snake reminded her of a dream she had had some time earlier. She and a man stepped into a body of water. There was a snake which bit him. She knew the name of the snake and this knowledge helped heal the man. The shape of the sand reminded her of a rib cage or of wings. Looking at the shape, the sand cast aside revealed a blue stretch at the bottom of the sandbox that reminded her of the roof of a mosque. During the review, she associated the well with the chakra of speech (a sensitive area for her) and the snake with the chakra located in the solar plexus.

Shaping the scene brought along a sense of relaxation. That time around, we did not go into detail with further associations concerning the well and the snake as guardian of a treasure.

The well indicates a gate to the unconscious where forgotten tragedy is buried. The head had been severed from the body. This could indicate a split between body and mind she had experienced on the basis of traumatic events in childhood. Disembodiment is an important aspect of trauma.

The snake most likely refers to the so-called 'reptilian level' of the brain, a part involved in the fight-or-flight response in life-threatening situations. Being bitten by the snake could also refer to the sense of immobilisation or shutdown one experiences when escape is not possible, a level mediated by the unmyelinated primitive vagus system establishing a connection with the enteric system or guts. The dream points to some knowledge she had about those profound levels in herself, she was able to name them, verbalise them, and therefore heal. In the healing process the instinctual layers of the brain are reconnected once again with the neocortical level of speech. Traumatic experiences may leave some individuals literally speechless – that is, they literally are in the body. Connecting instinct and speech is a transformative process. Her association between the well and the snake, on the one hand, and with the chakra of speech and the chakra in the region of the solar plexus, on the other, perfectly conveys her need to reconnect speech with a more instinctual level.

The white snake – as with white animals in general – symbolises a purified or spiritual aspect of the instinct. In the Brothers Grimm's fairy tale of the white snake, the white snake bestows on the hero the ability to understand the language of animals, thus connecting instinct to words. The specific symbol of the white snake that my client picked from my collection stems from the Japanese Shinto tradition. In Shinto lore, snakes are viewed as a lesser species of dragon. They may be potentially threatening but are considered as benevolent, righteous and wise. They are the guardians of a sacred wish-fulfilling jewel – the gold treasure that the figure with the two snakes protected. A white snake is often featured in the headdress of Benzaiten, the Japanese water goddess of fertility and flow. Benzaiten can also take the shape of a white snake. The figure she chose portrayed the snakes carrying in their mouths a round and slender object. I was told they represent Yin and Yang, the basic polarity of Daoism.

In our final review of the image, she associated the snake with the colour of the pearl. Accordingly, the snake partakes of the precious quality of the pearl and of the gold, which were also distinctive features of the beautiful earth goddess. The dream therefore presented the healing process as affecting the wounded masculine part in herself, represented by the man bitten by the snake. The picking of a white snake, a symbol rife with meaning, loosely reminded her also of the subterranean earth goddess of the dream, and she therefore unknowingly chose it as a figure suggestive of healing on an instinctual and subcortical level. In the Sandplay it faces the well, where, according to her associations, is the disembodied person. Thus, the healing potential symbolised by the snake is turned towards the disembodied part in need of healing. It is facing the well with the disembodied person, hopefully curing her.

In the following session, she discussed a dream image clearly symbolical of her own inner frozen part, a possible consequence of unresolved trauma. The dream had gone as follows: she had fallen into a deep crevasse concealed under thick snow. Unharmed, she had landed onto a snow-covered surface. Underneath it there was water. The snow then started melting. In the dream she had experienced a profound sense of helplessness. She had felt completely deserted. She was lost and did not know what to do. I suggested entering the dream in order to relive its emotional quality and to get in touch with the bodily sensations evoked by the image.

She first experienced a strong energy moving upwards from the breastbone. It felt as if it wanted to go up to the head and leave the body from there. Yet, the energy did not succeed in travelling any farther than the throat. She experienced a dramatic split between head and body. There was a feeling of sadness and a longing for the energy to leave the body. She felt a lot of heat in the head. Then, she suddenly experienced an incredible peace and bliss. She said: "I do not have to do anything anymore".

Fear had disappeared. There was a sense that she had broken through to a different level. The snow wall on her left was still there. She heard the sound of bells. It was like the sound of peace. Her body then felt very light. She felt warmth under her skin, all around her there was a warming light. She said: "I am completely inside my body, as if I were inside a big bright body". She felt as if she was lying on her belly, not on the ground, but on something invisible – she did not fall, though; quite the opposite: it was as if she was able to fly. Under her skin there was a very lively feeling, and she felt completely awake. It was a very beautiful state. Under her face there was an incredible heat, like fire. From inside she felt the shape of her face, but at the same time she also felt it from outside, like something which was being burnt. There was no pain. When a face has been in the snow for a long time, it feels as if afire. She felt free. The energy from above and the energy from below merged, there was no split anymore, no feeling that the energy should leave the body through the top of the head as she had felt earlier. She felt one with the energy. There was a sense that she could have stayed for hours in that state. She felt fully awake on her inside, pervaded by a deep sense of relaxation, with a sense of heat in the basin, feeling the whole space of her body from the top of her head down to her toes. Suddenly, also the snow wall on the left side vanished. She felt blessed by the experience.

Entering the dream and experiencing it on a physical level put her in contact first with an inner split between the lower part of her body and her head. If we think about the previous Sandplay process we could say that she became painfully aware of the split that was symbolically indicated by the beheaded person in the well. Staying present with the experience brought a sudden change in her feelings and sensations, a sensation of peace culminating in the feeling that she did not have to do anything. This non-doing was instrumental in enabling the wisdom of the body to become manifest. It was sufficient just to be present with her own inner states. By going through various stages while being mindfully present, the body manifested its inborn healing potential and enabled an integration of split parts resulting in a wide awake and intense awareness of the body as a whole. A frozen aspect in herself, manifesting in the cold snow wall of the crevasse, finally melted away.

In all likelihood, this inner journey had already been heralded by the symbol of the white snake in the Sandplay session, an indicator of the healing and transformative power on the level of the reptilian brain – notably, the brain stem. Wording her experiences even while she was going through them certainly also helped the integration of dissociated inner states, according to the model of neural integration put forth by Dan Siegel. Dissociated emotions – in this case, mainly sadness, helplessness, and loneliness – eventually reconnected with the right middle prefrontal regions and also changed throughout the process. According to Badenoch, sharing these experiences with a sympathetic listener may give rise also to an integration of the left middle prefrontal regions resulting in horizontal integration. This integrative process seems to be indicated by the dream sequence with the snake, in which the knowledge of its name made the healing from its bite possible.

Confronting a childhood trauma

Later on, she brought some of her childhood drawings she had found (Figures 4.12 and 4.13).

We examined the drawings together and we were struck by the phallic shapes on the drawings, as we can see in the previous picture (Figure 4.12). Some of the shapes reminded her of a scrotum with a phallus. As I had found her to be capable of tackling difficult topics before, I asked her this time, too, to pay attention to her bodily reactions to the images. She immediately fell into a state where she felt a separation line in the region of the throat. The heart was beating and the lower part of the body felt numb. At this point, I asked her what may be of help in this situation. She replied: "Imagining to be lying on grass belly down".

Then she approached the sand. She would stir the sand with her hands, reaching deep into it. She said: "Feeling its coolness feels so good. It feels as if I could disburden all of my sorrows onto the sand". There was an experience as if she could slip under the covers of the earth as if it made a

Figure 4.12 Childhood drawing with phallic shapes

Figure 4.13 Childhood drawing with flying phallic shape

protecting sheet. The deeper she went, the stronger the sense of protection she felt. It was as if the sand might help her better experience the boundaries of her own body. This eventually led her to connect with her self-determination. "I can assess by myself how much protection I need. I feel clothed and not naked". Working with the images which we understood to be visual traces of her sexual abuse in childhood, she experienced again the sensation of a dividing line in the throat, similar to the one she had experienced while working with the image of having fallen into crevasse under the snow. The first impulse to get out of it, and the subsequent panic caused her to feel as if her body was lying on the grass. Then, the earth element of the sand helped make that first impulse tangible and led her to the important realisation of her body boundaries in stark contrast to dissolution, self-determination to helplessness, feeling clothed to nakedness and exposure. Thus, she managed to reverse the remnants of trauma left in her body memory and to develop a new sense of being able to protect herself.

Taking care of herself on an emotional level

In a later session, she told me about a car crash she had had in the meantime. She was in shock about the event. It had been, however, both touching and practically helpful for her that 'B' had offered to help her. In the session, we relived step by step both the accident and her feelings in response to it through a meditation exercise. She realised a lack of ability to take care of herself emotionally – and this, alongside a long-standing feeling of sadness. She had developed a tendency to look after others, but less so to look after herself. Strong feelings accompanied this realisation.

Then, she created a scene (Figure 4.14), and a cave in a hill emerged. She placed a small fur trim into it. She placed the figure of the mother monkey with cub she had used earlier into that warm and sheltered nook. She reported that she recently had had a dream about wandering through underground network caves where she had felt protected. Farther away, behind the hill with palm trees on, she placed a dark-coloured wooden figure of an African fertility idol. In the foreground, on the right, she placed a shell with a nacreous surface.

She felt the image to be very archaic and representative of a deep inner level. In her body she felt a wide expanse. She tried to express this sense of expansion by stretching out her arms, allowing them to swing, with the back of the hands facing upwards, then outwards, and then joined together. While performing this gesture in the air, she felt the absence of resistance, space around the arms. However, when her hands started to move in the sand, there was a sense of being carried. It was the experience of being able to take care of herself she had been longing for. Also, the African idol conveyed a feeling of protection.

She commented that the shape of the sand was similar to an ear. She saw in it a clarion call 'to listen to the inside' (in German: *Nach Innen Horchen*). I

Figure 4.14 Taking care of oneself

Detail: monkey and cub on fur trim

was touched by her reference to listening to oneself, as it was aligned with a recurring theme in Etty Hillesum's letters I was reading at the time. Etty Hillesum – a Jew who had been a victim of the persecution by the Nazi regime and had been deported to Auschwitz – had developed a deep sense of being able to rest in herself by taking the time to listen to her inner voice on a daily basis. Towards the end of her letter, she worded her deep experience in this striking sentence:

> *Hineinhorchen* – I so wish I could find a Dutch equivalent for that German word. Truly, my life is one of hearkening unto myself and unto others, unto God. And if I say hearkening, it is really God who hearkens in me.

Likewise, the image in her Sandplay showed how, in her own way, by listening to the unspoken voice of her body through Sandplay she was able to find a deeper sense of safety within herself.

There followed two more sessions focusing (among others) on the exchanges she had had with her aged stepfather and on her ever-increasing understanding of the origins of his difficulties, rooted in his biography and in tensions within his family. She felt that her budding ability to feel safe within herself and independent from the opinion of others had also been helped by 'B', who displayed himself such an ability. After a dream analysis, at home she saw an image of a luminous figure similar to a Buddha which very well expressed her ideal of being able to 'rest in oneself'. Perhaps this had already been heralded by her first Sandplay featuring Buddha, which allowed the old lady to let go and rest.

Completion: the jester can tell the truth

Then, in her last Sandplay session, the figure of the jester appeared (Figure 4.15). The jester tells the truth, as he knows what happens behind the scene. This was a fitting symbol, in the light of the fact that in her own childhood she had been denied the truth about her own paternity.

After shaping the sand and moulding a central elevation remindful of a torso with two spirals on the left and on the right, she placed the figure of a jester on the edge closest to her. Opposite it, she placed a white feather. Also, along the far side of the sandbox, left and right, she placed two mirrors and two roses. While building the scene, she felt a calming effect which radiated from it.

She recalled that in an end-of-year play during her childhood she had played the role of a jester in a version of the fairy tale *The Emperor's New Clothes*. In the tale, weavers had told the king that they were able to make clothes invisible only to people who are unfit for their positions, such as stupid or incompetent individuals. Actually, they had not made any clothes at all, but had succeeded in making the king believe that they had clad him. Not seeing any clothes at all, he did not say anything, least he should appear

Figure 4.15 Feeling free to tell the truth

incompetent or unfit for his position. For exactly the same reason everybody else did not dare to admit that they did not see clothes while he was parading completely naked in front of them. In the version by Andersen, it was a child who finally exclaimed: "The king is not wearing anything at all". Both children, in their unspoilt innocence, and jesters, who are granted liberty to speak out whatever they may think, are able to transcend appearances and speak the truth.

In an earlier Spanish version of the tale, the king was deceived by weavers who claimed to make clothes invisible to anyone who was not the offspring of the presumed father. While tracing the origin of the tale, I was astonished to run across the episode of the client who was made to believe that the step-father was her real father, when in fact he was not. As early as her childhood, my client had therefore cast doubt on her ancestry when comparing her own complexion to her the supposed father's. Undoubtedly, upon playing the role of the jester in the play, she did not realise how close the story was to her own situation, and had to wait until she was told the truth.

In her Sandplay scene, the jester would look into the mirrors which reveal the truth. When in the review of her Sandplay process we discussed the figure of the jester, she told me that her partner loved humour, and therefore they could play the fool together. This situation was in stark contrast to her childhood, where there was no room for humour, as her stepfather was very sarcastic. The jester and the feather in the Sandplay, by contrast, evoked for

Detail: the Jester

her a sense of lightness. In the review, she said that she certainly intended to give way to humour. She also reported that at work her boss had suggested that she should be more light-hearted. This helped her face her work-related challenges differently, as with the use of music to create the right atmosphere to address larger groups.

In the review of her Sandplay process, she commented that the middle line extending from the jester to the feather evoked a spine. Thus, the jester appeared to be placed in the location of the sacrum, while the feather was closer to the upper part of the body. When I enquired about the reason for placing two mirrors, she said one was for the right, and the other for the left eye. She also saw in this an expression of the need to connect the two hemispheres of the brain. I certainly share her view concerning the two hemispheres of the brain. I feel that in her Sandplay process – along with the focus on a felt sense of the images and dreams – she had achieved both horizontal and vertical neural integration by bridging cognition, emotion and bodily sensations. This certainly had proved helpful in freeing various levels of blocks on a physical and emotional level due to traumatic childhood experiences, which resulted in an increased self-confidence. On this basis, she was able to experience renewed trust on an interpersonal level with a partner (an important aspect of interpersonal neural integration) and more light-heartedness at work. The way she had succeeded in integrating different levels of body and mind, in meeting her inner animal and the feminine, the way she had reached deep into inner levels of the Self (or transpirational neural integration) etc., reveal at the same time the depth of the process of individuation she had embarked upon.

Notes

1 P. Levine, *In An Unspoken Voice*, p. 36.
2 E. Neumann, *The Great Mother: An Analysis of the Archetype*, Pantheon Books, New York, 1955.
3 Ibid., p. 272.
4 E. Neumann, *Die Grosse Mutter*, Rhein Verlag, Zürich, 1965, p. 110, Figure 6.

Part 2

The method and the group

Chapter 5

Prelude

Luciana Battini

The train calls at the little station, only a few passengers get off. I wonder which road I should take, and realise I am still keen on the customary one, quite an uphill walk but which makes a shortcut to the village. Still, it is quite a climb and a fountain was aptly built there in the middle of the last century for passers-by to freshen up and quench their thirst. As I walk up the hill expending a great deal of effort, the green and golden roof of the church bell tower comes into view. The house where we meet up is located on its right, on top of the hill. Its very sight kindles emotions in me, as if I were coming home after wandering the streets of distant, foreign countries. The large dark green entrance door bearing a peculiar carving is always open in my imagination – and it almost unfailingly is, even in real life, at least during the day. A little bell announces the guest crossing the threshold, always heartily welcome.

The central part of the house, which is the oldest, used to be an important watchtower for the nearby town. Legend has it that, subsequent to a fire that had destroyed many houses in the village, the thick green door survived the flames, and so the old house, as well as its inhabitants and contents, were spared.

The tower is the place where we meet now, the physical space for our research. As soon as you walk past the door, you are immediately immersed in a unique dimension, as if time had decided to suspend, within these walls, its ceaseless weaving of worldly matters, thus enabling one to retrieve the scent and the warmth of a reality imagined rather than experienced, relished in dreams or in the stories that belong to other lifetimes – not only older times, but ancestral ones. As I reminisce and write, I feel as if I could smell the comforting scent of the wood burning and crackling in the fireplace, something not directly experienced in the house, but closely linked to the sense of warmth and cosiness felt upon progressing further into the house, to ever more intimate and private spaces and until reaching its heart, the watchtower. My limbs warm up and relax, leaving outside of these walls cold and tiredness. My breathing becomes deeper and calmer, my soul feels heartened as it's no longer besieged by doubt, uncertainty, judgement or proof, but feels welcomed instead in a space characterised by total freedom and complete protection.

DOI: 10.4324/9781003163503-7

Freedom and protection are the most solid and fundamental feelings of our experience in the tower. They enable us to look at each other beyond the veil of shame and fear so that a glimpse of our fragile innermost Self may be caught, rediscovering its poetry through sharing. We realise one another's richness, no longer just sensed or potential, but very real as it slowly unfolds, starting from the images that come from the patients' sandboxes, as their souls intertwine like threads with ours. A colour or a shape coming from these images links to the dance of our ability to feel, and then turns into movement and speech, colour and poetry, body and emotion.

Until it reaches a different sensitivity, a wider awareness that glimpses the weaving of an impalpable and at the same time robust fabric, born from warp and weft that intertwine thinking and feeling, matter and spirit, generating a new perception, more integrated and aware of the wholeness of being.

The thick door to the watchtower now closes to foster the thoughtfulness we need in order to pursue our quest, gathering after gathering, with never ending wonder and amazement at the beauty and the meaningfulness born from psychic suffering. We need to follow the rhythm of opening and closing, closing to the outer world and opening to the world of inner Self, the eternal rhythm of the tide, of our choosing, time after time, to be present with the freshness and passion of a shared and authentic love.

Chapter 6

Like a ritual

Michele De Toma

The Zollikon house

At number 8, Hinterzunen Road in Zollikon, in the old fifteenth-century house, there's a room with the sandboxes and the objects Dora Kalff used for the Sandplay Therapy she had herself devised. That very same house is now home to her son Martin, who works there and has reinterpreted her method in his own personal way; additionally, it is also the place where psychotherapists from all over the world gather and conduct research.

The house exerts a strong fascination on us, a group of Italian therapists who have periodically gathered here for more than ten years now[1]. What Chiara Bottari states, which I'm reporting in full, holds true for us all:

> Coming back to Zollikon feels like coming home – our own home.
>
> We arrive burdened by our toils and concerns, worries and afflictions – both our own and our patients'. We sometimes arrive here also at peace with ourselves, self-content, or with our soul yearning for peace and solace, just like when you get home in need of some rest and restored energy. The old house, now so familiar to us, welcomes us, with its spacious rooms, the arched stone doorways, the creaking floorboards, and Martin's smile that never changes through time, his wife Sabine discreetly by his side. You feel as if the past had come alive in that place.
>
> We are greeted by autumnal melancholy, it's a little cooler than where we came from, the sky is greyish and nature looks listless, like our soul when it 'withdraws' within itself. However, we do come back in the springtime, when we enjoy the caress of the wind, the arrival of the plants and their flowers, of the light on Lake Zurich. We feel the rebirth of life, the energy we deemed lost flows again, strong, in our psyche and our body.
>
> At least, this is what I feel every time I come back to Zollikon for an important session with people that I feel particularly in harmony with. I think that what really, deeply, moves me is the fact that we all know we have a Shadow, as Jung would call it, a dark area of our

DOI: 10.4324/9781003163503-8

psyche and, as we become familiar with ours, we also come to terms with the other's. A feeling of mutual trust then arises in the group and helps us through our work.

Ritual moments of our sessions

A building in the garden, by the house, has been turned into a Buddhist temple; Buddhism played a crucial role in the establishment of Sandplay Therapy.

The house and its many implications, the Buddhist temple, Martin Kalff's complex personality – shaped by Divinity studies, Jungian Psychology, and Buddhism – and the way in which the different moments of our sessions unfold – all of these contribute to an atmosphere where we sense our transformation into a small community taking part in a *ritual*. An important ritual, one that empowers us to access ourselves, prepares us to the sacredness of an encounter with the Other, and reminds us of the reverential respect we owe to our patients and of the deep relationship we have with them.

Our ritual consists of a few different moments:

◯An *initial guided meditation*. Kalff encourages us to listen attentively to the motives behind our choice to take the counselling and therapy career path, letting the Shadow latent in each of us emerge through our work, and he asks us all to focus our attention not only on the here and now, but also to how the burdens we carry in our life impact on us. Thanks to relaxation in a sitting position, with feet firmly planted on the ground and the feeling of the body in its joints, we can progressively let go of all the tensions, both mental and physical, churning inside of us, and let a sense of blank set in, as the indispensable premise to the real encounter with the Other.

In sacred rituals it is customary to don a ceremonial garb, as a requirement to transition from the secular to the sacred. Our meditation has a similar function on a symbolic level: we leave behind the burdens and conditionings of everyday life and just plunge into ourselves as we open up to the dialogue with the symbols that will be dealt with in the following phase.

◯An invitation to *pick a symbolic figure from a bag*, to investigate the resonances with our subjective being, to freely disclose it to the others and, finally, to *place* the object onto a small table by the window.

◯The *reading of the minutes* of the previous meeting, and a feedback with thoughts and impressions from those who had presented a clinical case during the previous sessions. Each of the participants report whether the group work has had an impact on the therapy, and discusses in what ways, other than the difficulties and the issues experienced.

◯Kalff's *presentation* of new research related to Sandplay Therapy (work on trauma, new ideas from neuroscience) and the discussion around thorny issues which have become matter of debate, and which pertain to Sandplay Therapy.[2]

◯The *selection* and *scheduling* of the cases we intend to review within the study group, prioritised on the basis of the urgency ranked by the therapist according to the severity of the patient's problems.

◯Before we begin to review the cases we have chosen, we practice *meditation* by drawing attention to our own breathing, in order to become aware of and leave behind our own bodily tensions as a preliminary phase to taking in the contents, the emotions, the feelings and the conflicts expressed by the images in our patients' sand scenes.

◯The meditation is followed by the actual *review and discussion of the cases*, during which we explore and *amplify* the images emerging from the sandbox through different media (colours, proprioceptive sensations, music, individual movement or movement in pairs, group dramatisation).[3]

◯ *Mealtimes* and *short breaks* contribute to the creation of a serene atmosphere amongst us.

◯ The *final meditation* helps us review the work done during the whole workshop.

◯ A *final moment* of thoughtfulness, each of us with our symbolic figure: the awareness of its symbolic value has remained a constant presence during our three-day workshop, and it may even be present and guide us later on, in our daily work with patients.

The picking of the symbolic objects

Our method consists of different phases and may be likened, to some extent, to sacred rituals. Here, too, we always have an *initial phase*, during which we leave behind our daily cares, and the *repetition* of gestures that form the ritual, and which have to abide by previously agreed-upon, binding rules. Whereas religious rituals ease the establishment of a relation with the sacred, our ritual eases the encounter with one's own Self, which is considered the hub of psychic life in psychoanalytical theory. Indeed, meditation practices shift our attention from Ego to Self, and help us forge a profound relationship with other group members. This in turns makes us more open and receptive to the symbolic significance of the images that emerge from our patients' sandboxes.

One moment above all embodies the ritual aspect of our sessions: the act of picking a figure from a bag, something with which we subsequently establish a relationship. One has to relinquish all of the Ego's demands and cast one's own rationality aside to be able to imagine that a figure randomly picked may ever end up revealing one aspect of our own psyche! And yet, it is precisely this simple gesture, alongside our imagination, that proves our work. We can rightfully claim that in this phase we are utilising active imagination, an approach that Jung experimented with the drafting of *The Red Book*, and which proves particularly effective in setting consciousness in dialogue with the unconscious.

This initial moment is characterised by the acceptance to take part in the game with the authentic child-like spirit that has always marked the activity of playing a game: the anticipation, the delight of the surprise, the frenzied expectation of wish-fulfilment. It feels like being taken back for one moment to the time of our childhood when gifts would be bestowed from above (by Christ Child in some southern Italian regions, Saint Lucy in northern Italy, Santa Claus across the country, etc.). In all our meetings, this ritual is emotionally charged – a clue, maybe, to the fact that our childhood is not completely lost at any stage of our life, even though now it is no longer our parents that make choices on our behalf. It's our adult Self – as we are now mothers and fathers ourselves – that carries out the random pick, thus playing along with what destiny has in store for us.

We each pick a figurine (an animal, a human being, a sacred image, etc.) and share with the group the emotions, feelings, and thoughts that it provokes. Eventually, we place our figures onto a small table by the window. The arrangement of the figures on the table reminds of a mandala[4]: they are no longer separate entities, but are now connected to each other. They symbolically represent the rapport we build afresh within the group at every session. The sharing of our experiences and the psychic images elicited by the figure almost represent the gift of Self, and the figures on the table transform into the Self of the group, so to speak. This eases for each of us the process of accessing a transpersonal dimension and of feeling part of a larger whole represented by our small community.

The centrality of the body

According to Erich Neumann, proto-rituals among primitive societies would take place in an atmosphere of mystical sharing and would almost exclusively affect the unconscious. In time, with the development of individual consciousness alongside the achievement of greater autonomy from the group on the part of the individual, the meaning of the sacred ritual has been internalised on a personal level.[5]

A similar process takes place in each of us throughout our three-day workshops: in a similar way to what would happen in ancient times, our rituals strengthen cohesion amongst us and create an intense feeling of belonging to a community so emotionally charged that we perceive it as "if not outright sacred, certainly solemn".[6] However, in contrast with what the outcome of sacred rituals would be in ancient times, the individual becoming part of a community does not determine the dissolution of our individual personalities, but rather enhances in each of us the awareness of our personal individuation process. "The outcome of the ritual therefore is the transformation of our own inner world".[7]

Being aware of this transformation is key to establishing a closer relation with the patient's private reality, as expressed by the images that appear in the sandbox.

As is often the case with rituals, the body plays a central role in ours and, if we ask the body questions, it will answer them. When we look at the images appearing in the sandboxes, at the beginning we pay attention to the sensations the body feels as a result of the emotions we feel, and only subsequently do we express feelings and thoughts. We put into practice some form of conscious regression to physical sensations which, unencumbered by the primacy of thinking, enables us to establish a profound rapport with the images we observe. One could argue it is the same physiological process of integration moving from the body to the mind that we follow when we shape an image in the sandbox.

Shared supervision

In the same way as every ritual relies on an officiant, we also have a mentor that wisely guides us on our journey: Martin Kalff. However, our mentor has gone beyond the traditional hierarchy applied to supervisory work, encouraging peer-to-peer discussion within the group: on the one hand, he has put himself at the service of each and every participant and, on the other, he has always met our contributions with enthusiasm, thus achieving a new, 'shared' approach to supervisory work from which shared research has also issued.

The ritual aspect of our sessions, which he presides over with expertise, has proved vital to our research, and has helped us gain deep personal insight and become receptive to the sacredness of our encounter with the Other – where the Other has been, respectively, the patient, the colleague, and the supervisor.

The ritual dimension of our sessions can be viewed as a large receptacle, some kind of alchemical vessel[8] for the group, in which we feel safe; inside of it, we have got a chance to divest ourselves of useless defensive superstructures and to authentically open up to the exchange with the Other. In this way, each one of us has succeeded in broadening our perspective and increasing our own therapeutic *background*, while feeling profoundly regenerated into a *new therapist*.

Notes

1 This chapter, by Luciana Battini, effectively conveys the fascination that house exerts on us; the same holds true for the following contribution by Chiara Bottari.
2 We discussed the following, amongst other subjects: the 'background' each therapist needs to acquire through their education, the assessment criteria for the duration of a therapy (once the symptoms that initially brought the patient to us have disappeared), the attention the therapist should pay to the patient's close family and the resources at hand to help the patient, the suffering caused by abrupt

interruptions of the therapy, and the realisation of the extent to which these interruptions may severely damage patients once unshielded by therapy.

3 An amplification medium, for example, is the resonance that the colours showing up in the sandbox has on each of us. The resonance is expressed individually through the drawing of shapes or the abstract use of colour in its traits, density, tints, shades, tones, and fields on sketch paper; later, the work produced will be presented and shared with the others. The twofold contact (both emotional and intellectual) we establish through these activities results in mutual exchanges that create an atmosphere of empathic sharing. This leads to the integration of emotional and rational contributions from everyone and to a more insightful interpretation of the images in the sandbox.

4 In Hinduist and Buddhist tradition the mandala is a symbolic representation of the cosmos; made of threads interwoven on a loom or with coloured powder on the ground, sometimes painted on fabric or frescoed on the walls of a temple.

5 Translated from Italian: E. Neumann, Il *Significato Psicologico del Rito* in *Il Rito, Legame tra gli Uomini, Comunicazione con gli Dei,* E. Neumann, A. Portmann, G. Scholem, Edizioni Red, Como, 1991, p. 36.

   Original text: *Zur psychologischen Bedeutung des Ritus* from "Eranos Jahrbuch", 1950, Bd.19, Mensch und Ritus, herausgegeben von Olga Fröben Kepteyn, Rhein Verlag, Zürich,1951.

6 Translated from Italian: C. Widmann, *Il Rito*, Edizioni Magi, Roma, 2007, p. 11.

7 Translated from Italian: E. Neumann, *Il Significato Psicologico del Rito*, p. 21.

8 A sealed vessel in which alchemists would endeavour to perform matter transformation processes, an activity that Jung would liken to projections of the individuation process.

Chapter 7

The importance of the group

Maria Teresa Pasolini

It is customary, before we start our work together, for each of us to pick one of the figures kept in a cloth bag. Our hand will pick the object, guided exclusively by the sense of touch and by the attempt to answer the question of the meaning that we are trying to attach to our life, from both a professional point of view and an existential perspective.

Martin Kalff draws closer to each one of us with a blue cloth bag decorated with stars, from which to randomly pick a figure. We don't know what will come out of the bag, our hands guide the action – the very same hands that, in Jung's words "Often [the hands] know how to solve a riddle with which the intellect has wrestled in vain".[1] These are the same hands that, as they come into contact with sand, become the means of expressing those psychic nuclei often buried deep in defensive oblivion, and in front of which speech proves utterly ineffective. Thus, we welcome the picked figures within us and feel their symbolic significance: they will guide us through the communal work awaiting us.

Kalff exhorts us to mind our body and express where we can feel the strong emotion arisen from the encounter with the symbolic figure. We give ourselves the time to feel in silence, and then we share with the others the meaning of our own emotion. This moment leads us to shift the attention to the inner world, and sharing our experience eases the relationships in the group.

The symbolic image takes each of us, in this session, to inner places that call out to be inhabited. Every time, to our amazement, we experience the encounter between the need to find a meaning and the image that helps us through our quest for an answer. Words that carry emotion and the embryo of thought then emerge: acceptance, protection, care, soul, meeting, affirmation, space, overcoming barriers, an ability to recognise and be recognised, a sense of impermanence, limitation, becoming, rootedness and displacement, disorientation – all of them help us move forward. And every time, like a miracle, the overlap occurs between what is inside of us and what is reaching for us but is still outside of us.

These are examples of some figures picked out of the bag in one of our sessions: a stone, heavy but smooth and light at the same time, round and warm; a snow globe symbolising concentration, but also the blank that can be

DOI: 10.4324/9781003163503-9

filled with new energy; a small statue of the Virgin Mary, an invitation to accept and keep on thoughtfully waiting; a pelican with its strength and lightness; a celestial globe, which looks as if its creation was time-consuming and seems to herald the possibility of expansion; a Chinese dragon, symbol of rage but also a grotesque mask; Saint Claire who brings light; a woman reading with a cat snuggled at her feet, standing for integration between instinct and intellect; a monk riding an ox, symbolising clear knowledge; an Indian man surrounded by children, tell-tale symbol of hope for acceptance; a pebble to indicate the meaning of the essential, solidity, simplicity and calm, which should accompany us in our daily life and in our work. These images stay with us during the three days of our session and help us carry out our work.

I feel – and it is a common and shared feeling – that every time it makes for a beautiful and emotional moment, the moment when each of us discloses to the Other – through the symbolic meaning attached to the picked image – some parts of their self. This is not the only time when we happen to share some intimate traits of our psyche with the group, perceived as a psychic locus including and protecting without passing judgements, without criticisms. It helps us grapple with imperfections and biases, supports us in accepting the manifestations of our Shadow, fosters the awareness that human nature needs to be embraced and nurtured, with all its weaknesses and idiosyncrasies: it's only then that the encounter with our Shadow can be appreciated in its transformative and evolutionary power. We all feel harmony flowing amongst us, the perception of a thread that links and supports us in our journey towards meeting the Self. It is as if the common journey prompted and exhorted each of us to confront our fear of leaving behind the safe harbour of rationality and to take up a challenge that may sometimes prove disorienting, but mostly enriching. It may be the same fear that our patients experience when we help them tackle it. Mutual recognition and acceptance encourage the free expression of our own feelings within the group, in a similar way to what occurs in the analytic setting; during a session, the therapist – who is ready and willing to empathise with the patient's essential needs, disregarded thus far – champions the carving of a space for their representation. Our diversity, far from being perceived as a threat, becomes by contrast the nourishment of our common work. The metabolising and transformative ability of the group is the reason behind its own functioning and enrichment.

Within the group, it becomes therefore possible to identify the transpersonal aspects of the psychic experience. We all respond to the evidence that, within this shared experience, we take a common path, each by our own individual choice and within which everyone's idiosyncrasies integrate.

I am strongly convinced that the main theme and recurrent motif of our sessions has been the way in which we have endeavoured to reach the goal of being together, our accepting the Other outside of us by welcoming the Other within us, even while we all share the common duty of taking on our patient's burden.

The new method Kalff has propounded revolves around one central idea: it exhorts us to prepare for resonance, as well as to let our body be touched by and be resonant with our patient's images. In our group sessions, we are invited to 'enter' some Sandbox images by letting our body respond to them. Our body, because of its immediate response is the starting point in a journey towards an authentic understanding of the patient's problems, along a path that starts from sensations (bodily perceptions), moves on to feelings and then reaches thought: the body that feels and finds expression is the earliest communication medium for our experience. The emotional awareness we achieve when our senses come into contact with the images from the sand scenes becomes our primary source of information and the instrument for understanding the energy that the objects represent for our patient, and what unconscious nuclei they stand for. This understanding issued from our own body enables us to encounter the patient exactly at the place where they mostly need to be seen and understood. 'Entering' the Sandbox with our own body is key to identifying the exact locus where the problem is at that given moment, at that obscure level of the psyche from which the patient is calling out for help and guidance. The emotional-sensory giving in to the images arising from the sandbox fosters an experience of sharing which forms the foundations on which to build both, as well as to jointly take the path to healing. To say it with Jung: "For the important thing is not to interpret and understand the fantasies, but primarily to experience them".[2]

The attention paid to our body provides us with the means to identify our own potential and our own wounds. In effect, it is only by recognising him/herself as a wounded healer that the therapist can finally detect the patient's wounds and guide them along the path to recovery.[3] The act of minding the 'body's felt experience' makes it possible for the therapist to become aware of the resonance within him or herself of the patient's suffering and to grasp its transformative potential.

Sharing the experience of our body's responses to the images from the sand scenes within the Zollikon Group has helped us identify our own wounds, compare them amongst ourselves, grasp the transformative potential lying within them – as a consequence, the healer's wound has made the viewpoint from which to observe, feel and interpret the images arising from the sand.

Notes

1 C.G. Jung, *The Structure and Dynamics of the Psyche*, CW, VIII, 1969, § 180.
2 C.G. Jung, *Two Essays on Analytical Psychology*, CW VII, 1967, § 342.
3 D. Sedgwick, *The Wounded Healer: Countertransference from a Jungian Perspective*, Routledge, London-New York, 2017. According to Sedgwick, in order to heal the patient the therapist needs to identify their own wound and make contact with their own Shadow.

Chapter 8

Body and movement

Ezia Palma

In the Zollikon research group, discussion of selected clinical cases studies takes place not only on a verbal level, but it requires us to step right in – both as therapists and as human beings – by being especially mindful of the role our body plays in the relationship with the patients and amongst ourselves. In order for the reader to form an understanding of our method – which has brought about a new theory of Sandplay Therapy – I am about to go over the milestones of our work, while lingering on the key role bodily perceptions and movement play in it.

The initial phase

Our work always starts with a short meditation, in order to focus our attention on our breath, to free the mind, and to feel in closer contact with ourselves and our body, so that we can 'make room' for the work we will do at a later stage. The aim is to achieve that emptiness inside of ourselves that Marie-Louise von Franz described as 'creative potential', and which proves crucial to ensure the possibility to make room for 'the not yet existing'.

We then move on to the choice of a figure among those used in Sandplay Therapy and that Martin Kalff selects and bundles in a blue bag. The selected figure triggers in each of us images and fantasies that we get a chance to share with other fellow therapists, calling forth new inner experiences also in the other members of the group. This sharing creates a harmony that paves the way for the entire work of our three-day workshops.

During this initial phase we try to develop and further the ability to mind our inner experiences and to open up to those of others. We try to pay to ourselves and to our colleagues that attention that, as Simone Weil pointed out, is essential in order to be able to really take care of the Other. The exercise we perform on ourselves thus prepares us to open up to the sorrow of our patients and our fellow therapists, which will be matter of concern and reflection for us throughout the rest of the meeting.

For a therapist, paying attention means comparing their own experiences with the patient's not only from a cognitive perspective, but also from an

DOI: 10.4324/9781003163503-10

emotional one, that is, by calling emotions and feelings into play. Approaching the Other as a therapist therefore implies a deep involvement that requires empathy, and at the same time, the ability to prevent feeling overwhelmed by the experiences of the Other. In the research group we have found that calling attention to bodily responses provides us with a solid ground on which to build the analytical relationship. To establish a connection with the world of the Other, it is crucial to learn to heed one's own physical sensations even before when faced with emotions and feelings. Being in touch with one's own positive and negative feelings enables us to prevent emotions from clouding rational thinking processes, as well as to avoid forming hasty judgments about the psychological situation of our patients.

In order to put the right distance between oneself and the emotions one experiences, it is therefore essential to focus one's own attention on what Martin Kalff calls 'the body's felt experience'. The body's responses, identified through meditation and attention paid to the breath, in fact precede the formation of emotions and lay the ground for emotions to be felt without overwhelming those who are experiencing them.

Working on a case

The review of a clinical case starts with an account of the situation, followed by the observation of the patient's sand image, projected onto a wall. Together we look at each image in silence, and we let the colours, shapes, figures and their positions, the empty spaces and the spaces that are occupied, resonate within us. Immediately after this, we turn to 'inner listening', eyes closed, paying attention especially to the sensations felt in the body, and only after this do we focus on feelings and emotions. Eventually, we share with the others what the images elicited in us. We pay special attention to the first sandbox installation, which very often contains in embryo everything we will see in the later ones.

While reviewing the other sand image subsequent to the time devoted to inner listening, we express our body's felt experiences using different creative means of expression such as movement, dance, music, painting and poetry.

To sum up, our analysis of sand creations goes through four different key moments: the silent review of the sand image; the attention drawn breathing and to bodily sensations; the identification of emotional experiences; and their expression through artistic means.

In our experience, emotions, affections and psychic complexes that emerge from the sand image are more clearly understood when we relive that experience on a psycho-physical level through a creative movement. When we draw our attention to the body, we often detect a response intrinsically embedded in a body part or a specific organ: feeling warm or cold, stiff or relaxed, pain or pleasure. These feelings can help pinpoint some of our patients' cruxes which may have escaped our consideration before, and identify new opportunities for transformation. At a later stage we then turn our attention to such emotions as sadness, rage, peace of mind and happiness, occurring in us as a result – to some extent – of those sensations.

The dialogue within the group, the comparison between our different bodily experiences and feelings, always bring to light new evidence which we utilise to interpret the sandbox installation. The creative/expressive moment, for example, can replace the sensation of heaviness derived from grief and trauma with that of lightness. This lightness furthered by the group proves, at times, an utterly new discovery for the therapist presenting a clinical case, and may even foster in them the awareness of alternative unexplored paths to healing for the patient. During an individual session, this awareness may be conveyed, through countertransference, to the patient.

Attention to bodily responses and experiences can also help discern one's own emotions without being dominated by them, and at the same time enables us to avoid overly externalising our feelings or externalizing them too quickly. Excessive externalisation tends to empty emotion of significance and impoverishes it by depriving it of its transformative abilities. Empathy can help feeling closeness to the person in our care, but cannot not lapse into identification.

It is by paying close attention to our 'bodily sensations' that we gain full awareness of the boundary our skin makes between inside and outside, as well as between the Self and the Other. Bodily sensations help us find the correct empathic attitude, with a balanced distance between therapist and patient. Again, a clear understanding of bodily sensations guides the appropriate evaluation of the quality of the analytic relationship from the standpoint of transference and countertransference. Sometimes a sudden headache or stomach ache may let out something about our relation with the patient, and the same holds true for the patients themselves. For this reason, in some cases it may be helpful to ask the patient – while reviewing the sand image – to describe bodily sensations while switching the attention from the object to the subject, from the image of the self projected onto the sand to the physical self.

As mentioned earlier, attention to bodily sensations plays a key role also within the research group. We frequently dramatise, using different techniques, some of the scenes shaped in the sand. It often happens that only after physical dramatization do we become aware of certain experiences which were potentially visible in the scene, but which we did not initially perceive: the catatonic sadness embodied by an empty corner of the sandbox, the sensation of warmth underlying a volcanic stone, the loneliness of a seemingly boundless desert, fear and courage represented by an unknown deity. This is when the *movement of the body* leads us to a deep understanding of a scene shaped in the sand. We sometimes work in pairs to enact a conflict or an alliance; at other times we move as a group in silence or guided by a drum roll. Accordingly, the peer-to-peer relationship shifts from a merely verbal mode to a physical one, evoking yet unexplored experiences felt by the body, and engaging our conscious and unconscious selves. Thanks to the movement of one's own body and that of the others in the group, the therapist presenting the case can explore new potential processing strategies and catch a glimpse of further possible developments, which he /she had failed to consider before and that can then be put to use in therapy.

This fresh approach to conducting supervision spawns a creative energy that affects, in turn, the group, the single therapist and their patients.

The importance of the body in therapy: a few theoretical remarks

In the course of our supervisory sessions, it has often become apparent that during the reviewing of the sand creations our body can help identify patterns, aversions, problems and resistances initially undetected.

The importance of the body in therapy has been a matter of debate on a theoretical level, notably as far as it concerns Sandplay Therapy, which is characterised by two aspects. The former, which is immediately apparent, is the patient's movement of the hands while creating the image in the sandbox as well as while moving about in the room to pick up the figures to be placed (again, in motion) into the sandbox itself. The latter is that the figures and scenes in the sandbox embody aspects – sometimes concealed – of the patient's own physicality: stiffness, tension, relaxation, fragility, sense of security.

It is often the case that, when a patient cannot word their experience – as is frequently the case with traumatised individuals – bringing the body into play may serve the purpose of untangling the speechless narrative of a traumatic experience which is not otherwise utterable. Images connected with trauma are almost unfailingly so deeply buried in the unconscious that processing and then uttering them may take a long time. Sandplay work often proves the means through which images can emerge without actually being uttered.

As a more general observation, the role of the body has long been emphasised within the theoretical framework. I will mention only three contributions to theoretical thinking on movement, which have proved beneficial to my own therapeutic practice.

C.G. Jung highlighted the important role that bodily experience plays in depth psychology in many of his writings. His early psychological studies included observations on unconscious motor processes, and in his commentary to *The Secret of The Golden Flower*, he maintains:

> Among my patients I have come across cases of women who did not draw mandalas but danced them instead. In India there is a special name for this: *mandala nrithya*, the mandala dance. The dance figures express the same meaning as the drawings.[1]

In 1916 Jung argued that the expressive movement of the body is one of the several ways in which to shape the unconscious,[2] while in his seminars on Nietzsche, he wrote:

We cannot say the side of the spirit is twice as good as the other side; we must bring the pairs of opposites together in an altogether different way, where the rights of the body are just as much recognized as the rights of the spirit.[3]

Mary Starks Whitehouse (1911–1979), a pioneer of dance therapy, studied the role of movement in the psyche while performing the movement itself. With respect to what she defines as "authentic movement" or "movement in depth", she made a distinction between "I move" – the clear awareness that I am the subject performing the movement – and "I am moved" – the sudden and abrupt movement in which the Self gives up control, stops choosing, stops making requests to 'their' own body. This way, the Ego allows the Self to take its place in moving the body. This is an unpremeditated lapse of control on the part of the Self, which cannot be either explained or repeated in the exact same way in which it spontaneously occurred.[4] In the experience of movement, the sensations of moving and being moved sometimes occur simultaneously. When this occurs, the subject experiences total awareness, the combination of something I am doing with something that is happening to me.[5]

Joan Chodorow from the San Francisco Carl Gustav Jung Institute compares the movement in dance therapy to the way it can be used in Sandplay Therapy. In Chodorow's opinion, upon observing the sand creation it is important to give in to the urges to move they communicate to our body. If we allow these sensations to become a physical entity within us and move with them, we develop active imagination in the same way as we do when we pursue a visual phenomenon engendered by our fantasy. The therapist experiences their own Self and the psychic content emerging from the sand image and partakes in what the patient themselves experience in creating the scene. The partaking of the inner world of the Other, triggered by movement, furthers the understanding of the deeper meaning shining through the sand image. The therapist's inner images interact with the patient's, in a relationship in which the analyst becomes a witness/participant encouraging psychic transformation.[6]

Notes

1 C.G. Jung, *Alchemical Studies*, CW XIII, § 32, Routledge, London, 1968.
2 C.G. Jung, *The Structure and Dynamics of The Psyche*, CW VIII, 1969.
3 C.G. Jung, *Nietzsche's Zarathustra: Notes of the Seminar Given in 1934–39*, 1988, p. 235.
4 M. Whitehouse, *Physical Movement and Personality*, in *Authentic Movement: Essays by Mary Stark Whitehouse, Janet Adler and Joan Chodorow*, edited by Patrizia Pallaro, Jessica Kingsley Publishers, London-Philadelphia, 1999.
5 M. Whitehouse, *The Tao of the Body*, in *Authentic Movement*, 1999.
6 J. Chodorow, *To Move and Be Moved*, in *Authentic Movement*, 1999.

Chapter 9

Countertransference in the analytic couple

Eleonora Tramaloni

My extensive experience in the research group led by Martin Kalff has enabled me to hone my listening skills and increase the attention paid to the emotional experiences and physical sensations sparked by the vision of sandbox scenes. We have tested a new approach to it which triggers not only thought, but also all of our psychological functions, and enables the connection between emotional and physical contemplation, on the one hand, and mental and verbal observation, on the other. As Kalff himself explains in the opening contribution to this volume, the new method he has devised (ERCS) gives a key role to the body, or to what we physically experience when confronted with a sandbox scene. The use of different media – such as colours, free movement, dramatisation in pairs or groups, enables one to feel with their own body what cannot be perceived through sheer observation.

I am deeply grateful to my colleagues – with whom we have formed a really close-knit analytic group – and to Martin Kalff for the constructive and valuable experience we have had the opportunity to share, as well as for the enriching personal and professional experience he has contributed to the group.

A journey for two

What I have always felt and experienced in the therapeutic rapport is its fundamentally transformative nature: the encounter between two worlds that draw close to one another by developing a mutual understanding and get to know each other until the establishment of a healing alliance fostering that inner journey on which the patient – accompanied and supported by the therapist – can finally venture. It's a special and unique relationship, unlike any other in our daily life, a deep friendship which comes into existence and dwells in the analytic arena, between two allies endeavouring to give voice to the subconscious which has content and purpose in store for them.

The space and time of the analytic work are set apart from the life outside of the psychotherapy practice and are placed in an alchemical vessel in which the 'whole' personalities of both therapist and patient meet, get in touch with each other, and undergo a process of transformation as a consequence.

DOI: 10.4324/9781003163503-11

Such a journey is embarked on by the patient with a view to disentangling crippling complexes, finding a life path consistent with the patient's lost authenticity and healing emotional wounds and traumas, but also a joint journey with someone, which transforms and engages both protagonists. This is the only way in which something can really happen and be conveyed through an interaction to which each contributes one's own whole subjectivity.

Unrepressed unconscious and implicit memory

Since the dawn of civilisation, ancient cultures like the Babylonians, Sumerians, Greeks and Jews were interested in the oneiric world as they felt it was of paramount importance to human beings. More recently, our founding fathers Freud and Jung highlighted the importance of dreams as a manifestation of the unconscious, as a guide to and amplification of consciousness. The attention to images surfacing from an individual's inner self – which Jung warmly encouraged – thanks to Dora Kalff's work has found a means of expression even in wakefulness through the images dwelling in the sandbox.

During this type of analytical treatment, the body – through to the hands playing in the sandbox – accesses the symbolic game, which enables unconscious contents to emerge and bridges the gulf between the patient's inner world and the outer world through the tangible presence of earth, water, figures, and the therapist's empathic presence. Only after the image – which conveys deep emotional contents – has been projected onto the sand will the patient be able to describe it in words, carefully listened to by the therapist. As with dreams, through Sandplay images the unconscious reveals alternative approaches to solving the inner conflict and reaching self-realisation, which are present in embryo in each and every individual. In my training the integration of body and psyche has always proved a necessary condition and I discovered (many years ago now) in Dora Kalff's workshops an analytical practice which is capable of reactivating areas that would otherwise be off limits, insofar as they belong to an *unrepressed unconscious* [1] which we now know to be linked to the implicit memory formed in the first two years of life.

The explicit memory resides, like speech, in the left hemisphere, and develops neurologically only after the second year of life; its contents can be consciously recalled, spoken and, therefore, also removed. By contrast, implicit memory is located in the right brain hemisphere, which is mostly concerned with emotions and the processing of past experiences, of which the individual is not aware, cannot put into words, and therefore cannot even remove.

Implicit memory collects all the emotions which the child experiences in their own environment and, notably, with their own mother. Researchers posit that implicit memory could date back to the last few months of pregnancy, during which the foetus lives in a very close relationship with the mother, with her heartbeat, her breath, the sound of her voice: this experience is believed to be a steady fact, as well as a model for the development of rhythm and musicality, which lies at the core of the early representations of the child's inner world. The memory of these primary emotions, pre-verbal and pre-symbolic, will only reach the conscience via imaginative non-verbal experiences. These mnemonic traces, stored in the implicit memory of the unrepressed unconscious, will form the base structure, personality and character of every individual and will impact their affective, cognitive and emotional life.

The *unrepressed unconscious* contains pre-symbolic experiences which cannot be recalled or expressed with words, because their dimension is non-verbal. However, these early experiences do condition our life and can emerge in non-verbal communication, symbolic images, outbursts, dreams and the transference relationship – that is, the affective relationship that is established between therapist and patient.

The analytic relationship can transform these pre-verbal and pre-symbolic aspects into experiences that can be expressed verbally and are accessible to the conscience, by paying attention to dreams and to the imaginative activity which is key to Sandplay therapy.

The countertransference

The research conducted on children and the so-called 'infant observation'[2] have made it possible to confirm that the development of mind and of self-awareness is based on a process which is basically relational. For this reason, the transference relationship of the analytic couple is one of the key factors to the healing process and can help, in the 'free and protected space' (Dora Kalff) of the sandbox, the transformation of contents emerging from the patient's unconscious.

I would like to reflect in particular on the analyst's countertransference (also known as 'co-transference'[3] or 'shared transference' – a name aptly coined by Marco Garzonio[4]) as well as on the importance of observation and attentive listening therapists should devote to emotions, thoughts and soma-tisation occurring within themselves throughout their work with a patient. The objective is to make the elements that emerge from that context, that 'alchemical vessel' that patient and analyst share.

This type of attention is of primary importance in Martin Kalff's work, whose teachings dictate not only a special focus on emotions, feelings and thoughts, but also on the bodily experience *per se*, which he has termed 'the body's felt experience'. In the transference relationship in general – and, most notably, in Sandplay therapy – the patient's body is engaged and so is the therapist's. The research group, according to this fresh approach, furthers the occurrence of countertransference from a basic physical level – that is, what we perceive within and through our body – all the way up to the emotional level and, eventually, to the rational one. Comparing the different transference responses from each member of the group opens up in presenter's psyche a number of unexplored paths communicated via countertransference to the patient's, too. The act of minding what we feel and perceive, of highlighting the differences or of detecting commonalities with what the patient perceives, is similar to the work of *rêverie* [5] that every 'sufficiently good' mother does with her child, and that, starting from a 'containing symbiosis', eases the achievement of those partings underpinning both individuation and growth.

The analyst is not only the place and object of projections on the part of the patient, also a subject and an individual as completely absorbed in this dual relationship (further 'burdened' by their own personality and counter-transference experience) as the patient is – the only difference lying in their clinical and personal training enabling the (toilsome, yet indispensable) processing of the interpersonal dynamics and of the experience issued from the analytic relationship.

The analyst is not only expected to listen attentively, observe painstakingly, and detect connections, but also to be an individual undergoing seamless transformation and development, committed to a never-ending individuation process and, in consequence, always engrossed in the close observation of the inner self with a view to identifying their own dark sides and weaknesses. These dark sides and weaknesses are often stirred during the transference work with the patient, thus compelling the therapist to ceaselessly work on themselves. In consequence, the journey with the patient offers ample opportunity for their own never-ending transformation – a precious gift of self-fulfilment.

An example

As a result of the clinical supervision work carried out in Zollikon, we noticed that the new psychic experiences which were shaping us had an impact on the work with our patients, too, as if they could sense on an unconscious level our new stance. This is clearly visible in some clinical cases reported in this volume and contributed from personal experience.

Once a fellow therapist presented the case of a child whose father had died of cancer, a very sad case which deeply moved us all. In the following session, the same therapist stated that – thanks to the exchange with us on this case – he had been able to fully perceive and come to terms with the deeply buried grief of his own personal loss: the lack of an authentic relationship with his own father, a deprivation that this time he was able to feel in his body instead of perceiving it as a painful rational realisation. He told us that this new awareness had helped discern the projection of his own suffering onto his young patient:

> It was this suffering that has enabled me to make a clear distinction between my young patient and myself as a child. Thanks to this clear distinction, I finally felt unhampered and free in the therapeutic relation-ship with the young patient and felt his strength and courage in full. After two months of therapy, the young patient gave indications to be

ready and willing to do something else in lieu of our sessions. The resolution of the therapeutic relationship and the grieving process were now possible even though the price to pay had been a little suffering on the part of both. This step enabled the young patient to fully process the grief for his father's death and to internalise his father's positive image encouraging him to continue his life by relying on his strength and courage. By virtue of a metaphorical system of communicating vessels, the therapist was finally able to heal and sooth his own personal wound.

The example shows how countertransference can help the therapist in their own personal individuation process as well as in fully understanding the patient's suffering.

The analytic couple

The deep exchange and fertile relationship between the analytical partners foster changes and new energy in both parties.

Jung writes to that effect in 1929 in his book *Problems of Modern Psychotherapy*:

> By no device can the treatment be anything but the product of mutual influence, in which the whole being of the doctor as well as that of his patient plays its part. In the treatment there is an encounter between two irrational factors, that is to say, between two persons who are not fixed and determinable quantities but who bring with them, besides their more or less clearly defined fields of consciousness, an indefinitely extended sphere of non-consciousness. Hence the personalities of the doctor and the patient are often infinitely more important for the outcome of the treatment than what the doctor says and thinks (although what he says and thinks may be a disturbing or a healing factor not be underestimated). For two personalities to meet is like mixing: if there is any combination at all, both are transformed. In any effective psychological treatment the doctor is bound to influence the patient; but this influence can only take place if the patient has a reciprocal influence on the doctor. You can exert no influence if you are not susceptible to influence. It is futile for the doctor to shield himself from the influence of the patient and to surround himself with a smoke-screen of fatherly and professional authority. By so doing he only denies himself the use of a highly important organ of information. The patient influences him unconsciously none the less, and brings about changes in the doctor's unconscious which are well known to many psychotherapists.[6]

Furthermore, in *Psychology of The Transference*, Jung illustrates his view of the patient-analyst relationship as the relationship between two fellow initiates deeply involved in a psychological lab, a bond as strong as that between two chemical compounds altering each other through bonding. "

It is inevitable that the doctor should be influenced to a certain extend and even that his nervous health should suffer. He quite literally 'takes over' the suffering of his patient and them with him".[7]

I believe it is important not to fear one's own emotions, one's own responses, be they positive or negative; on the contrary, they should be viewed as important pointers towards a fuller understanding of the Other and the self. It is important to overcome the sense of shame or insecurity that often poses an obstacle to the enriching experience we may gain from a bolder analysis of our responses to the analytic work. It is the same attitude we always ask of our patients, and which proves difficult also for us: getting involved and taking up the challenge, without losing sight of our own personal limits, of our personality and within an ethically valuable context that can be adapted to our needs and the individual patient's needs. The context should not be a rigid cage, but a flexible framework of reference.

In this context, would it prove useful to share with the patient our feelings towards them, that sentiment technically referred to as 'countertransference'? To what extent should we verbally share within the intimate relationship between patient and therapist?

I don't believe there is a set rule when it comes to this decision, and would argue that it is something to be assessed every time in the light of the idiosyncrasies of each specific relationship, with respect to the observation and processing of the previous sessions which can help understand what and to what extent we can share some insights with our patient.

However, there is something in a therapist's 'art' that is impossible to communicate on a cognitive level, and some of its aspects depend exclusively on that: sometimes it feels as if the Self may really take over and guide our work, prompting words and thoughts which we fully perceive as not simply coming from our Ego. In these circumstances, I believe we are the medium for a transpersonal energy that inspires our work and to which we may want to pay more thought.

Projecting our own complexes: a risk to avoid

The work we have been carrying out within the Zollikon Group encourages the comparison between the individual's and the group's point of view, and this can help avoid the risk of seeing ourselves reflected in the images issued from the patient's unconscious, and which possibly represents the patient's own self-healing process. This is a concrete risk: we, as therapists, are always inevitably stretcher-bearers of a wounded patient who may still need narcissistic nourishment and that could determine attention-seeking behaviours and lead to an illusion of indispensability. There is the risk of falling prey to our own undetected complexes.

The meditation practice led by Martin Kalff and the psychological debate amongst us has enabled the group members to work on our own dark sides, thus furthering a spiritual stance that makes us feel closer to the Self – both ours and the patient's – and transforming the complexes of the Self in the light of this transpersonal dialogue.

The last few years of supervisory group work we have experienced bears witness to the fact that countertransference – both emotionally felt and rationally processed – is the most effective tool we have to tackle the patient's problems, while at the same time it contributes to the therapist's psychological transformation.

Attention to one's own somatic emotional responses

It may be argued that in Sandplay Therapy it is important to listen to our own mind state and to the sensations our body conveys from the very moment the patient arrives and we wonder what we are feeling and perceiving while the patient is with us – sensations elicited by the patients themselves and by the scenes shaped in the sandbox.

In the analytic relationship, psychic contamination – of which we may be utterly unaware – often proves unavoidable and manifests itself in us through somatic emotional responses. For this reason, it is important to adopt a self-reflecting attitude which helps tell, within the transference relationship, the patient's answers from our own.

By analysing my reactions, I have noticed how sometimes, during a session, I develop physical somatic reactions, such as pain in the chest, sense of oppression, sudden tiredness, lethargy, headache: these are tangible signs in my body of emotional blocks and deep repression that, however, pertains to the patient's life.

The attention paid to the body's felt experience propounded by Martin Kalff has endowed me with fuller awareness and attentiveness in listening to somatic emotional responses and it has proved easier for me to feel and recognise them, as well as to link them to the patient's situation.

My defences, still difficult to come to terms with, are sometimes activated when with some patients I experience exhaustion from tackling negative feelings. Under those circumstances I don't feel like facing the next session or taking charge of the patient, because of the foreboding of the suffering that patient will cause me, or the apprehension that the patient's suffering – a burden which I am expected to share with them – may rub salt into unhealed wounds, chafe still sensitive or hurting parts, maybe healed, but still abiding in my body.

I remember feeling overwhelmingly moved while being confronted with the cold detachment with which horrible tragedies were being reported to me, symptomatic of an extreme defence mechanism clamping on the bereavement they were not ready to accept, but which the therapist is expected to get burdened with and bear on behalf of the Other as well as standing by the side of the Other, helping them cope with the void and angst derived from the loneliness where bereavement had left them. A sorrow may be first conceived of and begotten in the heart and the mind of the analyst, who later gives the patient the chance to accept and feel it within themselves thanks to the sharing underpinning this twofold relationship.

In these cases, it is important to be able to embrace what comes from the patient, but also to differentiate it from what belongs to us by understanding which psychic contents we have empathically allowed into ourselves insofar as still unconscious in the patient, but which may have reopened old wounds within ourselves. It is also important to listen to and ponder over the sensations experienced, detect projective identifications, introjections of the patient's psychic states so overwhelming as to breach into us through our weaknesses. It is important to recognise them as belonging to what the patients cannot yet show to themselves or to us, clues to a vulnerability which is often disowned and masked under opposite behaviours, yet given away by symptoms that are often crippling and uncontrollable.

I have sometimes become aware of the way in which my unconscious compensates for the inferiority complex my patient experiences by suddenly filling me with awe and countertransference, during which I perceive and feel in perfect harmony and have a great deal of empathy for the client, his or her states of mind and emotions.

I am particularly alert to the dreams where my patient appears, and I ask myself whether their appearance expresses any new psychological aspects which may have been stirred by the analytic relationship.

In conclusion, I strongly believe that in Sandplay Therapy the patient's intrapsychic process of self-healing is eased not only through the painstaking attention to and close observation of the transference aspects of the analytic relationship, but also through the awareness of the importance of the sensations of the body and of the emotions we experience. Minding the sensations of the body proves invaluable in drawing a separation line between our own experience and our patient's.

The analytic relationship accordingly results in the strong bond, the therapeutic alliance, and the special friendship that supports patient and therapist in reaching the common goal to transform and fulfil the self.

Notes

1 The term 'unrepressed unconscious' was first used by Mauro Mancia, Professor of Human Physiology and psychoanalyst. According to Mancia, the unconscious is a deposit inside the memory of the emotional representations, the defences and fantasies stored since the beginning of life and, for this reason, memory and the unconscious cannot but be intertwined. The neuroscientific discovery of the existence of two memory systems, explicit and implicit, encouraged the researcher to posit the existence of a double system of the unconscious, active within each individual since birth.

2 Psychoanalytical observation technique of the mother-child couple from birth to the second year. Observation takes place in the family environment (Marta Harris, Ester Bick, *The Tavistock Model: Papers on Child Development and Psychoanalytic Training*, Karnac Books Ltd, London, 2011).

3 The word 'co-transference', coined by Jungian analyst Kay Bradway, draws attention to the simultaneity of the transference implicating both patient and therapist.

4 Marco Garzonio, founding member and teacher at AISPT (Italian Association Sandplay Therapy), member of ISST (International Society Sandplay Therapy), member and teacher at CIPA (Italian Center of Analytical Psychology), professional journalist and writer.

5 Psychoanalyst W.R. Bion in *Learning from Experience* (Jason Aronson, USA, 1994) uses this term to indicate the mother's ability to receive the emotional and sensorial impressions from the new-born and to process them in a way the child can assimilate and use. The concept of 'rêverie' is also used by Bion for defining the mental state of the analyst during a session.

6 C.G. Jung, *The Practice of Psychotherapy*, C.W. XVI, 1966, § 163.

7 C.G. Jung, *The Psychology of the Transference* in *The Practice of Psychotherapy*, § 358.

Chapter 10

Sandplay and meditation

Creative grains of transformation

Maria Polidoro

The encounter with Sandplay Therapy

Fulfilling one's own existential journey, abiding by its truth, and emphasising its spiritual aspects, make lifelong commitments that may be pursued along different routes.

I was studying for a university exam when I came across Dora Kalff and Sandplay Therapy for the first time. The essay on her theoretical approach was one of many others among my reading lists,[1] but it was the only one that particularly piqued my curiosity. The discovery of the use of body language and play in the analytic setting caused me to yearn for a more in-depth exploration of her psychological and spiritual research.

A few years passed. After my postgraduate studies, I came to learn of Martin Kalff's training sessions in Zollikon only upon participating in a workshop on Sandplay recommended by my own analyst. I immediately contacted him and expressed my interest in becoming a member of his group, and he didn't hesitate to take me on board. I could not even imagine then the impact this encounter would have on my life.

One month and a half later, on a fresh July morning, I stood in front of the green door, left ajar, of a fifteenth-century house, previously owned by Mrs Kalff and now inhabited by her son Martin.

Thick walls, stone flooring on the ground level, a narrow creaky wooden staircase leading to the upper floor, a small waiting room with a fireplace, the meeting room, the windows overlooking the garden, neglected in some corners and dotted with hydrangeas and roses in others, a cat curled up by a birch tree and totally indifferent to the nearby building, the Zollikon Buddhist Centre. A house of a distinguished simplicity and of distinct echoes from the past.

In the Sandplay room, you immediately find yourself in the fascinating world of play and creativity. It felt so emotional being in a place full of things meant to quench the thirst for transfiguration of the woeful landscapes of the soul, as well as to channel the creative instinct that, when deployed, enables the fulfilment of one's own individuality, uniqueness, the unstoppable emergence of awareness from the sea of the unconscious, and the healing from

DOI: 10.4324/9781003163503-12

their contraposition. It allows, therefore, to establish a deep harmony between the inner and outer world, to offer one's best contribution to the world, "to do each of us his little bit towards transforming the spirit of the times".[2] Digging the sand with one's own hands, digging matter, represents going back the original substance, to the unconscious depths, "we might truly say from the realm of the Mothers where the creative work arises"[3] which constitutes the "widest, most important answer, the most meaningful, less direct and less specific to psychological suffering".[4]

It is in this very room that symbols prove capable of eliminating neurotic dissociations, as maintained by C.G. Jung: "They are the remedy with whose help neurotic dissociations can be repaired, by restoring to the conscious mind a spirit and an attitude which from time immemorial have been felt as solving and healing in their effect".[5]

Here, thanks to play, unconscious contents and images can find expression in symbolic representations, Ego and Self are brought together and restored to wholeness again, a contact with one's own centre is established and, along with it, a new order is found that becomes a rainbow of psychological transformations and healing as with mandala creations – which will be touched upon later.

The former group

When I started attending Martin Kalff's seminars in Zollikon, the group was open and no two sessions in a row hosted the same participants. The work focused on the supervision of clinical cases and on theoretical debates. Supervision was carried out through the analysis of the Sandplay images, the discussion of their contents, of their symbols, of the psychological significance that objects take depending on where they are placed in space. The procedure would mostly involve intellectual understanding.

The activities carried out during the sessions proved invaluably educational. Accordingly, Martin's proposal to restrict participation in order to form a permanent group meeting up twice a year for longer seminars, was met with enthusiasm not only by the participants, but also by other fellow therapists who had never attended. The group's novelty would lie not only in its formation, but also in the ground-breaking work procedure characterising it. This marked the beginning of what in time has become known as the "Zollikon Experience Related Sandplay Study Group".[6]

The new group

What made the latter group different from the former one?

The objective was (and still is) to provide therapists with specialist background in Sandplay Therapy, alongside training them in in-depth theoretical studies. With respect to the work procedure, Jung's four psychic functions (thinking, feelings, sensation, intuition) are key to unscrambling the message conveyed by the Sandplay images. Moreover Kalff states that "it is wise to arrive at an understanding which opens spaces, leaves questions open rather than closing the discussion".[7]

In this context, a key role is played by the attention paid to the body's felt experience of which one becomes aware through meditation. The proposed approach harmonises intellectual processing with its distinctly patriarchal stance, with the inspiration provided from matriarchal awareness, in which "[t]he ego's actual achievement lies in one's readiness to accept the emerging contents of the unconscious and to put oneself into accord with them".[8] "We need – Kalff points out – an approach which combines careful analysis with a 'knowledge of the heart', an understanding which does not only rely on concepts, but arises [also] from introspection and silence".[9] This understanding has nourished him over 40 years of practice in meditation based on the application of mindfulness.

The word 'meditation' therefore spreads within the group, quietly at first, then in an increasingly pervasive way. The word itself comes from the Latin verb *meditàri*, an iterative form of *medéri*, 'to cure', and shares its root with *medicare*. Meditation as medication, ointment for the wounds of the soul, but also a slit through which we can catch glimpses of new horizons of transformation. Through meditation, the rush of thoughts, emotions, and dreams that crowd the mind and heart, slowly comes to a halt. Wide expanses of silence open up and in them it is possible to meet our own shining essence. The dark cave is left behind, and the derived awareness is the most valuable treasure one can ever find in life, the only one we cannot be deprived of insofar as it comes from the inside.

What an intellectual curiosity is ignited within ourselves, what a remarkable challenge is offered to us! We are asked to shift our gaze from the outer world to the inner one, and to witness what happens within us in a:

> state of alertness and mindfulness so that an awareness of our natural state of mind emerges. This is a state of mind in which awareness is not afflicted by memories and thoughts of the past, nor is it afflicted by thoughts of the future, anticipations fears, and hopes. Rather our mind remains in a natural and neutral state.[10]

According to Kalff, awareness amounts to staying present with what arises in the present without any judgement – a similar description to Jon Kabat-Zinn's, who views "mindfulness as a lens, taking the scattered and reactive energies of your mind and focusing them into a coherent source of energy for living, for problem-solving, and for healing".[11]

The present is the only reality we own. "Yesterday", writes Indian poet Kalidasa in his *Salutation to the Dawn*, "is a spent dream, tomorrow is only just a vision". Living in the present, therefore, is the path along which Kalff leads us in our group work.

This path is not unfamiliar to me. In the last few years, Kalff has held workshops at the Monastero Camaldolese della Santa Croce di Fonte Avellana (Serra Sant'Abbondio, PU, Italy). I took part in some of them and I understood the relevance of meditation in building one's own awareness, knowledge of Self, identity, and notably the unconscious identity which often determines our behaviours and causes deep suffering. Through meditation, our focused attention – our mindsight, as defined by D.J. Siegel – increases. It, in fact, "encourages openness, observation, and objectivity. We are able to see with more depth and precision".[12] It unleashes the potential to become more receptive to any image that comes to consciousness, made free from expectations and automatic behaviours, and helps relativizing everything.

Kalff's work method encourages us to pay attention to the experience of 'here-and-now', while freeing ourselves from the urge to take action and hush the hubbub within ourselves. It is "a bell that reminds us to stop and silently listen",[13] a privileged locus where we can get in touch with our true nature and catch the calling of beauty, love, and life.

The group at work

Henceforth, the ringing of a bell will announce the beginning of each and every activity. Our journey will be guided from now on by "non-judging, patience, a beginner's mind, trust, non-striving, acceptance, and letting go",[14] being unbiased witnesses, accepting the naturally slow ripening times of any fruit, which we now observe as if we were seeing them for the first time, trusting ourselves without expectations.

The review of clinical cases starts in this way, from the body, the heart and the mind, which are now new vectors of knowledge. We begin by focusing on our breath, physical sensations, feelings, emotions, and thinking, which then find a special outlet for expression in writing, painting, movement and dramatization, sound and dance.

We start working by dwelling in our breath. Life is to be found within the breath. We mind the flow of the tactile sensations engendered by breathing in and out, gently and open-mindedly. The attention is purposefully free from any mental analysis. Feeling our breath in our own belly, chest, and nostrils, proves a soothing experience, an activity that restores balance, purifies the mind, and brings stability and concentration, essential ingredients for the work we are about to do.

In the poetic words of Samyutta Nikaya, reported by Bruce A. Wallace:

> Just as in the last month of the hot season, when a mass of dust and dirt has swirled up, a great rain cloud out of season disperses it and quells it on the spot, so too concentration by mindfulness of breathing, when developed and cultivated, is peaceful and sublime, an ambrosial dwelling, and it disperses and quells on the spot unwholesome states whenever they arise.[15]

In every session, meditation is the conscious rediscovery of the needs of the soul. When at the beginning of our work we proceed to pick a figure from a star-patterned bag, we feel great astonishment at the answers that it gives to questions – be they implicit or explicit – that churn within ourselves.

Once again, this time through our hands, the body talks to us. It is the healing from deafness to our body's voice that originally inspired 'body scan', a technique we utilise to call attention to every part of the body and to recognise different sensations: warmth, cold, stiffness, fluidity, relaxation, heaviness, lightness, pain.

Listening to the language of the senses, to their wisdom, is tantamount to breaking free from the bridles of conceptual thinking. The drum, the powerful sound of percussions, also helps us access a dimension of greater freedom, less control, and enables us to tap into ancient contents, elements of "implicit memory"[16] which we cannot otherwise detect solely by looking at the sand. Everything is echoed in the relationship between patient and therapist: the scene in the sand, silence and drum, breath and meditation, the silent language of the senses and of the emotions.

And let's think of the effects that movement triggers under the watchful eye of a member of the group after gazing at a Sandplay scene. "The movement makes the sand come alive, enables us to reach the depths of our patient's sorrow, helps us identify both strengths and weaknesses, and infuse energy that may jounce back to the patient" (Eleonora Tramaloni).

The exploration of a Sandplay image within our group also goes through the phase of spontaneous gestures that make the means to contrast any resistance to the contents of the sand.

We imagine a safe harbour inside of us, and we then allow images and movements to come to us, without dwelling on the most obvious aspects of the patient's history, but getting to its essence instead.

The energy from a Sandplay scene uncovered through meditation finds its expression in polychromatic drawings, which we make with watercolours and pencils: we still discover unconscious bays full of questions, unconfessed emotional venations within which the answers already arise. Poetry also comes to our aid – like dramatization and dance do – shedding further light on the secret motives of the soul through these windows.

Over the years Kalff has given meditation an ever-increasing role in our meetings and has extended it to empathy, compassion and goodwill. His exhortation is for us to open our heart, and fill it with love and compassion for oneself and the others. All beings yearn for happiness, for freedom from suffering. It is important, therefore, to seek happiness and freedom from suffering for ourselves and for others.

Empathy is an indispensable feeling in interpersonal relationships, which are the bedrock of psychic balance. Minding physical sensations is the ground on which empathy is built, which is "a 'feeling with', a sense of how another person is feeling: happy, sad, fearful, and so on".[17]

The group is repeatedly trained on this. Recent neuroscientific studies have proved that "meditation may change brain function and structure in the direction of greater integration, it can be a powerful agent of neuroplasticity and it might even offset some detrimental brain changes associated with aging".[18] These studies also observe that therapists practicing awareness show greater ease at opening their heart and empathizing with patients. Empathy, which is crucial to being able to resonate with the emotional experiences seething in other people's souls, poses the risk of identification and, therefore, of the impossibility to build a relationship which, by contrast, compassion ensures. Through empathy, one suffers seeing others suffer – an experience of great distress:

> Contrary to empathic distress, love and compassion are positive states of mind, which reinforce one's inner ability to confront others' suffering and to care better for them. [...] Without the support of love and compassion, empathy left to itself is like an electric pump through which no water circulates: it will quickly overheat and burn.[19]

Training a loving heart, compassionate towards both our and the others' needs, is what we strive to achieve through meditation on goodwill. Wishing happiness for us and for the Other: good practice for all of us, who are confronted on a daily basis with a life burdened by grief, conflict, and sadness.

In time, the different types of meditation practices described earlier in this section have become the main tool for detecting transformation in Sandplay processes. Through these practices, psychic contents inaccessible to mere thought finally become accessible. Meditation practices therefore increasingly prove a vehicle for a different knowledge which begins its journey from silence and opens up new horizons ahead.

Verbal pondering is never neglected, serving the purpose to synthesise each and every participant's emotions, sensations and feelings.

In conclusion, the operating procedure of the group seems to embody Jung's tenet according to which "the important thing is not to interpret and understand the fantasies, but primarily to experience them".[20]

Resonance in the group

The new method proposed for ferreting out the meanings of Sandplay scenes initially aroused perplexity in some of us. The group was confronted with embarrassment: fear of disclosing and bringing into play each member's personal dimension. Casting objectivity aside felt scary, but the group soon realised that even the traditional analysis methods used in Sandplay Therapy are marked by projective interplay, and therefore confront participants with complexes as well as with their Shadow. The new method is characterised by similar aspects, but its main upside is the therapist's increased awareness while conducting the analysis.

We soon realised that the difference in our responses, emotional experiences, feelings and thoughts makes it a unique heritage for each of us.

It then became clear to all of us that this kind of exchange results in the relativization of one's own personal standpoint, the avoidance of biases, and the acceptance of one's own limits. This experience enables us to widen one's own interpretative field; it also furnishes new tools enlightening the therapist and, through the therapist, their patient.

As I mentioned at the beginning of this contribution, each of us is called to an individual journey which progresses between detours and halts, back-trackings and advancements.

The path to awareness through meditation which Kalff guides us through, is an answer to the calling, and it fosters transformations within ourselves on a personal and a professional level. We all have noticed changes in our way of doing things, in our life, in our being with ourselves. Every day "we approach our here-and-now experience with curiosity, openness, acceptance and love (COAL)".[21] We try to set ourselves free from preconceptions, from harsh judgements, lack of kindness, and try to renew our relationship with ourselves and become our own benevolent friend. This way, we tap into a source of wellbeing and health.

Practicing meditation on awareness in group becomes fruitful training for its application to everyday life. Our journey together provides us with the means to experiment with a "living psychology: one of the oldest and most well-developed systems of healing and understanding systems on the face of the earth".[22] It is a type of psychology that paves the way for new intuitions, new possibilities that pervade and transform our way of being and working.

We realise, with surprise and gratitude, that our work can heal the Other but also soothe the wounds in our soul. We are then therapists and patients at the same time. In order to understand the Other, we probe more in depth, thus fathoming yet unexplored parts of our being, such as our Shadow which may now be understood in its evolutionary function.

The Butterflies' Nest

I mentioned previously in this essay my first encounter with meditation during Kalff's workshops at the Monastero Camaldolese della Santa Croce di Fonte Avellana, held at the same time as our seminars in Zollikon. They both resonated so deeply within myself that, a few years later, I felt the urge to continue my experience with meditation, which I considered a fecund source of self-knowledge, water into which to plunge weariness and grief to actually pull out regeneration.

Spurred on by this need, and further encouraged by some dreams, I conceived the idea to offer a space for meditation to others. This is how *The Butterflies' Nest* came into being, a small group of friends that is ever-increasing. At the beginning, we would meet up once a month, then more and more frequently. We are guided in our practice by Kalff's teachings delivered at the Monastery and in Zollikon, but we also explore other forms of meditation as paths towards our inner selves, peace, and vitality places. Dancing (in a circle or swirling) and meditating while creating mandalas, become vibrant experiences within our meetings, enhanced over time by silent retreats.

A small yellow house in the countryside surrounded by an olive grove and an orchard, chestnuts trees and a vegetable garden has become our *nest*. Gathering around its fireplace is our *homecoming*.

The moment when we sit down in a circle, look at each other, and smile, is always emotional. We are together, once again, happy to share this space where our heart immediately lightens. It feels as if all of our pain had preferred not to step into the house, but moved away through the fields where horses are grazing.

We meditate, and we come in contact with ourselves, with the Other, with the world. This feeling of unity is emphasised by the dance. We hold each other's hand and we move in a circle around a centre of light, in delicate or lively choreographies, or we swirl in a Sufi dance. In each dance, we feel as if we were in "the mandala dance",[23] as we swirl around a centre or around ourselves. We try to reach out the "inner, sacred precinct, which is the source and goal of the psyche and contains the unity of life and consciousness. The unity once possessed has been lost, and must now be found again".[24]

We try to do this even more incisively through the creation of mandalas, a meditative space which is particularly important in our encounters:

> Age-old magical effects lie hidden in this symbol, for it is derived from the 'protective circle' or 'charmed circle', whose magic has been preserved in countless folk customs. It has the obvious purpose of drawing a sulcus primigenius, a magical furrow around the centre, the temple or temenos (sacred precinct), of the innermost personality, in order to prevent an 'outflowing' or to guard by apotropaic means against distracting influences from outside.[25]

I have always been fascinated by studies on mandalas. It is a form of expression that stirs childhood memories. On the occasion of the solemn Procession for the Corpus Domini celebration in the village I come from, a small village in Southern Italy (San Donato di Ninea, near Cosenza), it was customary to raise by the door of shops or cellars some altars covered with white lace. However, the most exciting work for me was the process of laying a carpet of flowers right before the altar.

At dawn, women and children would walk down to the riverbanks and gather fragrant broom, daisies, poppies, rose hips, aromatic herbs, and on their way back they would also pick begonias, and carnations, reaped from the vases on the balconies. And then they (along with some particularly devout men who would not infrequently join them) would lay a silent, spontaneous composition of enchanting and mysterious mandalas, fated to be swept away by the treading procession. We were all deeply touched by this. It was difficult for me to cope with their destruction. To me, these compositions were something precious and inviolable.

Precious in fostering psychic forces, self-awareness, and balance restoration are the mandalas made by our group (Figure 10.1). I agree with Giuseppe Tucci on his claim that:

> a mandala is the framework of disintegration from one to many and reintegration from many to one. Working with it is like a journey back to one's mysterious essence, to the divine seed, to the light that burns inside each of us, expanding and propagating.[26]

The creation of a mandala is the place where "the worshipper is compelled to follow a ritual way from the periphery to the centre, the shrine"[27] – the sacred shrine within oneself.

All participants pay special attention to the setting of the material with which the mandala will be made. They also perform the dances that precede it to its slow, meticulous, silent fulfilment from which transformation and individuation radiates. "Mandalas are birth-places, vessels of birth in the most literal sense, lotus-flowers in which a Buddha comes to life".[28]

We perceive in them a powerful impulse towards a new order, often heralded by confusion, conflict, and agitation which firmly urge us to take the reins of our life back. The positive experience of silent meditation retreats guided by teachers of the Center for Mindfulness in Medicine, Health Care and Society, founded by

Figure 10.1 Mandala

Jon Kabat-Zinn, has prompted me to share my experience. In the group, we value silence and we realise that listening to silence makes possible the blooming of the flowers of awareness, whose seeds sit in unfathomed depths of our soul. We see them blossom in our everyday life.

A yet further event occurs. During a meditation retreat with Martin at the monastery, I have a dream: I am in an imposing hall with stone walls and no furniture, with a sandbox at its centre: around the sandbox some scientists and monks are standing in a circle. I study my dream. In it, I find my consorting with the world of physics, my passion for psychology, Sandplay, and my interest in spirituality. My life flows among the valleys of *Physis* (Nature) and those of Psyche, along a spiritual quest. While I muse on these considerations, I chance upon a book by Wolfgang Pauli, *Psyche and Nature*, in which Pauli theorises "a deep analogy between complementarity in physics with the concepts of 'consciousness' and 'unconscious' in psychology, as any 'observation' of unconscious contents implies a practically indeterminable repercussion of consciousness on these very contents". I am also struck by the proposition: "meditation as active practice is akin to the setting up and the use of a spectrograph in physics".[29] Like a spectrograph, indeed, meditation analyses and categorises.

I wonder: sand, physics, monks, Pauli. My intuitive guidance tells me to move the sandbox, the spectrograph of our soul, to the monastery. Martin agrees on my proposal. In the same way as in our work group in Zollikon we had introduced meditation in order to understand the sand scenes, we decide to bring Sandplay in the meditation course at the monastery, to prepare and integrate the experience of meditation.

The combined practice of Sandplay and meditation displays its effects at the monastery as well. We witness a transformation process inviting us to nurture hope.

My training on awareness meditation and Sandplay Therapy over the last few years has definitely changed my life, my relationship with things and people. From them I have received creative stimuli that have led me to places of unspeakable beauty, to the most spiritual aspects of my inner self, and to an unexpected strength, which ultimately enabled me to confront merciless diseases and heart-rendering losses.

Echoes in the analysis room

The experience with the Zollikon group inevitably reflects on our professional activity. Our being in the analysis room changes, we learn how to suspend, to wait, not to rush. We rediscover the importance of silence, of meditation, of minding the body as a medium to access the dark, troubled and invaluable seas of the unconscious. Loving-kindness meditation becomes an unfaltering friend opening our heart, nourishing us, giving us strength and protecting us from the risk of contamination by emotional states.

Meditation boosts the therapeutic journey. Raffaella's story bears witness to this.

Raffaella

Raffaella seeks help after a yet further failed sentimental relationship. Her low self-esteem and the unrelenting feeling exclusion with roots in her childhood, contributed to pose a threat to the stability of her relationships.

Her past has been marked by one important relationship, characterised by love but also not devoid of suffering, misunderstanding and repeated separations. After a few turbulent years and only in view of the rejection subsequent to the pulmonary transplant her partner had undergone, did Raffaella settle on moving in with him and even entertained the idea of getting married. Her partner, however, worsened and eventually died. For many years to come, Raffaella would swing between troughs of despair and peaks of hope. She tries to weave new relationships, but every time her grief undoes them.

The path with Sandplay combined with meditation becomes an important journey across the rough waters of her soul. After taking part in a course at the monastery with Martin, she says:

> All-absorbing experience. Time in the monastery comes to a standstill, vital rhythms slow down, attention shifts to our inner world. My time there was magic, even though tiresome. All the grief I had always carried inside of me has come out and found a shape through meditation with a view to overcoming difficulties. I visualise a kitten removed from his mother. I am that kitten. I feel fear, exclusion, the heart beats faster. Following the teacher's indications, I try to understand what the kitten wants. I feed him with nectar out of a shell. And the kitten eats and eats, and when he has had enough, he licks his whiskers and begins cleaning himself. He grows into an undefined flower, then a sunflower, and finally a big white fragrant rose.
>
> It was not a rational awareness; I made it to my existential void, my despair and my rage at an emotive level. When I was back home, I felt at peace and balanced and in a short while I found love, a rebirth for me.

Meditation practice has reshaped Raffaella's inner and outer world.

The man she now shares her life with is a positive person – sound, unclouded. He is the father of the child that Raffaella, now 44, is expecting. She writes:

> There is my child, a gift from above. He arrived when I had lost all hope. It's an indescribable joy. I feel he is also the result of the journey that enabled me to reach the deepest side of me, carving a space for it and giving it a right to exist.
>
> During the meditation session I felt the energy that emanated from the group, an energy that everyone welcomes inside of oneself and gives back, revived and stronger. I shared part of this energy with my child, a small

seed bringing life and happiness. The sand creations, silence during meditation, dance, mandala – they all took me to him, to my tiny Seed!

The following Sandplay scene is the last one created by Raffaella (Figure 10.2).

Conclusions

Each of us has a journey to undertake prompted by the voice of the Self, which, if listened to, slowly reveals it. To abide by its truth is a commitment that accompanies us throughout our lives and takes paths which are nothing like the noisy motorways of conformism, but narrow and toilsome trails blazed in solitude. The encounter with Sandplay Therapy and its creative leaven within the group led by Martin Kalff marked a fundamental milestone in mine own. Thanks to the work carried out in Zollikon and the spiritual

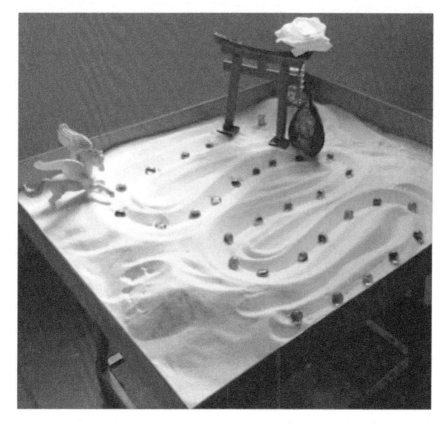

Figure 10.2 The path of joy

space carved there, we have been able to make progress in the process of individuation, to awaken the creative breath from its primal slumber, and to hone the ability to plunge in depth into the human soul. One's own and that of others.

Awareness achieved through meditation, a primary focus for the group in sand analysis, has been our greatest challenge over the last few years. Turning the attention to the inner self, minding one's own body, one's own heart, and one's own mind, makes a subversive act against the established order. Throughout our new journey we have discovered the great value of pausing, being quiet, living the present moment, feeling empathy, compassion, kindness – all extraordinary means to successfully grapple with conflict and other people's suffering even while easing their integration and processing. They are means by which we set ourselves free from the thrall of expectations, automatic reactions, one-sided thinking and, at the same time, they are catalysts for transformative energy.

The experience I lived with the Zollikon group was so intense and, probably, so resonant with my inner calling, that it became an imperative and unavoidable clarion call for a humble re-creation. That's how *The Butterflies' Nest* first came about. Meditation started to accompany my life and that of the butterflies hovering in the nest. We no longer meditate by the fireplace of the small yellow house of the beginnings, but at dawn by a sea reflecting ancient temples, in discreet farmhouses on foamy hills of wheat, in the silence of retreats held by the embrace of the mountains, in rose gardens that shyly bow to solemn churches.

We meditate at our places, with our kids, at work, at school with children, themselves beaches from which we hope to see grains of transformation raise.

Notes

1 F. Montecchi and A. Navone, *Dora Kalff e il gioco della sabbia*, in *Psicologia analitica contemporanea* (Edited by C. Trombetta), Bompiani, Milano, 1989, p. 391
2 A. Einstein, *The World as I See it*, Snowball Publishing, 2014, p. 17.
3 C.G. Jung, *The Spirit in Man, Art, and Literature*, CW XV, 1966, § 159.
4 A. Carotenuto, *Trattato di psicologia della personalità e delle differenze individuali*, Raffaello Cortina, Milano, 1991, p. 533.
5 C.G. Jung, *Psychology and Religion: West and East*, CW XI, 1970, § 285.
6 M. Kalff, *Experience-Related Case Study: Like a Masked Ball*, p. 99.
7 Ibid., p. 100.
8 E. Neumann, *The Fear of the Feminine*, Bollingen Series, Princeton University Press, Princeton, 1989, p. 92.
9 M. Kalff, *Experience-Related Case Study: Like a Masked Ball*.
10 A.B. Wallace, *Genuine Happiness: Meditation as the Path to Fulfillment*, Foreword by His Holiness the Dalai Lama, John Wiley and Sons Inc., Hoboken, NJ, 2005.
11 J. Kabat Zinn, *Full Catastrophe Living – How to Cope with Stress, Pain and Illness Using Mindfulness Meditation*, Kindle Format, Bantam, Random House, 2013, p. 808.
12 D.J. Siegel, *Mindsight*, p. 31.

13 Thich Nhat Hanh, *Silence – The Power of Quiet in a World Full of Noise*, Rider, Ebury Publishing, London, 2015, p. 4.
14 J. Kabat Zinn, *Full Catastrophe Living*, pos. 1177.
15 B.A. Wallace, *Genuine Happiness*, p. 16.
16 D.J. Siegel, *Mindsight,* p. 149.
17 B.A. Wallace, *Genuine Happiness*, p. 66.
18 B. Badenoch, *Being a Brain-Wise Therapist*, p. 175.
19 M. Ricard, *Altruism: The Science and Psychology of Kindness*, p. 64.
20 C.G. Jung, *Two Essays on Analytical Psychology*, CW, VII, 1953, § 342.
21 D.J. Siegel, *The Mindful Brain*, p. 15.
22 J. Kornfield, *The Wise Heart: A Guide to the Universal Teachings of Buddhist Psychology*, Bantam Books, 2009, p. 3.
23 C.G. Jung, *Alchemical Studies*, CW XIII, 1968, § 32.
24 Ibid., § 36.
25 Ibid.
26 G. Tucci, *Teoria e pratica del mandala*, Ubaldini Editore, Roma, 1969, p. 40.
27 E. Neumann, *The Great Mother*, Bollingen Series XLVII, Princeton University Press, Princeton, 1972, p. 9.
28 C.G. Jung, *Alchemical Studies*.
29 W. Pauli, *Psiche e Natura*, Adelphi Edizioni, Milano, 2006, pp. 37–39.

Part 3

Clinical experiences

Chapter 11

Story of a child who would not talk

Chiara Bottari

Foreword

Within Martin Kalff's Zollikon-based study group we have perfected a method to help us better examine sand scenes as well as understand more insightfully and in-depth our work as therapist therapists. Each of our patients' sandbox scenes is presented alongside movements, silence, drawings, poems, music and meditation – all meant to help us unearth the deep meaning of the scenes, in the attempt to figure out what the patient is trying to say in the unique and idiosyncratic way each patient expresses it.

The case study we are about to examine is about a child who, for a long interval, only expressed himself through images and not words. The case was analysed and approached in compliance with this work method.

The images M. produced, while locked in his silence, *spoke* in this way to us therapists. In the group, we gradually examined what we felt, we relived and enacted what he was giving shape to through his hang-ups, inertia, silence, but also his great energy and vitality. The trauma, which couldn't find a verbal outlet, found expression through Sandplay scenes and – through them – an emotive resonance in the therapist who would listen, observe, and accept while taking part in the Sandplay work.

In November 2011, after about a year of therapy, something began to change. M. began to 'talk' to me by moving his lips – even though without making a sound – thus breaking open a new communication channel. After a further two years, at the end of a journey during which he had made 55 sand scenes, M. eventually found his words.

From M. I have learned to keep quiet, wait and embrace the rhythm of silence, which can tell us many things. I believe that, without Sandplay Therapy, for M. leaving his silent world would have been very difficult – if not impossible. The journey with him was long, incredibly beautiful, and it may have been utterly different, had it not been for the Zollikon-based group which helped me put up with this lengthy process, characterised by moment of silence and vacancy, which M.'s psychic transformation called for.

DOI: 10.4324/9781003163503-14

The journey through the sands

M. had started attending playschool aged three, and had been quiet hence-forth, except in his own familiar domestic environment: he was then diag-nosed with elective mutism. Since the very first encounter with his parents, I wondered which trauma had stunted his development.

"Mutism is a condition which does not allow a human being to commu-nicate using the voice and words". The entry on DSM-5, the Diagnostic and Statistical Manual of Mental Disorders (American Psychiatric Association, 2013), describes it as "a condition affecting children of infant or primary school age, who don't speak at school and in other spaces outside the domestic confine". It is worth noting that DSM-5 classifies elective mutism as a separation anxiety disorder. It suggests it may be viewed as a post-traumatic disorder or as the result of an unresolved psychic conflict. According to this view, a trauma at some point 'froze' the psychological development of these children, originating a psychic or emotive inner block, in such a way that they perceive the external world as so hostile to preclude communication.

We know that the earlier the trauma occurs, the more it interferes with the child's psychosomatic development, as children then protect themselves through defensive and obsessive rituals. My hope was that *playing*, and notably Sand-playing, with its therapeutic benefits, may eventually reopen the blocked-up energy channels to allow the Self to resume its harmonic development.

M.'s parents had contacted the Operational Unit of Child Neuropsychiatry and Developmental Age Rehabilitation at the Don Gnocchi Foundation in Milan in September 2010 – that is, the time when we first met. I had been informed that M. was an only child, born in November 2004, and had just started attending primary school. His medical history detailed that he had been delivered by vacuum extractor. His development had been normal, with regular sleeping patterns. However, M. had had trouble falling asleep until the age of three.

M.'s mother resumed work when he was eight months' old and, since then, he had been in the care of his maternal grandparents. Since preschool, M. had quit talking whenever he was outside of his domestic environment, and had also had difficulty eating. In 2009, he had undertaken psychomotor therapy, however without achieving any significant results. I vividly remember my first encounter with his mother, and notably her desperate cry: she could hardly speak, similarly to her son, due to the grief his mutism caused her.

M. was a handsome fair-haired child, with sparkling – albeit somehow elusive – eyes, a piercing look that observes and scans the Other in silence. He embarked on his journey with Sandplay Therapy in September 2010 – again, in silence.

Every therapist, upon meeting a patient, experiences mixed emotions and feelings: fondness, fear, dislike, impatience, empathy, etc. I noticed that, espe-cially at the beginning, I felt disoriented by M.'s silence, but I also felt intense, profound empathy.

The alliance with M.'s parents, and with his mother especially, was of fundamental importance – so was also regular contact with his school teachers, with whom I talked regularly on the phone and also saw in person, in the presence of both of M.'s parents. Within this context, Sandplay Therapy enabled us to achieve results which had been unimaginable at the start of the therapy.

The following pages show a selection of sandbox scenes and episodes from my sessions with M., which were nearly all shared and *re-lived* with the Zollikon Group.

M.'s Sandplay journey may be divided into three stages. The first stage includes the last months of 2010. The first three sand scenes belong to the first phase, marked by the alternating presence of blocks and movements. The second phase shows important unblocking episodes, related to the birth of a younger brother in 2011. In the third phase, which took place in 2012, split-off aspects and the reconstruction of Ego became visible.

In the first meeting, M. created a volcano, thus making apparent the intense transformative and expressive potential of his psyche (Figure 11.1).

The volcano is a representation of strong energy, it is something explosive, it erupts and ejects, it is fire and Eros.

M. touches the sand, working in silence, representing in this way energy, rage that he cannot curb, and impetuosity. He then looks for a sheet of paper and draws a volcano.

Figure 11.1 Expressing rage

In the research group, by minding our own sensations, we perceived on a countertransference level impetuous force, vehemence, energy, warmth, aggression, and fire. We all felt overwhelming rage, the presence of contents difficult to bridle, but which were finally able to find expression. We deeply connected with M., with his mutism, his potential explosiveness, his vitality that could not be channelled, his blocks, but also his great energy.

How much rage does this child feel? How strong, dangerous and difficult to keep in check, like fire, is it?

With the help of Sandplay and drawing, M. also expressed great energy and finally his *rage* was able to find means of expression. Hands and body, through Sandplay, drawing and movement, conveyed those sensations that words could not express.

In the second sand scene (Figure 11.2), in lieu of a volcano we find an empty circle. We could argue that it may stand for the volcano after the energy has flown back. We wonder what may be born out of here, what can be built on it. On the right, some heavy-duty vehicles appear, some halted trucks, ambulances, and police cars, but also airplanes and helicopters that can potentially take flight.

This circle seems to represent the beginning of 'something' that may potentially move, but at the same time is still frozen. Perhaps the stationary cars, which will often be found in his sand scenes, act as a defensive and

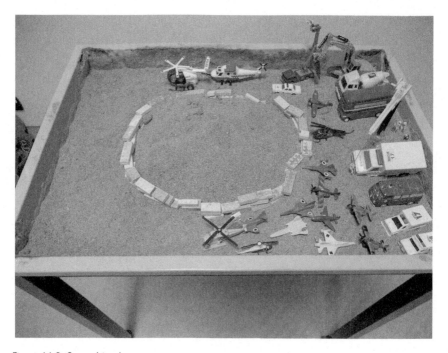

Figure 11.2 Something loosens

obsessive ritual, the symbol of a trauma which occurred in the earliest years of his life. Along with stuck vehicles we also find, from the very start of the therapeutic work, emergency vehicles like ambulances, police cars, airplanes and helicopters which may represent a chance of development and opening-up.

During the third Sandplay session, at his request, we worked together and we created a sea. M. added some boats and a large stranded ship. I asked him "Do they move?"; he shook his head to mean "no" (Figure 11.3).

The block is still there, but the boats can be interpreted as bridges, unconscious means to embark on a journey. It looks as if M. needed to go through every stage of pre-verbal communication. I find it noteworthy that on the edge of the sandboxes two sailors made their appearance, observing: perhaps a clue to his dawning awareness.

These first few sand scenes fulfilled a diagnostic function by clearly indicating the presence of a trauma, of a block of the psyche; they also fulfilled a prognostic function by indicating that movement and removal of trauma could possibly be expected. Here we can see the tendency of the psyche and of the body to find their own bearings, as Dora Kalff and Carl G. Jung posited.

Upon looking at these sand scenes, I felt M. was endowed with an extraordinary amount of inner energy and that he would be able to overcome the wall of silence; I expected this to happen in the short term, but I would be

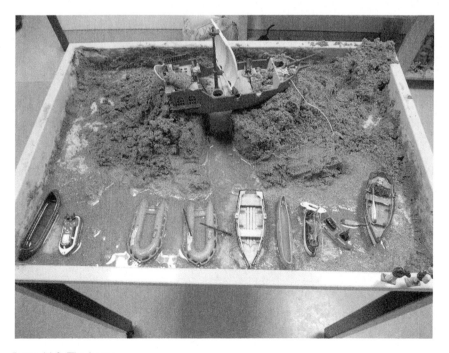

Figure 11.3 The boats

proved wrong, as the journey ahead was still very long. Thanks to my colla-boration with the Zollikon Group I found a time that was not originally mine, and probably not M.'s either, but was the kind of slow and stretched time of the psyche and of its inner journey. In the group, every time we examine a scene, we mind our body, and try to feel – even before understanding – the sensations elicited by our looking at the images, and to perceive, through our own movement, blocks and defences. Sharing my work with the Zollikon Group, the work we did together through creative approaches, with colours and body movements, helped me understand M.'s silence and the images from his sand scenes resonated more clearly within myself and my unconscious. My approach changed and I would address M. less frequently, I would not fill his silences with my words in order to feel more at ease in its awkwardness, I would accept this slow pace and develop patience.

After the first three sand scenes, there followed a time when M. started repre-senting conflict; the moment when the representation of conflict arises is impor-tant insofar as it loosens some defensive ritual blocks and portends the dawn of a new energy. These months were difficult, as the blocks marked by defensive obsessive rituals were still strong (the cars were still in a row and were still stuck).

I, too, feel a block. I ask M., once again, "Are these cars not moving yet?"

"No!" he shakes his head.

I can hardly conceal my impatience and I am projecting onto him an unti-mely resolution of the block. I must bear in mind that, as Jung says, the psyche's natural rhythm should not be forced.

Let's move on to a new sand scene. This is #11, made in February 2011 (Figure 11.4).

Two completely separate areas may be noticed – one on the left with cars, a concrete mixer, ambulances, and one on the right with airplanes, cranes, and a human figure. Empty space in between. You perceive a sense of movement, of work in progress, but on the left we still have rage that halts development. M. is unable to access the masculine dimension of words and thoughts.

The question is, "What could possibly help him get out of this block?" Perhaps the discovery of warmth and emotions, which are frozen as yet. What are my feelings when confronted with this scene? How does the group feel?

We all felt the coexistence of two parts, one motionless, stuck, maybe waiting for something – and our bodies, in dramatization, felt the same way: inhibited, blocked, unable to move. We first experienced movement, slow at the start, then more paced, and then a sense of something working and moving, of energy slowly, but eventually breaking free from a lock. Are we not in a similar condi-tion? Blocked but also moving, inhibited but also full of vitality, living oxymora?

Thenceforth, M. started making two scenes per session: the focus was still on the alternation between block and movement, between still cars and air-planes ready to take off, while ambulances were still present.

Let's take a look, for instance, at installation #14, created in March 2011 (Figure 11.5).

Figure 11.4 Paralysis and movement

Figure 11.5 The crossing

Here we see a top part with some toy cars, which M. wets with water. The side which is closest to him, and from which M. looks at the sandbox, is divided into two parts by a small brick wall, which he patiently and painstakingly builds – telltale sign of the extent to which his approach to the work with sands has changed. There are also many aircrafts which he says are still, but have the potential energy to take off. This time the two halves of the sandbox are joined by a pathway, a small sand bridge; accordingly, there is exchange, communication.

Finally, we also began to communicate and make progress towards mutual understanding. I witnessed a small miracle: thenceforth, M. would speak in whispers, in order to explain and tell me about the scenes in the sand. The sand was moulded through the movements of his hands and body, which had become less rash and hectic. Now his gestures were slow and meticulous, the dirt was being shaped with more energy and participation on the part of his body. At this stage, M. began to whisper also to his school teachers.

I feel these two scenes stand for a connection, but also for a split that resonates, at a deep emotional level, inside of me, a split I find hard to stand. The prevailing perception in the group, though, was that something might happen or come to light: the colours in our drawings and the movements of our bodies expressed a hope for the future, an expectation of something about to happen in the psyche. The experience of the group helps me as a therapist – a great deal.

In the months from March to May 2011 the same working rhythm continued uninterrupted – two scenes per session. M.'s body stance was slightly more relaxed, we now communicated in a very, very soft voice.

During the months of May and June, impetuosity and vehemence came back; the sands scenes were often flooded with water, the toy cars were as stuck as before, or even more, nothing seemed to move, energy did not flow.

I wondered why we were witnessing the return of such a strong block. Why – in response to a therapeutic relationship that I perceived as strong, intense and positive – was nothing evolving in the sand scenes? "What is still blocking you, M.?"

In June, I ran across the answer to this question during an exchange with M.'s mother: she was expecting a baby, they had known for a month but had not told M. yet. However, he knew about it anyway! This was the reason behind such restlessness and angst. M. was afraid of this prospective event and would protect himself by exacerbating his defensive rituals, among which stuck out the orderly, almost obsessive lining up of cars.

I now realise how fundamental the last months of inaction and repetitiveness preceding the news of his brother's arrival had been. It was thanks to his obsessive defences that he was finally able to find some sense of safety. As his therapist, I found that the blocks and the split represented in the sand were resonating in me.

An important step was taken in scene #24: it was now July 2011, just before parting for the holidays. In this sand scene M. represented, maybe for the first time, conflict properly speaking, and he consequently started to show what he was unable to speak of his trauma (Figure 11.6).

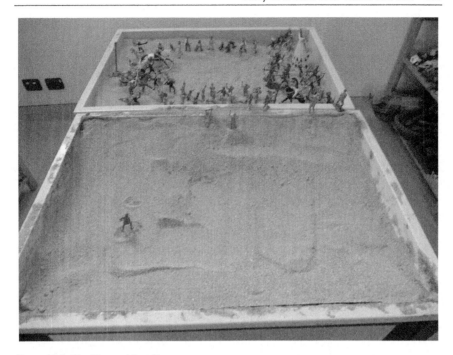

Figure 11.6 Conflict and loneliness

Women with babies

As it is had become customary by then, he expressed himself in two different scenes.

The image emerging from the first scene is that of men fighting, the clashing of male forces. There is also the presence of feminine energy. He sets up a tent with two women and a child.

"Are they two mothers with a child?" I ask.

"No", he whispers, "this is a mother with a child".

He probably feels the need to protect the primary relationship which he feels threatened right now. Is he afraid of losing his mother to the baby on the way? I wonder if the trauma could have happened with respect to the attachment relationship with his mother.

The second scene was marked by a sense of emptiness, of solitude. He was alone in a battle, a little warrior clearing the field of land mines; he was also struggling alone to carve a space for himself.

While looking at this scene, I felt moved and upset by a very deep emotion; I remember that, on that occasion, both his parents came to pick him up after the session and he asked them both to have a look at his scene. The image, also in this case, spoke louder than words.

The loneliness of the little warrior was communicated to the group as well, and we attempted to represent it through some poems. I have chosen two of them:

> Water, air, wet sand and dry sand, a small soldier in the middle,
> mute because of the deafening sound of the explosion, too strong for his hands, for his smile.
> Where are you, I cannot see you.
> Where are you, I cannot hear you.
> Grey is around me and you are silent.
> There are no words, I have no words.
> Only one wish: to be with you.

M. is still whispering to me; every time he arrives, I can hear that, outside my office, in the waiting room, he is speaking at a normal pitch with his parents, and when he comes in he only whispers; the same happens at school, where he communicates with the teachers by whispering.

After the summer, we entered the third phase, that would last one year – from September 2011 to September 2012.

From September to the end of October, I noticed an evolution in the movement of the scenes, as is shown in scene #26 (Figure 11.7).

The scene is not so motionless here, there are some buses and some trucks moving around, and red is the dominant colour – perhaps indicating the thawing of his emotions.

In December, his little brother was born. In January 2012, I witnessed a new important development in the scenes in the sandboxes. M. was obviously staging his own trauma!

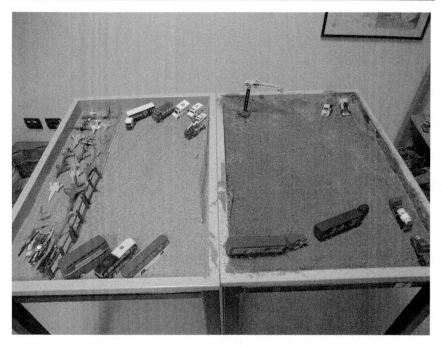

Figure 11.7 Movement and emotions

In scene #37, he portrayed a terrible accident (Figure 11.8).

Cars were arranged in a circle, some within a green fence: in the middle there was an accident. There was a strong sense of motion.

It was as if the accident could now take place in a confined place: nothing was sent to smithereens, nothing got shattered. M. hinted that the cars were moving – for the first time, there was no block.

I was touched, so I hugged him.

I learnt to better cope with silence and the importance of taking one's time. In the group, I managed to process this new awareness; without the thorough work on my inner self with the help of the Zollikon Group, I would not have been able to understand and control my reactions, my doubts, my countertransference.

M. is a wonderful child capable of talking through images in the sand.

Scene #36 is dated January 2012 (Figure 11.9).

The theme of the accident is the same here, yet this time there is an overturned truck. M. whispered to me that the police were involved. There were casualties. Now that the trauma had found an outlet through some strong and meaningful images, maybe something was stirring within the healing process.

A few more months of standstill followed; nothing noteworthy happened, either in the sand images or in actual life – until April, when, scene #42 heralded a significant breakthrough (Figure 11.10).

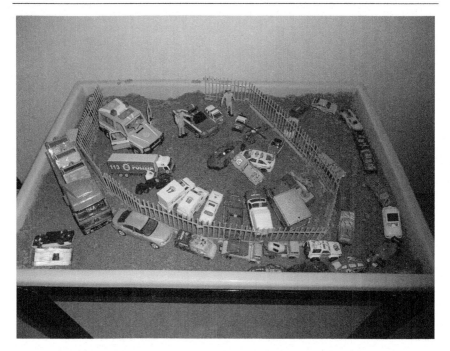

Figure 11.8 The accident

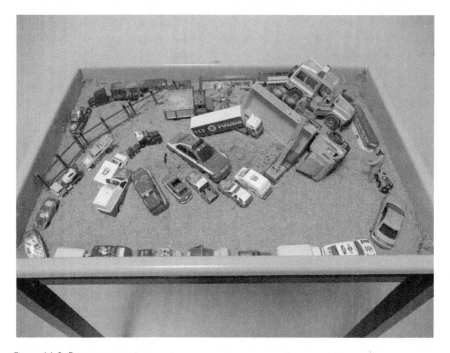

Figure 11.9 Rescue operations

Figure 11.10 The rebirth of life

The scene is arranged vertically, the accident takes place at the centre, amongst some small trees in bloom. At the beginning, that space had been taken by the volcano; now there was life, a life that was thriving. For the first time, M. used pine trees, trees in bloom and green with foliage – the block was no longer there.

After portraying the trauma, the psychic energy reappeared, blooming, renovated, luxuriant. As Dora Kalff argued, the reappearance of the vegetation is the first stage at which the Self takes shape, the first moment in which order and harmony begin to surface.

M. was working calmly, thoroughly, with participation, slowly; I hugged him. Words can't express the intensity of our deep emotions.

In scene # 43 (Figure 11.11) – created, once again, in April – vegetation shows up even more harmoniously than before, the centre is occupied by trees and there no longer is any accident. Life is blooming and beautiful. There is a red truck passing by, but it doesn't either crash against or destroy anything; there are little red mushrooms, and wooden sticks; in the middle there is a pink tree, maybe representing the Self.

At this time M. is still whispering to his teacher, yet he takes to greeting other children's mothers.

From May to July 2012, there is an ongoing evolution and an ever-increasing significance in the sand scenes, of which I will present two. In our group we

Figure 11.11 Life, again

observed them, analysed them, and each of us tried to compare, within ourselves, the initial stillness and motionlessness to the extraordinary vital and
transformative energy that these images elicit.

The cars eventually made room for animals and plants (sand 44) (Figure
11.12); the sense of movement emerged, almost like a dance, which we
expressed in our group through dramatization.

In scene #46, dated May 2012 (Figure 11.13), something new occurs within
M.'s psychological processes.

The sand was piled up vertically again; he was working in silence, engrossed
in his task. He placed trees on the left, built a bridge made of wood, piece by
piece, branch by branch, with painstaking precision. He then added some
animals, clear sign that his instincts were reawakening within himself. He
added a tiger and a panther, which could represent his aggressivity, but also a
she-bear, which stands for a highly positive maternal symbol.

And lastly … he adds Mowgli! Mowgli, in the novel by Kipling, is the
Indian child who goes lost in the jungle, is raised by a family of wolves, and is
helped by Bagheera the panther and Baloo the bear. He does not speak the
language of humans, but he can communicate with animals. In the popular
cartoon adaptation by Disney, he then meets Messua, a little girl that can
speak human language, and follows her.

Figure 11.12 Dance

Figure 11.13 Communication with animals

Finally, I think, M. is born, or rather, born again as Mowgli. When is he going to revert to speaking our language again?

We both experienced this sand scene in an intense way. From this scene onwards, the evolution was uninterrupted, and the following images *spoke* of men working and digging, of an energy that had finally resumed flowing. Horses, farm animals, entire animal families began to show up in his work.

Around this time, his mother texted me: "He reeled off times tables at a normal pitch, and then he read softly. We are happy!"

The last scene before the holidays is #48 (Figure 11.14).

The setting is the seaside, edged by banks and stones; there is a crane and a boat that he has put to sea with a sailor on board. M. is now the captain capable of steering his own boat; his Ego, his personality is no longer stuck, energy can freely flow, the sails can finally be hoisted.

It was now September 2012. M. had had a lovely summer. He was growing more handsome every day; he smiled, he no longer looked stuck. We resumed our work together, his sand scenes were rife with characters and motion; livestock and pets are the predominant presence now, always arranged in families, with the almost constant presence of horses that have now replaced cars. The horse is the representation of psychic energy par excellence, it stands

Figure 11.14 Crane and boat

for unpredictability within nature and, at the same time, for the element that leads to the enlightenment of awareness.

It is Saturday and M. arrives as usual with his father. I am talking about working mums and ask him, "And where does your mum work?"

M. replies, as loudly as me: "At the grocery store".

I felt a deep emotion, so I could not help hugging him.

He then approached the wet sand and shaped it briskly, intensely, in order to have the colour blue stand out.

I timidly ask: "Is that a river?"

"Yes".

"It's all true", I think, "he is speaking!"

I cannot find the words to express the intense and deep emotions I felt at that time.

While he was so working, we talked normally, as if we had always done so. Thenceforth, he spoke normally.

This is the sand he created on 29 September 2012, when M. spoke for the first time (Figure 11.15).

Figure 11.15 Wading horsemen

In the sand, there are two horses with two riders wading across the river; a one of the man is riding a horse and the other is mounting. They are travelling, it is a life journey. M. can now ride away across the world that is opening up in front of him. With some white stones, he says, he's building a house.

M. began his journey in silence and ended it speaking, arousing in me a deep sense of empathy and emotion as he managed with his little hands to shape deep and transformative scenes which, in the span of three years, enabled his words to gush forth. I am grateful to M. and the Zollikon Group for helping and supporting me throughout the process.

M. has changed me as a therapist, has taught me the *time* of silence, how to wait, how to be patient. I now feel that my work is similar to that of a farmer, sowing seeds in the field and then waiting for the harvest.

Chapter 12

Perceptions of the body within the research group

Iside Piccini

Foreword

My work with Linda was presented to the Zollikon Group in November 2014.

We follow the supervision method developed by Martin Kalff, in which the bodily sensations evoked by images and the awareness we derive from them guide us towards a deeper understanding of the significance of our work with patients.

Introduction

Linda is two years and seven months old when she is referred to me at the suggestion of her nursery teachers. She likes playing on her own, her exchanges and interactions with fellow children and adults are very limited, she hardly ever makes eye contact. Her language skills are retarded: the child uses one-word sentences that often are completely out of context, as is the case with her imitation and repetition of phrases spoken by cartoon characters or when she speaks in falsetto.

During the preliminary consultation with her parents, who had already had a daughter, they reported that Linda's arrival had been utterly unexpected. The mother's predominant feeling during pregnancy was extreme anxiety – a feeling mainly ascribable to the fact that Linda's sister (two years her senior) had been born after some miscarriages that had proved traumatic for the mother. This, on top of the fact that the woman had endured the loss of her own mother not long earlier.

The parents expressed their concern about the child's behaviour: she was a selective eater, she would never seek her parents' attention upon their return from work of her own volition, she could be so engrossed in her own games as not to even hear her parents' calls.

The mother also reported her difficulty upon leaving the house unassisted with her two daughters, as Linda seemed totally incapable of recognizing danger.

DOI: 10.4324/9781003163503-15

The therapeutic work

During my first observation sessions, I noticed her limited participation in two-player games and her eye contact avoidance. Body expressivity and mimic gestures were virtually non-existent: she seemed unable to express emotions such as happiness, discomfort, fear through her body; she was more interested in structured games (jigsaw puzzles, shapes …) than in spontaneous and movement-based games popular among her age group.

After working together for three months, a time during which I tried to respectfully 'be a part' of her games, Linda finally approached the dry sandbox. It was a discovery for her: she showed her curiosity, touched it, picked it up and felt it with her little hands. It was a very intense moment marking her first meaningful contact with me, by means of the sand: Linda looked at me and smiled!

After the summer holidays, our work together was still mainly focused on her strong interest in feeling and shaping the sand.

Linda touched the wet sand and began to shape a small mountain she called 'snowman', then placed into this container a monkey, a macaque, a bear, elephants, tigers, a nest-tree.

When the research group reviewed this sand image (Figure 12.1), before looking at the image we had been encouraged by Kalff to enhance our own

Figure 12.1 The Kind Monkey

awareness by letting ourselves 'slide into our own body' to fully experience the emerging sensations and emotions.

The experience took me back to a dream I had had two days before Linda's first encounter with Sandplay.

> I am at home, and I am surrounded by an orchard with fruit trees. The atmosphere is pleasant and peaceful, the light and air are those of a late spring day: suddenly, a monkey shows up. I am worried and distraught, the unannounced guest steps into the house and steals a banana from the fruit basket.

While reminiscing about the dream, I felt a surge of empathy and *compassion* for Linda, who populated her sandbox with a monkey and a macaque bearing a monkey infant on its back. This was a particularly strong experience which, thanks to Kalff's suggestion, paved the way to a more cognizant co-transference with Linda.[1]

After reporting my dream, the group participants made short remarks about their own experiences. A second look at Linda's sand image prompted the possibility that the snowman might 'melt', thanks to the 'kind' monkey carrying an infant on her back, tenderly and warmly. The snowman could be viewed as a kernel firmly encased in a nut hard to crack open, and impervious to contact with the Other on Linda's part. The more straightforward and deeper communication Linda and I have established, represented by the macaque with infant or the kind monkey, may open the way for the conscious processing of the fear experienced by her mother during pregnancy.

In a later session, while Linda was playing with wet sand, she made a small mountain with a hole at its centre: she only uttered the word 'a clown'; she then placed a red egg made of stone and a white bear (Figure 12.2).

Kalff suggests we should visualise the image and rivet our attention on what it stirs within our body. I feel as if the felt experience of the group formed a mandala of perceptions, feelings, images, so diverse and creative as to expand my visual and interpretive horizons and activate new energy in me, thus enabling me to detect shapes and connections in the sand that I could have not detected so clearly without the experiences my fellow therapists shared.

The colleagues' contributions highlight the great intensity of the hand movements, the slow motion of the bear,[2] the contact with the earth, the time of waiting and the need for a hug. The egg evokes sensations of cold, stiffness and closure; the clown, only mentioned by Linda, represents a different identity concealing something and is perceived as the mother's grief, perhaps the trauma of the past miscarriages she had gone through.

On an emotional level, some of us feel pain and difficulty in 'trusting the mother-body'. I sense that the act of hearkening the sensations and the feelings that each of us felt in the context of this experience, will make it possible for me to get to know this child more authentically within the vital and

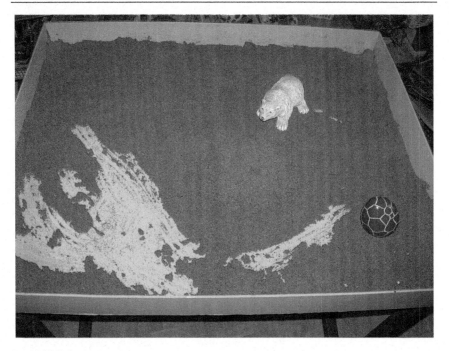

Figure 12.2 A clown

creative playground of the sandbox, where the wisdom of the body and the knowledge of the heart provide staple food for thought.

After this sand scene, Linda drew a red and yellow rainbow and her body grew increasingly alert to sensations: she stumbled in the room, and for the first time she let out an exclamation of pain, "Ouch". Eventually, there was a smile on her face and her eyes met mine.

The Rainbow, appearing after the flood, links the sky to the earth – I therefore sense that a new contact might have been established.

During the same session, Linda played with dry sand, where she placed snakes, eagles and frogs. She brings out the water surface with neat and clean-cut strokes (Figure 12.3).

Upon being confronted with this image, the group felt as if something was coming into existence.

The approach to a more instinctive process heralds the possibility of opening up; the frog and the eagle stand for an evolutionary progression that enables Linda's inner world to access a higher level of differentiation. It is this development that makes the encounter with the deepest and least known nooks of the unconscious possible with lesser fear.

In the dry sand, placed vertically, we find frogs, dinosaurs, owls, snakes, Tinkerbell, a mermaid, a space rocket and an egg (Figure 12.4).

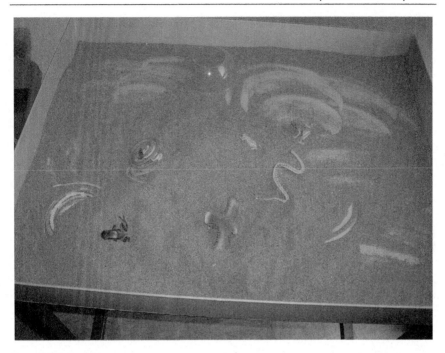

Figure 12.3 Instincts

Figure 12.4 Light and heaviness

Before discussing the sand scene, Kalff chairs a session in which we each come in contact with our body, and focus our attention on our breath in order to achieve an enhanced awareness of our body. Only after the practice, do we study the sand. The commonality of the resonance emerging from group discussion is, this time, strength: a natural and instinctive aggressiveness seems to gush forth, a deep energy from which we could expect the development of the 'No' which is indispensable to differentiation.[3] In the dimension of play, two opposites manage to come together:[4] the lightness of the winged girl, not completely embodied yet (Tinkerbell and the mermaid), meets the heaviness of dinosaurs.

In the following sand image (Figure 12.5) Linda selected a red dragon, a two-headed dinosaur, a crocodile, a green dinosaur, a Pokemon figure (she calls it 'space rocket'), Yoda (to Linda this is her father), a dodo (a turkey), Batman (a bat) and Colette Tatou, the figure of the *Ratatouille* cook holding a bowl and a hand mixer (to Linda this is the crocodile's mother), and placed them into the dry sandbox.

The attention and concentration of the group on the sensations in the body and on the free flow of its energy enabled me to visualise the image in the sandbox with a fresh (and more creative) set of eyes.

The egg we had found in the previous sand scene was now replaced by a red dragon: it looked as if a new energy was emerging and a new evolutionary

Figure 12.5 Dad and Mom

direction was being taken. For the first time, Linda uttered the words 'father' and 'mother'. The parents she never turned to in actual life had now come into existence in her inner world, and she was able to name and represent them through Sandplay.

In the last sand image I showed to the group (Figure 12.6) we find a red egg, a golden egg and an elephant.

The experience of 'inhabiting one's own body' and 'taking (in)' our breathing made it possible for us to plumb the depths of our emotions and feel, as a group, moved to joy for this pair of eggs.

The red egg conveys a vital energy which achieves peace and soundness thanks to the proximity to the golden egg. Dinosaurs have been replaced with the elephant, a more evolved animal, with its trunk raised as if to announce something: now there may be a chance for Linda to open up to the world, a new psychic birth that may help her establish a firmer presence in her relationships and to effectively word her communication intention in the encounter with the Other.

The deep feeling expressed by the group is one of a new process of opening up and changing.

It feels as if our group, by looking at Linda's sand scenes, had been on an inner journey and, thanks to the emotions and deep resonance within our

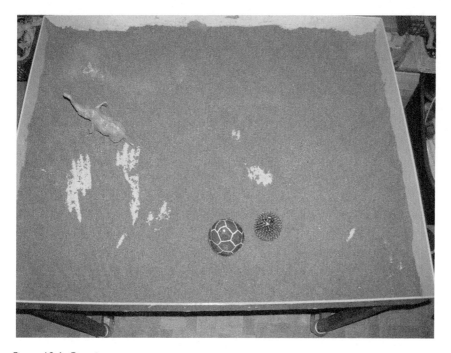

Figure 12.6 Opening

body, we each feel the urge to 'name' emotions and deep resonances through poems which have made the understanding of the steps taken by Linda even more authentic and creative.

The exchanges with my colleagues, on both a bodily and a symbolic level, let me into innermost depths within myself that I had never reached before, and this new awareness has given me the chance to form a more insightful and complete picture of my own living experience, as well as of Linda's.

The journey with Linda continues. Now, she doesn't often play with the sand and prefers involving the body as well as painting, and she actively makes eye contact with me and seeks my participation and contribution. It is now possible for her to share what she is feeling, as if her body had opened up to let out her rich inner Self.

Linda increasingly seeks interaction with similarly-aged children and with adults, and calls for attention in order to take part in other people's activities. Her verbal and bodily communication is now more complex and suitable to the context she is in. She has now started attending primary school and her teachers are very happy with her social and cognitive skills.

Notes

1 Carl G. Jung claimed with regard to transference: "For two personalities to meet is like mixing two different chemical substances: if there is any combination at all, both are transformed. In any effective psychological treatment, the doctor is bound to influence the patient; but this influence can only take place if the patient has a reciprocal influence on the doctor.... Nothing less than that the doctor is as much 'in the analysis' as the patient". C.G. Jung, *The Practice of Psychotherapy*, CW XVI, 1966, § 163.

2 J. Hillman in *Dream Animals* (Chronicle Book, San Francisco, 1997), with regard to bears, argued that the attachment to their offspring is such that they hug their babies until the very last and grieve them with the most heart-breaking wails.

3 In the primary relationship (which in *The Origins and History of Consciousness* (1954) E. Neumann called 'Ouroboros Stage') the child lives as if they were only part of a whole: the inner and the outer world, as well as psyche and soma, are undifferentiated. Progressively, a harmonious development of consciousness results in an ever-increasing differentiation. Thanks to the newly-acquired ability to say 'no', the child achieves separation from the mother as an autonomous being and therefore prepares for a rebirth through the development of the Self and its own identity, necessary prerequisite to the Self-Other relationship.

4 "Jung insists that the reconciliation of opposites be achieved through the positive activity of letting things be as they are by accepting within oneself the opposites as necessary coordination principles.... The term *conjunctio oppositorum* defines the reconciliation achieved through convergence of the opposites, and is borrowed from alchemic literature and used metaphorically". P.F. Pieri, *Dizionario Junghiano*, Bollati Boringhieri, Torino 2005, p. 301.

Chapter 13

Artwork in black

Drawing and therapy

Paola Gherardi

I learnt to recognise the symbolic and creative significance of colours pertaining to their therapeutic effects during the years of my training with Maria Rosa Calabrese[1] and within the research group chaired by Martin Kalff in Zollikon.

The following case is the story of a therapy session in which the use of colours proved a key means to the healing process.

Chiara's parents had heard of my therapeutic approach and had consequently contacted me in October 2010. I met them only once during the preliminary consultation. They told me that the child had recently gone through an ordeal, as she had been sexually abused by an older cousin, himself a minor at the time. The parents had been in the dark about this although it had taken place in their very home; it had been Chiara herself that, shortly after the fact, had opened up and told them about what had happened.

The parents also said that, as a baby, Chiara would often cry, and added that, later on, she showed an odd characteristic: she would frequently stumble and fall. When Chiara was two-year-old, she had been admitted to hospital because of a concussion and a laceration on her forehead.

Chiara was six and a half years old when I met her; she had just started attending primary school. She was born on 27 March, 2004, with an emergency caesarean section, due to placental abruption, even though her delivery was at term.

When I met her, I saw a quiet observer, perceptive to the world around her; she moved about the new environment freely and briskly, immediately accepting to establish a relationship with me, with the space surrounding her and with the objects in the room as well.

From the phone calls I had with her teachers, I came to understand that the girl at school was rather withdrawn, reluctant to participate in group discussions, and yet achieving great results in all subjects.

During our first session, Chiara openly and spontaneously admitted to knowing the reason for which her parents had enrolled her in therapy, but she did not add any further detail; she only informed me that during our sessions she would like to have fun and play.

My study is equipped with a variety of art materials: coloured pencils, water colours, oils and gouache, coloured chalks, oil pastels, hard materials

DOI: 10.4324/9781003163503-16

such as marble, alabaster, wood, iron, stone slabs; some soft material such as sand, clay, wax, fabric, coloured wool yarn, strands of cotton yarn, felt.

In the first two sessions, Chiara enacted a symbolic game where she carefully prepared some food for herself and her father, and did not speak until the end of the game.

Starting from the third session, I noticed that she showed a liking for black-coloured materials for all of her works: from the shelf, Chiara retrieved black gouache, black pencils, black chalk and, without uttering a single word, she spent the time allotted to her making two drawings (Figures 13.1 and 13.2). She eventually handed them to me without translating their contents into words. During the session she had used all of her time retrieving black materials and wielding them painstakingly; every gesture was performed with utmost concentration and strong emotional charge.

In our fourth session, still using black drawing material, she filled a page and explained she had drawn a tornado that had killed three people (Figure 13.3): there is a little girl whose knickers, as well as t-shirt and trousers are being removed (on the right side of the picture) by a tornado, a little boy wearing a nappy (in the middle, between the others), and a man swept away by the tornado (the figure on the left-hand side, whose head and arms only are visible).

The fifth session began with Chiara preparing food with toy pots and pans, and then settling again on black drawing material. She played in silence during the session. In her drawing, however, some colourful beads made their appearance (Figure 13.4).

Figure 13.1

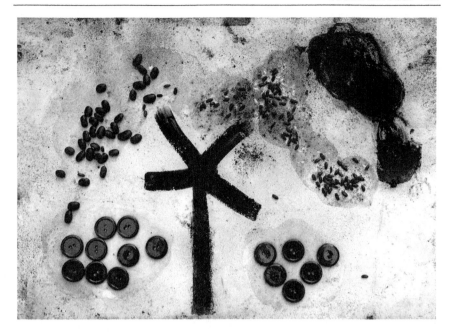

Figure 13.2

Figure 13.3

Figure 13.4

In the sixth session, a change occurred: Chiara felt the urge to use colours. She took colourful gouache, rolled some paper balls and then painted them in different colours: she felt they were precious, hid them in her pocket and smuggled them home stating she would not show them to her parents.

Our seventh session was entirely spent drawing a picture which is again mostly black, embellished by a few coloured grains of salt (Figure 13.5).

During the eighth session, Chiara drew a huge heart with a smaller purple heart on top; a big black arrow pierces through the red heart (Figure 13.6). During this session, without my asking, she claimed she felt good. She did not mention her drawing, she just handed it to me. In the drawing, I noticed the dominant use of bright red for the heart which, however, embraces and somewhat limits the smaller purple heart.

Chiara looked more serene, I noticed it myself and so did her parents, who confirmed it during our second and last encounter. We contacted the teachers by phone and they confirmed our impression. I explained to the parents the importance for their daughter to be given the means to express herself manually and creatively without external constraints: to her, space is a 'workshop' that enables her by means of drawing and painting materials to establish a contact with her sorrow in order to manage to overcome it – or, at least, to try.

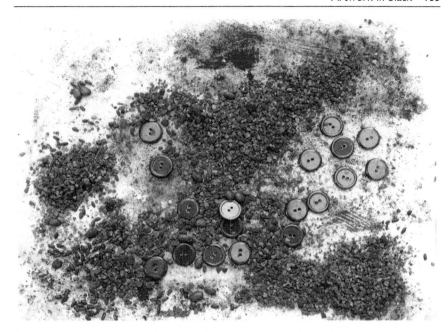

Figure 13.5

Figure 13.6

In the short time we spent together, I had a chance to notice how important it had been for Chiara to draw and paint using mostly black materials. As with alchemy – which Jung studied for many years – work and play with black materials enabled Chiara to experience the beginning of a transformative process. Black material enabled her to come in contact with her deep sorrow; through drawing and 'working' with her hands – a creative action – the child would recover each time a part of her Self which had been previously removed.

Chiara is now in third grade. I am in touch with her parents, who tell me she is making progress at school, has a regular social life for her age, and is open both at home and with same-aged friends; she also plays basketball with dedication.

In conclusion, a few brief remarks on my responses, on what is technically known as 'countertransference'.

Undoubtedly, drawing was the chief means for Chiara to become acquainted with her inner distress. I was surprised to see her resolution in choosing a diversity of materials: she would seek a specific gesture to convey or freeze an inner moment … that movement was bold. I would feel it in my body that I could not say or do anything, I was left speechless by her every adamant and incisive gesture. When she was working, I would sit close to her, motionless and quiet, breathing slowly. I felt emotional, at some points I felt tears rolling down my cheeks. My body was present, silent, attentive, still, and involved in her work. I could feel her gestures, the use of black and of the other colours, of the different media, the traits on the paper – they were resonating in my body, bearing witness to a descent she was undertaking into her own depths, but which I was also undertaking into mine.

Note

1 Maria Rosa Calabrese (1954–2016), Jungian psychoanalyst, Sandplay Therapist (ISST and AISPT member), in her theoretical and practical work with colours drew inspiration from Goethe's theories. She taught the course 'Archetypes of Imagination and Art Therapy Practices' at Accademia di Belle Arti di Brera, Milan.

Chapter 14

Body and sand

Dramatization

Emilia Canato

Sandplay Therapy in a department of mental health

The training experience within the Zollikon group did not only offer me the opportunity to experiment with nonverbal language through Sandplay Therapy, but also to expand the reach and scope of my struggle for meaning, and increase my openness to the symbolic dimension of experience, thus nurturing a creative approach in my work as a psychotherapist committed also to rehabilitation.

In my capacity as psychologist in a Department of Mental Health, I worked for many years on psychosocial rehabilitation of patients affected by mental disorders.[1] For many years, nonverbal group strategies have been utilised in this field, including the use of colours, mosaics, music, theatre, movement and dance, in the belief that these may favourably impact relationships, and may prove valuable in restoring skills lost as a result of psychological disorder or trauma. Bringing the body into play is a way to promote interpersonal exchange and the expression of inner emotional aspects preceding verbalization.

Being admitted to a Psychiatric Centre for Diagnosis and Treatment automatically results in an interruption of the patient's personal relationships and of the orderly unfolding of their daily life. Once the initial disorientation phase is over, it is important to help the patient rebuild their personal experience, cope with daily routine as well as with the relationship with the Other. In the Psychiatric Centre for Diagnosis and Treatment of the Rovigo Public Health Service, we have tested the assumption that sharing an artistic experience may help the patient reconnect socially and that this reconnection lays the groundwork on which to rebuild a sequence of experiences interrupted by the admission to the centre. Listening to music, dancing, acting: these are activities conducted in small groups which foster human contact within the ward, as well as decrease the risk of isolation and self-harming.[2] We have also noticed the importance of enrolling in rehabilitation programmes immediately after admission, to be carried on by local health services after discharge. This proves useful in reducing the dropout rates during

DOI: 10.4324/9781003163503-17

treatment and helps family and caregivers grapple with their emotional difficulties. Alternating moments of bodily expression, 'traditional' pharmacolo-
gical and verbal treatment sessions has ensured patients with severe or acute
symptoms better adjustment to the therapy also subsequent to the discharge,
while in the care of local services.[3]

Structured activities involving the body and conducted in small groups can
infuse daily routine with meaning and develop cognitive activation. What we
have ascertained in time through clinical trials, nowadays finds confirmation
also from a theoretical standpoint thanks to the discovery of mirror neurons,
which – as has been proven – are activated both when we carry out motor
activity and when we see it carried out by others.

With adolescents adamantly impervious to relationships, dialogue and verbalization, group approaches prove difficult to implement. This is the reason
for which I have introduced Sandplay Therapy among our range of techniques,
as it provides a privileged channel of communication to the unconscious and is
accessible also to individuals particularly averse to relations with the Other.[4]

As Rosa Napoliello Balfour[5] points out, Sandplay Therapy promotes the
contact with *implicit preverbal memory*, which forms as an emotional attachment during the earliest years of life – this cannot easily access the symbolic
understanding of reality, but can be awakened by relational experiences conveyed by play.[6]

The nonverbal approach typical of Sandplay enables the therapist – who is
empathically involved in co-transference or counter-transference dynamics with
the patient – to take an active part in the process, thus increasing the chance of
new openings and narrations on the part of the patient, as I had the opportunity to witness myself in a clinical case I shared with the Zollikon group.

Sandplay and dramatization

The clinical picture I reported to the Zollikon group a few years ago was very
problematic for me at that time; I was in need of a constructive dialogue in
order to overcome the stagnation of my relationship with the patient. The
case concerned a young woman, aged 34 when I first met her, a graduate
running a private practice in the medical profession. The first encounter took
place at the Public Health Service clinic, but later the psychotherapeutic
journey would continue in the form of Sandplay Therapy at my private
practice.

From the beginning, the request for help was confused and the therapy
began after an assessment confirming the urgent need for intervention in
response to diffuse anxiety. This was due to dissatisfaction with her job, which
in turn impacted her emotional relationships.

The woman was the youngest of four siblings in a family of farmers, she
was brought up in contact with nature and within an extended family that
included uncles and cousins. She did not recount much about her childhood,

but recalled hostile behaviours within the family. The tie with her family seemed strong nonetheless, and the siblings would often gather together for lunch to celebrate festivities. Amongst the few memories of her own childhood, she mentioned a strong relationship with an aunt. It was not easy to collect information from this young woman, as she was distrustful of the Public Health Service, where treatment began, due to the fact that she was familiar with the environment and a few people working there. After vocational school, she had enrolled at university to study arts, but had to drop out due to an unplanned pregnancy. After her son had been born (she is very proud of him today) she completed her medical studies with flying colours, she started a family with her partner and established her own medical practice.

Our sessions often ended on long silences and doubts over the scheduling of the later sessions, mostly pencilled in because of possible work commitments, usually unconfirmed. However, when she accepted to play with the sand, our relationship took a different turn: she showed interest and curiosity about our sessions, which then became more regular and more relaxed. Her way of handling the sand would arouse a pleasant sensation in me.

Upon shaping her first scene (Figure 14.1), the patient set to work by dividing the sandbox and the sand into two parts; she would touch the sand with an extraordinary responsiveness and made moderate use of water to mould a

Figure 14.1 The Universe

mountain on the right side. The final result was a forest with trees on the left side, while a hemisphere with a pyramid emerged from the blue side, joining the two parts at the centre; she placed a sailing boat in the upper right corner, and below that a set of stairs meant to convey a sense of scale and different proportions, thus creating a background effect. The hemisphere represents the moon: the patient placed a glass bunny on top of it, and on the left side she placed some dirt and trees. It was a representation of the Universe featuring a pyramid which, in her imagination, represented Egyptian culture. She would work very intensely and engagingly. She worked similarly also on the following scenes, two of which were made one shortly after the other.

In the second scene the patient set empty stretches in stark contrast to sand-filled one, with smooth strokes drawn at a steady, almost hypnotic, pace. The title she came up with was 'The Fire Bird and the Water Bird'.

The third scene was basically all drawn on wet sand and etched with the point of a small pocket knife. She called the resulting image 'Snake'.

In the fourth scene (Figure 14.2), I noticed the reappearance of some objects she had already fastidiously picked out from the range on the shelves. She shaped the sand with water to make it more supple, and it turned into a mountain that the patient shifted from its top and then from its centre; on the right, she added a trail of sand in the shape of rays, and afterwards she dug a round hole deep enough to uncover the blue bottom of the box. I had the impression to be able to detect an image into this (yin and yang), but she then continued and covered the hole by placing two insects. She looked for some

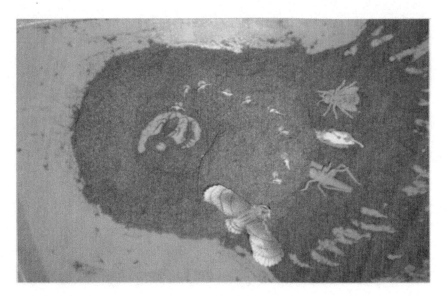

Figure 14.2 The Jellyfish

animals she was not able to find, and so she explained to me that the lambs represented sheep and the eagle stood for an owl. She lined up some toy soldiers on the edge of the mountain crater, but she was unable to say whether they were coming out of or were heading towards the central hole; she said she was dissatisfied, she added a locust and a bee to the rays, both upside down, and a cow resting on its side. Suddenly, she asked for the time and felt like leaving the session. She was not happy with the final result, she said it was a jelly fish and rushed out.

She agreed on my proposal to share her sand creations with the research group also in order to answer her questions on the meaning of the work. Her tendency to take everything to a logical and verbal level and to play down creative work, downgrading it to no more than a definition, did not, in my opinion, do justice to the images appearing in the sand.

Within the Zollikon group, after reviewing the first three sand images, Martin Kalff suggested listening to the body, first, starting from the attention to the breath, in order to be able to perceive the emotions and the energy radiating from the sand images, and to then expressing what we were feeling through movement.

In the following group discussion, using our life experiences as a starting point, we all sensed the presence of a block, manifesting itself as an inability to progress or a lack of energy. We also felt bewilderment and a lack of direction, the burden of being confined in a world of relations and encounters, of ambivalence, emphasised by the bewilderment of the toy soldiers unable to find their own bearings in the sandbox.

Kalff suggested we visualise an image that could help break that stillness and, amongst other things, the image of a holding hand was prompted, which conveyed a sense of warmth and energy. Someone felt that the patient could not climb out of the mire by herself. The therapist could be of help, but in order to do so she had to avoid identification and, in consequence, wallow herself in the same mire. The notes in the session minutes, taken to keep track of the significant moments of our sessions, interestingly read as follows: 'If the therapist does not manage to thaw what is frozen inside of herself, she is fated to confront the frozen block again in the following sessions'.

I must admit that the experience of reliving the scene through movement – mine and the others' – helped me thaw what was still frozen. I am convinced that, as Gallese and Guerra also argue, when we witness movement and behaviour performed by others, we notice a number of intentional contents – and, as such, significant – without resorting to language as a means of communication. Through *embodied simulation* we use brain mechanisms to map other people's actions. The very observation of other people's behaviours releases new potential and prepares us to deeply understand the other.[7]

In the following scene, the fifth (Figure 14.3), we find a central nucleus of sand, shaped the same way as on previous occasions, except in this case the centre widens and becomes a lake with three blue branches, and with an edge

Figure 14.3 Relativity

made of sand, broader and more rugged than the previous ones. There are two fish in the lake, while on shore, in the top right-hand side, a polar bear with her cub. In the sea, on the upper left corner, there is a squid; on the lower edge, a character with bow and arrows (Merida, main character of the Pixar movie *Brave*, awarded with an Oscar in 2013); then colourful birds, a fir tree and other scattered trees here and there. All around, in the blue section, crumbled polystyrene represents ice blocks. It looks like thaw season. The patient's title for this scene is 'Relativity'.

The group shares thoughts related to lightness, depth, intensity, dynamism, energy, contradictory elements difficult to arrange into a sequence. Kalff suggested we should express them by means of poetry.

I have chosen three poems which I feel best represent our collective feeling:

On an island in bloom again
life is reborn
the relationship is rekindled –
the relationship that heals.

The kiss of the polar bear to her cub
releases bright tenderness in the cold.

There is vitality being born
and pervading the body
and there is also freedom, and robustness.
Ducks, squids, tigers
are welcome
to the fight:
helplessness has vanished.

————

In lightness
in colour
in water
and in tenderness
the encounter takes place.
In cold
in warmth
I am alone.
Danger!
Perhaps I will find you.

As agreed with the patient beforehand, I handed her the page with the poems as a feedback from the research group: I would have never expected this may deeply affect our relationship. The patient wrote to me that the poems were priceless gifts for her, begetting emotions, tears and joy:

> These poems may have arrived serendipitously, who knows? The words 'perhaps I will find you' are like a sword through my heart, I have never found myself and I often wished someone had been looking for me.

After this, the patient gradually improved, our sessions went smoothly and her participation became more active and relaxed.

As our analytic journey was drawing to a conclusion, I felt the urge to share the last stages of the therapeutic process with the Zollikon group by viewing two sand scenes: one shaped immediately after the breakthrough, the sixth, and a more recent one, which made, in my opinion, a fitting conclusion to my work with this patient.

The first scene we examined after her reading of the poems is very wet, unlike the previous ones; the water she had poured spilt over the brims of the sandbox and wetted the floor (Figure 14.4). In the sandbox the patient created a vortex, which she experienced as an expression of energy. She said "The centre is the heart of the problem, I cannot stick my hands into that". She worked on the edges with utmost care and ended it by adding a candle which she lit and, while screening the flame with her hand, she told me, in a soft voice, of a dream that had to do with water. It was a recent dream in which she was the protagonist: in the dream she was at home and was very busy

Figure 14.4 The Vortex

mopping up water and drying the floor from leaks that had caused a flood on the ground floor. She needed to hurry up to prevent further damage to the wiring. The fear connected to electricity causes her to feel worried and anxious. She got very tired but managed to stem the damage caused by the flooding without too many consequences.

Kalff asked us to express our feelings through a drawing, turning to the sand scene for inspiration.

Upon comparing our drawings (Figure 14.5), we noticed that, despite using different colours, in every single trait a sensation linked to a spiral-like

Figure 14.5 Drawings

rotating motion could be detected. This motion released energy and vitality. A fresh energy also vibrated in the colour palette used, as well as in the warm light from the candle, which looked as if fuelled by the vortex ostensibly growing from the centre of the sandbox. Some actually identified a little dragon in the image, a slow prehistorical animal, scale-armoured, representing, maybe, the intention to hold back something that should come out instead.

Many months after she had made the sand scene she had called 'Vortex', she worked on another very unusual one. The patient had been prompted to work with sand by a dream in which the therapist was taking a picture of an undefined sand scene. So she stirred the wet sand energetically, and asked for an hourglass, but the one she found was unusable and she exclaimed, "It doesn't matter, I will change everything!" So, from her work with the sand, a tortoise emerged (Figure 14.6).

The patients said she had two tortoises in the garden and that maybe one of them had got lost, because she hadn't seen it for a while, although it was, she observed, hibernation time. She placed four ducks on each side of the tortoise and on top she placed a native American chief, two warriors, a totem and a tepee. To finish off, she drew, in silence, the 'shell' with a sharp tool. The drawing looks like the 'Aztec' illustration in the third scene.

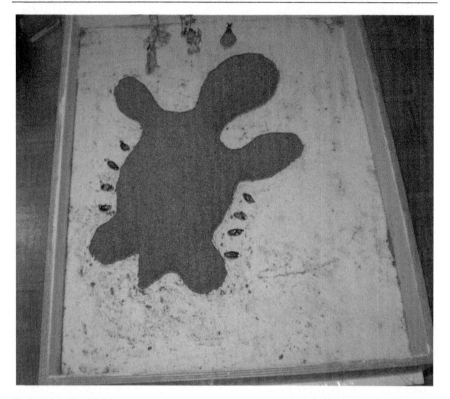

Figure 14.6 The Turtle

Within the research group we observed, together, the execution of this work from which we derived a sense of participation and which gave us a sense of deep, intimate tranquillity. From above, the tortoise looks light, but from the side it looks heavy and sturdy, a great mountain from which the ducks are leaving, possibly representing 'pilot fish', as someone conjectured, although their direction is unclear. The sand could be interpreted in a spiritual sense, maybe a reference to the mythology of the Creation.

Kalff then invited the group to move to the garden, so as to express our life experience through a collective dramatization in which each of us chose a figure to act out. The proposal was met with enthusiasm, it was a lovely sunny day and each us picked one figure to embody. Kalff and another member of the group would observe us.

In short, the dramatization went as follows: the tortoise, led by the ducks, found a landing place; the native American chief, in an exchange of hooks and lines in which the warriors were addressed, as well as the totem and the tepee, asked the others whether they wished to welcome the tortoise – and they did.

The dramatization ended by forming a circle, a symbol of inclusion and hospitality.

The experience of this dramatization was very intense for each of us. Some of us lent our voice and body to a performance that became a very meaningful event, and we all were amazed to feel so involved in the characters experiencing such intense emotions. Some also felt physically tired, a strong emotion connected to catching a glimpse of landing chance; at the start the young warriors were distrustful and on the defensive in front of something they perceived as an invasion. The wise words spoken by the chief, the welcoming tent and the supervision by the totem, caused the tension to dissolve and made it possible for the tortoise to reach the shore.

Our dramatization was instrumental in 'entering' the sand scene with our bodies, acknowledging the difficulty inherent to movement, our weak and vulnerable points, the value of struggle. Through the bodily sensations, we felt as if we were more attuned to aspects of the patient's psychology. In her quest for meaning, in our eyes, the young woman has become a migrant in need of shelter. We also felt this dramatization could acquire symbolic value in two different ways: on the one hand, from an interpsychic perspective it showed us the importance of being able to welcome our difficulties and integrate some aspects of the Shadow; on the other hand, in a social-historical context, it prompted us to pause and think about contemporary migration, and about the challenges of hosting the foreigner who reaches our shores from the sea.

Notes

1 E. Canato, *La riabilitazione* in *Medicina generale e psichiatria pubblica*, a cura di E. Toniolo, A. Grossi, Ed. Cleup, Padova, 2002.
2 S. Caperna and E. Canato, Teatro Sociale in Psichiatria, *Pedagogika.it*, XVII, Rho, Milano, 2016, 3.
3 L'utilizzo delle tecniche espressive e le attività di gruppo in SPDC, *Errepiesse rivista quadrimestrale*, updated International Ed., Anno IV, 2, 2010.
4 This therapeutic approach was introduced within the framework of a broader research project on major disorders in adolescents. The project was financed by the Veneto Region and involved the Health Services of Southern Veneto Region, coordinated by the University of Padua (reference period 2005–2009).
5 R. Napoliello Balfour, Sandplay Therapy: From Alchemy to the Neuroscience, *Journal of Sandplay Therapy*, 22(1), Walnut Creek, CA, 2013.
6 With regard to the importance of play, Jung maintains: "For as a grown man it seemed impossible to me that I should be able to bridge the distance from the present back to my eleventh year. Yet if I wanted to re-establish contact with that period, I had no choice but to return to it and take up once more that child's life with his childish games. This moment was a turning point in my fate, but I gave in only after endless resistances and with a sense resignation. For it was a painfully humiliating experience to realise that there was nothing to be done except play childish games". C.G. Jung, *Memories*, p. 208–209.
7 V. Gallese and M. Guerra, *Lo schermo empatico. Cinema e neuroscienze.*

Chapter 15

A rebirth

The story of a woman

Maria Teresa Pasolini

Stepping into the sandbox room is like stepping into a miniature world showcasing hundreds of trinkets on which the eyes linger, objects that beckon us, through the emotions and the associations they trigger. They urge us to tell the stories through which some parts of us – hidden away in deep and otherwise inaccessible nooks – can finally come out. And the eyes sometimes guide the hands, or are sometimes guided by them. Hands digging into the sand, stirring it, shaping it, picking and placing objects onto its surface, playing in and with it, building scenes and settings where split parts of our personality may possibly come together and integrate. This way images are engendered, images capable of conveying frozen, unutterable emotions.

The healing journey through Sandplay progresses step by step, each step representing a milestone along a lengthy inner journey. The earliest sand scene may be the expression of the patient's ailment in its entelechy, their complexes, the issues at stake and the directions which the therapy may take. It often takes some time for the changes portended by a sandbox scene to occur in real life. In later scenes, trans-personal or archetypal images may show up, images that ease the encounter between the Ego and the deepest layers of the psyche, and can restore the Ego-Self axis, and accordingly vent the energy that was previously stuck.

The sandbox is an important free and protected space, and equally important is what, by analogy, we call the analyst's inner space, capable of encompassing the meaning of the image without judgement, letting it resonate through its emotional quality and perceiving it, first of all, in the body – as we have experienced ourselves over the last few years within the Zollikon group. The analyst begins their work from the perceptions of and in the body, to later identify and acknowledge some contents which the patient's Ego is still unable to process. Only later on will they be turned into emotions and feelings that the patient will be able to acknowledge, as a milestone along the healing process. The body feels something before the mind can even understand it, and thus constitutes the starting point of a journey that leads from sensations to feelings, and therefore to thoughts, which are so rooted in the body. The body that perceives and expresses is also the first instrument we avail

DOI: 10.4324/9781003163503-18

ourselves of to communicate our life experiences. In order for us to meet the patient and understand them at the exact stage where they find themselves the moment when they are shaping their first sand scene – which is also the moment when they come in contact with their innermost selves – we, too, have to approach the sand through the cognitive potential offered by our own body.

May I offer as a way of example of this bodily process the story of a patient (whom I will henceforth refer to as 'Sabrina'), a story beginning in the sand-box and a story about a person who entrusted me – or, should I say, our therapeutic relationship – with the painfully confused story of her life.

Sabrina is 46 years' old when she makes up her mind to embark on a therapeutic journey, apparently urged by her difficulty in sustaining a spousal role she cannot identify herself with anymore. She has been married for 18 years to a man she has never really felt physically attracted to, but whom she settled on because she had thought he would prove able to ensure the supportiveness she associated with parental roles. Soon, however, in order not to succumb to her marriage, she had felt the urge to have affairs, which she would then look back on with deep guilty feelings[1]. She always took for lovers men she saw as 'important', and explained that they made her feel protected, however she always avoided any serious involvement and embarked on sexual liaisons she would dismiss as 'nonsense'.

When I met her, she asked me to help her make a choice between her husband and her then-lover. It looked patent to me that this was not the real problem, but the fact that the strands of confusion in which she felt entangled were a symptom of a deep-seated malaise associated to a different type of betrayal – the betrayal Sabrina had committed against herself.

In her family, male members had had a marginal role. Sabrina had used to live in a narrow matriarchal world. She describes her mother as a powerful, dominating and intrusive woman – *au fond*, depressed, and characterised by a victim mentality designed to make others feel guilty, presumably to manipulate them more effectively. Sabrina, too, is manipulative and seductive. One can at times glimpse the fussy child who tries to control others by means of seductiveness in an attempt to flee her past which has been with her for a long time, yet always disregarded. Her dependency on the other in order to build a fake identity for herself bears witness to this. Her therapeutic journey is haunted by the figures of the mother affected by abandonment issues and of the father who failed to guide her in life. Dependent on a fusional relationship with her mother and deprived of a positive relationship with her father, Sabrina had been for years in a sorrowful state of depression in which she felt any purpose and sense of direction had been lost.

I had liked Sabrina since the very beginning, I sensed that her suffering was the outcome of her unmet need for validation, as well the relinquishment of her own subjectivity. For too long she had identified with a self-image passed down to her by her mother, like a distorting mirror through which she had always seen herself as defective, and she had been trying to conceal the girl still alive inside of her, a needy child disguised as a manipulative woman. I liked the way she would live our analytic relationship, laying bare her 'blots' and her 'faults'; I enjoyed her wittiness and her irony. I perceived in her great spirituality, depths of feeling and thought that may help her in her journey towards individuation. I felt empathy with the deep suffering of the child that was still inside of her, a child who felt plain, unappreciated, unacknowledged, who – in order to compensate for her fears of abandonment – needed to believe herself a princess thinking she had a right to everything.

She would soon herself understand that her problem was not the choice between her husband and her lover, but rather choosing herself and identifying her actual needs and wants.

The opinion I had formed since the very beginning and that would accompany me to the end of the therapy – even though I didn't share it with her – was that she needed to meet and choose her inner lover, named Animus by Jung, which in a woman is determined by the contingent features of the actual father figure.[2]

Failure to establish a positive relationship with the Animus may engender insecure women, plagued by guilt, self-destructive, narcissistic, prey to a lust for power compelling them to be in control and command of the situation, or to take advantage of it. This is what had happened also to Sabrina, whose eyes had never met her father's loving look: in her, the masculine energy had been perverted to such an extent as to cause her to say her life was undignified and soiled by guilt.

In the course of her therapeutic journey, Sabrina would eventually realise her worth and find the strength not to betray herself anymore, and she would achieve this by overcoming her fear of rejection and abandonment – she has now learnt to choose and to pursue what she authentically longs for. She has finally met her inner lover, a gentle and respectful Animus that guides her and helps her understand that, in order to say 'yes' to herself, she must, at times, say 'no' to the others, even at the risk of losing them. She is now aware that the sorrow to avoid is the one that is felt when losing one's own identity.

Let's now move on to the pictures of the sand scenes making the milestones of Sabrina's inner journey.

The first time, she chose the dry sandbox but did not touch the sand, as she stuck some objects into it without either digging or disturbing it, keeping off from her own body and from what her body might have to say (Figure 15.1).

The black castle, the dominant element in the entire picture, located on the diagonal line between two opposite corners, seems to represent a demarcation line drawn onto this symbolic body between a fairy tale and child-like world, and a travel project. While looking at the sand, Sabrina said she did not know what she would do, but that she could catch a glimpse:

> This world fascinates and frightens me at the same time. I need someone to guide me, because this is a new world to which I can get closer only

Figure 15.1 A possible voyage

with the help of a guide. The castle is not the destination – the destination is a possible voyage, probably by sea, and that sailor will guide me.

I believe this was a good intuition: a male guide, an Animus, is asked to lead her through the unconscious in order to come in contact with her subjectivity.

In the research group, we prepare – after finding the silence within ourselves – to mind the body's responses to viewing the images of this first sand scene. First of all, we ask ourselves what kind of physical reaction we perceive, minding also where they are located in the body, and then we ask what kind of emotions and feelings we experience. Some of us reported feelings of rigidity and emptiness, others felt warmth and tenderness. By following this process, we began to feel, and then to understand, a few things about Sabrina: not only the most visible aspects of her personality, but also her dark sides, her naivety and vulnerability. This way, the body's perception – upon letting in the image of the sand scene – becomes the voice of the narration of the psyche and sows deeper the seed of a thought that authentically comprehends, and of a word that interprets. If you do 'enter' the sand scene 'with your own body', heeding sensations first, and then emotions and feelings, you will be able to encounter more closely the deep images that voice the unconscious.

Looking at this sand scene, we sense that Sabrina may already have enough energy to leave for the voyage she talked about, we feel this energy in the well – which, channelling deep waters, signifies the opening of a channel between sub-conscious and consciousness – and also in the flowering tree with its promise of new fruits. The presence of several children's objects in the sandbox causes us a physical feeling of disorientation. A small child, a woman's dress, empty and unworn, suggest a feeling of waiting for adulthood, an experience she doesn't seem to be yet ready for. We all perceive in our body the weight of the castle, the weight of this building that seems to hamper the flow of energy. Behind the castle we notice the painful area of the absence of subjectivity, a protected space, void of self, but filled with depressive symptoms. The castle, which is called upon to defend her child Ego, is maybe a reference to her marriage (represented by a bride and groom) from which, in real life, she periodically escapes, and protects her from the grief caused by emptiness. We sense that the space where Sabrina is hiding is the prison where she feels caged.

Looking at the sand scene, I felt a sense of oppression, of being locked in, of breathlessness, and especially the sorrow of the bird locked in the red cage – I felt it myself and also on her behalf, now that she was away. I was struck by the fact that – upon commenting on this scene – Sabrina had not noticed this element which – precisely because she had withheld it – acquires a special significance.

Sabrina may not have been aware of it, but the cage was there, her captivity was there, and these elements triggered in me a sorrowful emotion which, at that time, could not be either acknowledged or accepted by her. The grief I was feeling was the consequence of denied freedom, of an identity lacking authenticity, built to ensure other people's acceptance.

After crafting this scene, Sabrina told me there was a development in her extramarital relationship and that she was feeling less of a void, as she was accepting to be more deeply involved in a relationship.

Her second scene portrayed precisely this depth (Figure 15.2).

As she was drawing closer to the sandbox, she said: "I am following my hunches, I really don't know what I am doing". I think that this is truly the best way to approach the sandbox.

While contemplating the final result of her work, Sabrina described the imagined attitude of the young woman standing in front of the dragon:

> She defies the dragon, she stands there with a sassy attitude; the contest is between the two, however she can call on a warrior ready to help her. I sometimes have a sassy attitude, too, especially when I want to grapple with fear, I do this with men as well.

A glimpse of the young woman came to me in a flash – she was defiant and aggressive, striving to protect the frail and defenceless girl by hiding her and denying her existence. The sailor she had placed in the previous scene turned

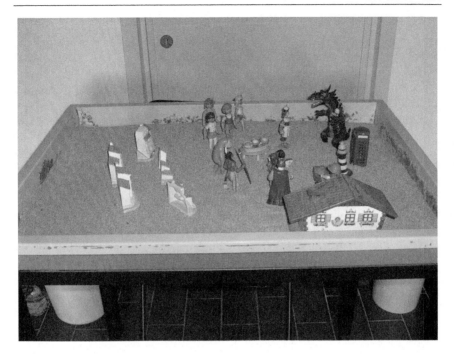

Figure 15.2 The challenge

into a strong native American warrior, the symbol of a powerful Animus linked to unconstrained and untamed instincts. Sabrina perceived him as a possible rescuer, investing him with a respectful and true protection. There is also the King, and Sabrina had him say: "You two, calm down!", thus investing him with the role of ordering principle. Finally, there was a mother with a child, a serene image of nurture and caregiving.

The defiant attitude of the young woman in front of the dragon, as well as the young girls behind her unafraid of the potential danger, reveal an attitude half-way between the childish and the omnipotent. Sabrina did not notice, however, that the dragon was holding a little angel captive under its hoof, with the angel being the mediator between the spiritual world and the material world, the bearer of good news for the soul. She was not able to perceive yet that the angel was the most authentic part of herself, held captive and needful of rescue. In Christian culture, every human being is assisted by an angel guiding their life and protecting them. As for the dragon, this is the symbol of archaic psychic contents, of regressive energies contrasting the journey which the Hero has undertaken to build his individuality, rescuing it from the deadly coils of a psychic system dominated by the mother's influence. It may represent the enemy which should be defeated with a mature and self-possessed attitude, in order to get a hold of the treasure represented by the angel.

After working on this scene, Sabrina was finally able to voice her anger against her father, who had been dramatically degraded by the women in her family: her mother and her aunts. She claimed:

> I am angry because he allowed himself to be put upon without putting up a fight; he and I were the weird ones in the family, however he did not teach me how to defend myself from my mother's intrusiveness, he abandoned me, so I am not at all sorry for him. I had to abandon him, too, when I grew up, and hold on to my mother, so I went on denying myself in order to feel accepted and loved by her.

In the third sand scene, Sabrina seemed to be leaving for the travel mapped out in the first sand, and seemed to be heading towards the places of her inner Self leading to the deep sea (Figure 15.3).

Guided by Kalff, we endeavoured to 'enter the scene' by feeling it in our bodies and feeling carried under the sea. We all felt a sense of depth and were able to perceive the images from the sandbox resonating inside of ourselves. Instead of the void, this time someone perceived a sense of enveloping fullness, the sea water, almost haptically felt on the skin. Only after sharing our sensorial experiences, did we come up with some hypotheses on the meaning of the animals Sabrina had picked.

Figure 15.3 Between Good and Evil

We were particularly struck by the huge spider placed in the middle of a flow between good animals and evil animals fighting against each other which seemed to represent a negative maternal complex that was clouding her and consequently making it difficult for her to discern good and evil. Sabrina had for a long time been busy building an image of herself which would be instrumental to feeling accepted rather than to representing her real self, and she was now confronted with her own ambivalence.

Captive to a fusional relationship pattern, she now found it very difficult to make responsible and independent choices, particularly when they involved conflict. Finally, she got to see that her problem was also an ethical one. The confusion between good and evil prevented her from authentically taking care of herself.

Between this sand scene and the following one, Sabrina had a dream about a journey in which she found a female character she associated to the 'close, reassuring, guiding' relationship she had with me, and a male character in the role of a helper, whom she connected with her father. Thinking back to her father, she was able to see for the first time some qualities and resources in him that her alliance with her mother had prevented her from acknowledging:

> My father was the only one in the family not to overdramatize, which was by contrast typical of the women of our family. Now I am astonished and ashamed to think back to my behaviour towards him, which was almost cynical.

Shortly after this dream, she talked to her husband about her decision of separating from him. She now felt the urge for transparency and truth.

The fourth sand scene (Figure 15.4) dug into a depth from which a white and compact underground world emerged, and which she described as:

> A closed world, with some elements of light and a lot of things thrown in at the centre – nothing that may prove harmful, but there is motion in the shells placed upright and representing perhaps male energy. Something came afterwards, the tips of the shells are not sharp and aggressive. It feels like a day after, elements thrown in the emptiness [the emptiness again]; this is a unique item, as if it was a heart, but nothing is haphazard: it looks like an internal organ, a heart or a pancreas.

I observed the movements of the hands and of the body as she was working on the sand, while attempting, with much effort, to arrange and hold together all the parts in the scene, and some shells kept on slipping away. The effort involved was considerable, however it did not stop her, and the strong emotion pervading her as she was working was patent. The shells could allude to split female nuclei, parts of her original Self which the Ego was trying to hold together.

Figure 15.4 Feeling her own pain

Through this sand scene Sabrina came to the lowest point of her grief – her hands had helped her unearth what the Ego would never have wanted to acknowledge. In the sand scene she saw the rigidity of her defences, the shield behind which she had used to hide. Suddenly, she burst into tears and said: "I feel like crying, I don't know why, but I feel like crying, I feel it is all that's left of me, everything is so piled up, layered, toilsome".

By bringing the attention to my body, I felt a dumb pain, a sense of breathlessness due to lack of air.

Sabrina sensed my bodily sensations and the emotions they produced in me, and said: "I feel locked up, without air, always on the defensive, piled up, without an objective, and overstimulated". The rigidity I felt in my body enabled me to understand that the heart Sabrina was talking about was an ossified, hardened heart, unable to carry out its function of receptacle of feelings and source of discernment. Until now, Sabrina's heart had not been able to secrete a feeling sufficiently able to discern, recognise and assess herself and others. Even the pancreas, the internal organ in charge of combustion and of transforming matter into energy, symbolically representing self-affirmation and the freedom of being what we are, looked ossified.

One day Sabrina rushed into my office and asked to work on the sand right away. She took some wooden building blocks and said: "I would like to build something vertical, as if I could defy gravity". I perceived this as an act of defiance, heavily conditioned by her Ego. She built something resembling a city and said: "I built a world, a turreted world" (Figure 15.5).

She then burst into tears: "I feel as if I were exactly like this, full of piled-up things, without any arrangement, everything scattered about in a precarious world; the slightest thing and, wham, everything comes down". And with a finger she toppled a tower. She lingered for a while, looked as if she was listening to the scene, and then: "It might also be ok like this", she says. "Why not? I like it this way as well".

I felt and thought that there was very little to add, that this was an important step: Sabrina no longer needed to build a strong image of herself, defended by a shield. All it took was a small gesture to underline the brittleness of the towers representing her defences. She had access now, to the inner resources that enabled her to look at the debris. Now it was time to rebuild.

After this scene, Sabrina's husband tried to talk her into giving up on the separation. This request confused her; however, she was lucid enough to understand that she would accept his offer only in order to fill the void she was afraid of, and so she decided to move forward with the separation. Some things changed during these weeks. She understood that her lack of assertiveness was caused by the fear of conflict and loss, and she became aware of

Figure 15.5 The collapse of the tower

how the rage she had been building up would be given vent to through argumentative behaviours – what she would call 'my maliciousness'. She began to enjoy the feeling of comfort experienced when she was true to herself. She began to understand that 'loneliness' does not mean 'emptiness'. She also decided to look for a different job to fully put her skills to use.

As our journey continued, one day Sabrina stepped into the sandbox room and said: "Today I want to build something". It is no longer defiance; it was a real urge to rebuild (Figure 15.6).

She started from a mosaic at the centre of the sandbox and built a house around that. She worked with great gusto and painstaking attention, and at the end she said:

> It is an open house, with many things to discover inside, two stories, symmetric and complex, but free from constraint, with its own rigour and coherence – it is protected. Could this be a description of myself? There is even a small shrine for prayer and meditation.

It looks like a space is actually clearing within herself for a spiritual/male energy. "I feel good, I am comfortable and I would like to continue to feel so, not to feel alone". It looks as if she had progressed from fragmentation and

Figure 15.6 An open house

shattering to a situation in which she was able to collect and hold together the pieces of her Self, to look after herself.

In the supervisory session, Kalff invited us to 'enter the sand' under the guidance of our senses. Different sensations gushed forth from each of us, but we all sensed overexposure: we perceived doors and windows were still missing from Sabrina's buildings. Our sensations helped us comprehend the unconscious energy springing from the elements that made up the images in the sand. They revealed to us the urge for cleaner-cut differentiation, for the establishment of more functional boundaries to decrease the need of paranoid defences, represented by a fencing that Sabrina describes as a decoration – a further attempt at repression. Once again, the attention turned to our bodily responses helped get further into the transference dynamics, and realise that her individuation process still needed to build doors and windows.

Later, in a talking session, I felt emotional when she told me that she had been thinking about the scene built during the previous session, and which had been the object of our supervisory work: "I paid some thought to it and I felt it was still too open, that I should have built doors and windows". It felt as if our feeling had resonated in her, resulting in the same awareness. Even though I know that the analytical relationship is also an encounter of subconsciouses, I am always pleasantly surprised and feel emotional when I live through those moments when the doors of the subconscious open up and allow for its circulation, and when the empathy with the patient reaches a deeper level.

In the meantime, Sabrina confronted her husband again with regard to the separation, which he was trying to put off so as to avoid a decision; however, she stood firm and asked him to start making arrangements to end their marriage. Before her breakthrough, she would have left the decision up to him, she would not have wanted to bear the burden of 'guilt', but the new Sabrina understood that she had to go through this to build her new identity.

Later, Sabrina worked on a scene in which earlier frozen blocks melted and turned into a red-and-pink flower, made of a very light material, on which she laid some shells open towards the depths of the earth and protected by the flower. The group observed the sand and we all felt a sense of lightness and light. The previous images had become something soft, aerial, colourful, a kind of axis or bridge between the sky and the deep sea, to which the shells refer. The scene seemed to indicate, in the light of both the colours and the shapes chosen, the activation of a creative energy. We felt as if led into a landscape at dawn that seemed to protect anything that might still be in embryo. We felt it was an important and delicate moment, which could be likened to the gestation and incubation of a new life, of a new femininity (Figure 15.7).

After this scene, Sabrina had a dream. "I held this new-born girl in my arms, in a family atmosphere, we were all happy". It reminded her of the sense of harmony she would feel when she was at peace with herself, and which she happened to feel more and more frequently.

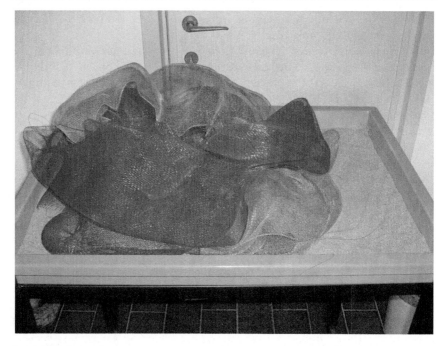

Figure 15.7 Pregnancy

> When I am at peace with myself, I feel good even with my birth family –
> but only when I am happy with myself, and this occurs when I am
> honest, when I don't hide things, when I don't manipulate or show a
> person I am not.

In the next scene, the eighth (Figure 15.8), similarly to the dream, she picked a
new-born baby girl in a crib and said: "She will need protection; that is her
authenticity and it would be a pity if it were to be suppressed!" She was now fully
aware of the mechanism she would re-enact to avoid pain and responsibilities.

In the ninth sand (Figure 15.9), an initial castling turns, melting, into a
cascade of pearls and red marbles that move towards the centre of the sandbox. She looks at the image born from her hands for a long time and says: "A
waterfall of pearls descends from the initial castling and at the end of the
descent everything shines". How much wealth hidden inside the armour,
which has finally been removed.

With reference to the following sand (Figure 15.10), Sabrina described

> a large beautiful forest, brimming with life, where everybody may stay
> where they please. The tree at its centre looks solid, firm and full of
> light – it is the centre of a beautiful world, rich and full of life, which

Figure 15.8 Authenticity

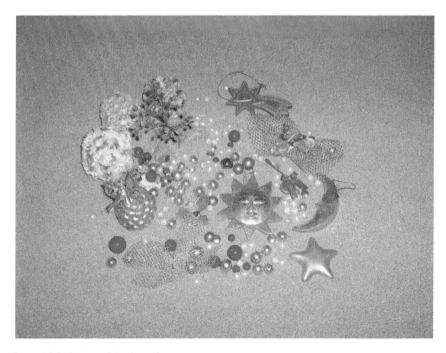

Figure 15.9 A waterfall of pearls

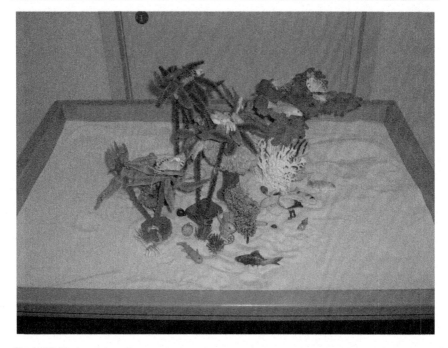

Figure 15.10 A centre

nourishes and is sun-kissed; it is a forest where elements of lightness and firmness harmoniously blend.

It felt like a representation of a moment in the psyche when she had felt free and safe.

However, there might still be some defences at play. A little while later, in a talking session, while I was listening to her, I had the impression that she was keeping me at a distance, that she was repeating words she had said before and I felt heavy and a little bored. My body sensed, in a countertransferential way, an awkwardness she was not able to voice. I asked her whether she felt like working on a scene, and she acquiesced.

In this scene (Figure 15.11) she placed the black castle again as a dividing element between the inside and outside. Something on the inside was different, however, and at the end of the Sandplay work, she commented: "A princess in her castle, at ease, with her things, her two guardian angels, her reflections into the sea (the marbles), on the outside there is a fountain, her musician, her carriage – in case she felt like leaving". It occurred to me that the sea of the subconscious she was always afraid to sink into had now become the mirror in which she could look at herself. I thought there was still more that the sand could tell us, and I asked her to observe it, to feel it in her

Figure 15.11 A fairy tale drawing to a close

body and then emotionally, to pick a part of the work in which her emotion was stronger. At that moment, her attitude and the overall feeling of the session changed: she concentrated in silence on some of the objects and managed to express herself freely. All of a sudden, she wept and a genuine response followed:

> The emotion is in the marbles, they bring light and you can read a whole world in them.... Then, if I look at it closely I feel everything is a bit unstable, like a fairy tale ... that it will end, that there will be an ending to it; she will get out or someone will step inside but she will leave.... It is a bit of a fake world, I perceive the sorrow of waiting for a blow that sooner or later will be struck.

Together we lived a moment of deep emotion: her perception manifested itself through her tears and her words, simple but truthful, which uncovered what had been removed before. Perhaps the image of the forest in the previous scene, so alive with a thriving and harmonious nature, had helped her cope with the sorrow caused by the evidence of the deception in which she had been lost before.

Sabrina was now ready for the blow that would eventually free her from the cage in which she had imprisoned herself. The sea was no longer something dragging her to the bottom and causing her to get lost, but had become a reflecting surface, giving out rays of light that brighten, illuminate and lead her to a new awareness.

In the last scene (Figure 15.12), we find a female Pope, an image of female spirituality, and an old Scotsman playing the bagpipe, a positive male image – both keepers of a farm where "the animals are happy and cheerful. No one is alone here, everybody has a mate, everything is in order, the man plays and watches over the place". The opposites are reconciled in a harmony that gives life and nourishes it. The man, with his music, symbolises feelings and with them the ability to acknowledge and put a value to things.

The new way Sabrina views herself, the value she puts to herself and to her needs and wants will help her make free choices and implement projects that will give back to her life the dignity which, when lacking, had caused her to suffer so much.

The subconscious tells us of a newfound freedom in the last dream Sabrina recounted just before the end of our journey together:

> In a trip with a girlfriend along the shores of a large lake, with mountains all around it, the sky is blue – to me, this is a journey in a new and exotic landscape, with large white nests from which birds have taken flight.

Figure 15.12 **A new feeling**

The little bird, locked in a cage in her first scene, was now free to fly in the sky. Sabrina seemed to have finally found her own way in life.

Notes

1 On guilt see P. Ferliga, *Attraverso il Senso di Colpa. Per una Terapia dell'Anima*, Edizioni San Paolo, Milano, 2010.
2 When this archetype – bearer of male energy in the female body, unconscious counterpart complementary to female consciousness – is not recognised and consequently accepted, it manifests by showing its destructive and negative aspects. As argued by M. Valcarenghi, when a woman is unable to recognise her own aggressiveness and cannot express her own assertiveness, she risks becoming resentful – that is, pedantic, rigid, exploitative, specious, polemic. M. Valcarenghi, *L'Aggressività Femminile,* Bruno Mondadori Editore, Milano, 2003.

Chapter 16

Acknowledging the wound

The story of a man

Paolo Ferliga

I am presenting the pictures of a sequence of five scenes reviewed by the Zollikon research group and which make the beginning of the therapeutic journey that Francesco (not his real name) embarked on when he was thirty-eight. The last image presented was shaped by the patient several years later.

Early in our work together, Francesco told me he would feel a 'lack of space' and that he would sometimes fall prey to such a strong feeling of anxiety as to feel breathless. A whirl of thoughts was spinning in his head: thoughts of death that would flow quickly, especially at night. He felt burdened especially by the death of two friends, a boy and a girl, who both, at different times, had committed suicide. He said he used to find it difficult to communicate with others and to identify his own feelings. He was not happy with the relationship he was in, and was dissatisfied with his job. He felt relentlessly tired and fatigued, a sensation that would prevent him from getting involved in things that interested him and doing things he liked. From the start, he had proved very good at recalling his dreams in detail, and had readily accepted my offer to try Sandplay.

Before we started with Sandplay, I suggested we should meditate for a few minutes, trying to concentrate on our spontaneous breath and to clear our mind of the cares and the worries from our daily lives. He would later tell me that he had found this initial moment very useful and we would often do so in our later sessions.

Before he picked the figures, Francesco kneaded the wet sand with his hands diligently and delicately and he immersed himself in the game without ever taking his eyes off his work, in silence. As I was observing him, I was surprised to notice that he had placed all the figures flat on their backs, including animals and trees. Francesco told me that this scene had rekindled the memory of a girlfriend who had committed suicide many years earlier (Figure 16.1).

When I shared this picture with the research group, Kalff asked us to look at it in silence for a few minutes and then to move about, minding especially what we were feeling in our body. I found it difficult to perceive my body to start with, for a long time I was motionless, and then I started oscillating

DOI: 10.4324/9781003163503-19

Figure 16.1 Everything is asleep

slightly. When I stopped, I felt all the weight of my body on my feet. I then felt the urge to open my arms and to whirl while taking all the necessary room to perform this movement. Others in the group also found it difficult to stir after viewing the sand and felt their body heavy, or experienced a sense of feeling imprisoned and having difficulty balancing.

Maria Polidoro described her experience as thus in her notes:

> I sense unbearable sleepiness and death. This compels me to clear the path bearing left and leading to the Holy Virgin of the obstacles posed by some black stones, to move the marbles forward, as one would do in children's games. This movement causes the holy image to get hoisted, so I kneel down before it and two tears appear in my eyes. Only after this encounter, can I go back and stop in front of the native American who is standing up and has begun looking around. I remain on the floor, motionless, the desolation confronting me is still too much to bear, but I know that the native American will do something, he will be able to raise the cattle and even the sleeping beauty. My feet also wake up, my heart is racing.

After describing their 'bodily experience', each of us shared some thoughts about what the sand image had stirred on an emotional level: tiredness and sadness, a sense of death and surrender, a regression into childhood, lack of contact with the body, with feelings, with life.

Everything is asleep. The sand represents the mechanism of dissociation in which wellbeing and peace come at a price: the absence of a relationship with one's own body and with life, and with a sensation of relentless tiredness. The lying characters looked as if they did not have the strength to achieve three-dimensionality. The sleeping native American did give us the impression of having some potential: a stifled rage, in which most of the energy that cannot be utilised at that moment is stored.

In the second session, Francesco settled on the dry sand. He took special care in drawing some footprints with his finger. He then placed three characters into the box: a mermaid, two fishermen and an eagle (Figure 16.2). He said he had stopped so as to avoid erasing the traces. He felt the eagle was headed towards him and he asked for permission to place a sieve into the box, then he threw some sand onto it.

In the same session he admitted to have trouble sleeping and to be afraid of allowing himself to yield to sleep; sometimes he could not perceive his own body and felt dissociated, impervious to contact with others.

Within the research group we endeavoured to feel what this scene stirred in us with the help of meditation: we focused our attention on our own breath

Figure 16.2 The tracks

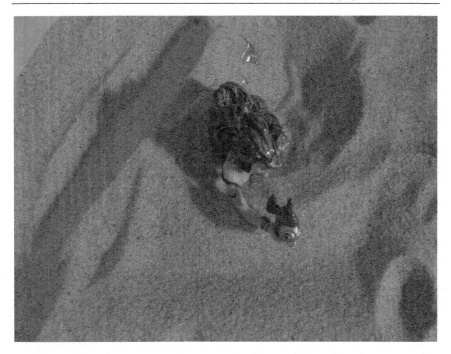

Detail: the Mermaid

and closed our eyes. Upon looking at the image, we closed our eyes again to feel how it resonated in us. We were struck by the lines of a fine, delicate movement, and by the possibility of looking down from above. The sieve attracted our attention as a symbol of Francesco's activity. This is a tool used by gold diggers and it was used for discriminating – it might help him sift out the traces of his personal history and of something important for his life.

Something precious may have wound up in the fishermen's net and lie protected in the subconscious depth. The mermaid, with a red starfish in her hair and a red and blue fish in her hands, seems to speak of emotions that have a hard time surfacing from the subconscious. The eagle, which has left behind the footprints, is the bird associated with height beckoning to a spiritual dimension. We tried not to overdo the interpretation of the symbols evoked by each figure: the fishermen, the mermaid, the eagle! Rather, we lingered on the analysis of what we perceive on a physical level, through our eyesight. In front of the light that showed the tracks of animals, we were stuck by the shadows that objects cast onto the sand. We felt the weight of the shadow and the presence of something which still awaited scrutiny. Someone felt the clash between the heaviness in the body and the push upwards, as if the sand scene was about verticality, about the tension between body and spirit.

Five months had passed since the first scene, and in these months Francesco recounted his dreams, his difficulties and his sorrow. Through the following sand image, he managed to express those things he had never managed to utter (Figure 16.3). In commenting the composition emerging from his work with the sand, he remembered that, outside that little church, as a child, he had been accosted by an older man and molested. He had remained petrified in the face of that abuse, completely unable to react. This image elicited strong guilty feelings about his powerlessness and submissiveness.

He now felt enraged by his passive attitude at the time and deemed as a failure the fact that he was unable to confront the old man and 'teach him a lesson' when he met him again at the age of 25.

He described the scene as a lunar landscape, with houses built in the rock that reminded him of the Meteora Monasteries in Greece. Two astronauts were bringing a message from the afterlife. The witch and the skeleton were disturbing characters he was obsessed with and which he had already retrieved at other times from the figures in the sand room. The church, which was instrumental to having the memory of the abuse resurface, evoked a spiritual dimension he felt attracted to.

After viewing this sand and allowing it to resonate in our body, we worded our impressions and came up with interpretations and hypotheses. On a

Figure 16.3 Death and Guilt

physical level, some of us perceived something protruding from their own bodies, like lumps or bumps, which then transformed into phantoms. Finally, Francesco managed to talk about his own trauma, which was probably contributing to keeping him stuck and passive, and which had always caused him to feel a sense of death and failure. The trauma often blocks the body, thus causing dissociative processes to take place. It was probably for this reason that Francesco sometimes was not able to perceive his own body.

Following the tracks of the previous scene and confronting the Shadow, that is, the dark side of his psyche, Francesco was finally able to utter what had scarred him. The message coming from the afterlife (alluding perhaps to his dissociated life experience) seemed to initiate him to a sense of death and evil, facing each other on opposite sides: the skeleton, which in the picture stands out as quite brightly lit, and the witch from the fairy tale of Snow White (sleeping in the first scene). Now it became vital for Francesco, who was still grieving over the suicide of two friends of his, to come to terms with death. Kalff reminded us of the main theme of the comment to *The Tibetan Book of the Dead*, in which Jung shows that a person directing feelings to the spiritual sphere achieves a sense of liberation. Meditating on death and its bridging function between the material dimension and the spiritual one might also enhance the process of vertical integration between emotions and rational awareness (see Martin Kalff's essay in this book), and therefore help Francesco in his own individuation process.

In the houses-meteors we seem to detect a phallic aspect that Francesco still found disturbing. The contact with the spiritual dimension could have, at this time, a protective function that might allow him at a later stage to experience in a new way both his sex life and his masculine identity. We all felt that his sand image represented a very important milestone along Francesco's psychological journey.

A few days after working on it, Francesco jotted a note about a dream in which he was paying a visit to the widowed wife of his friend who had committed suicide. Suddenly, he felt all the weight of his body, while lying on the floor with his mind working as if split from his body. Afterwards, in the dream, someone woke him and he found himself in a house where he could recover and feel good.

Guided by Martin Kalff, we attempted to live and feel, through the practice of mindfulness, the experience of the split between mind and body. Life experiences emerge, as well as feeling of head spinning, fright, fear, pain, descent into the netherworld of trauma, the urge to wake up, a sudden awareness of death.

Feelings and responses were different – which did not allow for an 'objective' vision, and thus compelled us to relativise our points of view. In consequence, we are all exhorted to confront individually our own projections and to detect their possibilities thanks to the life experiences and the point of view of the others.

After five months during which the dialogue with his own body – and, accordingly, with death and sexuality had become more stringent – Francesco asked me to work on a new scene (Figure 16.4). He worked on the sand in total concentration and silence (Figure 16.4). At the end, upon reviewing his work, he said he could identify a cat – perhaps his cat that was ill and which he had taken to the vet a few days earlier. He added that the snakes reminded him of some walks in the woods and in the mountains when he was young, in the company of his father. Those were happy experiences in which he felt his wild side might find an outlet.

Within the research group, we were all struck by the remarkable expression on the face, interpreted by some as a suffering human face. We tried and reproduced those expressions on our own face. We felt a strong tension amongst the snakes that seemed to want to move upwards with their jaws stuck downwards. Kalff reported feeling some discomfort above the eyes and on the forehead because of the snakes, which prevented the face from fully surfacing.

Perhaps Francesco was now able to see and accept the pain coming from the inner conflict between the need to control and the new stimuli emerging from the subconscious. The cat may be suffering and ill, but it is a very sensual animal and has a strong attachment to life.

Getting beyond the physical perceptions, someone posited that the snakes might stand for those processes of obsessive thinking which still beset Francesco.

Figure 16.4 The Sick Cat

After this scene, Francesco continued with his therapy, based on the analysis of dreams, which he would recollect in great detail, and on his life experience. Every now and then, Francesco felt the urge to work with the sand. I would leave it up to him to choose when, thus encouraging a proactive attitude on his part.

After the sand we called 'The Ill Cat', the images that would arise from the sandbox for a year or more became lighter and were sometimes characterised by an aesthetic principle, towards which Francesco had a special inclination. In his sand images, shapes and colours were carefully chosen, there was an emphasis on a highly symbolic geometrical style, and no use of figures of animals and plants.

Due to the choice – which is inherent in Kalff's method – to linger on the pictures of each sand scene, I cannot present all of the scenes Francesco shaped, and, after the first four of them, I have accordingly settled on the ninth (Figure 16.5), in which a strong change is noticeable.

The sandbox is populated by animals, two elephants, four (!) hippopotami, one of which is wounded and presented belly-up, small red stones, bushes, fruit trees and conifers, three ponds, a young lady in a seductive pose (Betty Boop) in front of two men, a monk and an elegant man. A rope runs on the sand, connecting some scenes, starting from the wounded hippopotamus and ending at the pond, surrounded by bits of straw.

Figure 16.5 The thread of life

The elephant drinking water with his calf reminded him of his father, who had passed away not long before, and he felt a deep emotion moving him to tears.

In the research group, as usual, we looked at the picture for a long time, in silence. Kalff then asked each of us to express with a short sentence what the image aroused in us. Here follow some thoughts that were spoken: 'The journey starts from the wound'; 'You are no longer alone with your sorrow'; 'I am slowly picking up the threads of my life'; 'I can finally drink'; 'Male, female and spiritual dimension can meet'.

When I saw Francesco again after the session at Zollikon, he told me of a dream:

> A girl, no more than an acquaintance to me, is hospitalised subsequent to a serious accident. Her friends and parents are in the waiting room. The doctors explain that her wounds are deep and that she has lost her flesh, and for this reason they have stuffed her wounds with gauze. I would like to draw closer to see her, but I know I would burst into tears and so I hesitate ...

It would take some time for Francesco to draw closer to the (almost) unknown woman, to recognise his own wounded soul in her. After a few years, thanks to a therapeutic journey that included the exam of his life

Figure 16.6 Meeting his own Anima

Detail

experience, together with dream analysis, active imagination experiences and Sandplay Therapy, Francesco eventually managed, as shown by the last scene (Figure 16.6), to meet and identify within himself the Anima, the archetype that enables a person to give sense and significance to their own existence.

Dora and Martin Kalff's Sandplay House in Zollikon

Editorial notes

This is the revised and extended translation into English of the original Italian text, first published by Moretti & Vitali (Bergamo) in 2018 under the title: *Ascoltando il corpo. Nuove vie per il gioco della sabbia.*

Editing: Maria Polidoro, Michele De Toma, Paolo Ferliga

Translation: Mariacristina Natalia Bertoli (Ph.D.) and Julia Dawson

The Experience-Related Case Study Group was formed in May 2007 and has met up ever since in spring and in autumn at Martin Kalff's house in Zollikon, a small village by Lake Zurich.

Current and former members who have contributed to the publication of this book are: Luciana Battini, Chiara Bottari, Emilia Canato, Michele De Toma, Maria Paola Drighi, Fabia Errani, Romana Fabbri, Paolo Ferliga, Paola Gherardi, Ezia Palma, Maria Teresa Pasolini, Iside Piccini, Maria Polidoro, Eleonora Tramaloni.

Special thanks to Alessandra Tabarelli De Fatis and Elvira Carolina Valente for proofreading the footnotes and looking up the original quotes from the *Collected Writings* and special thanks to Maria Magri for her valuable contribution in post-processing the pictures.

Biographical notes

Martin Kalff is a teaching member and co-founder of ISST (International Society of Sandplay therapy) and SGSST (Swiss Association of Sandplay Therapy). He works as a Sandplay therapist, teaches Sandplay Therapy and is a meditation teacher in Zollikon, Zurich, Switzerland. He holds a Ph.D. in Comparative Religion, and pursued his studies both at Zurich University and at the Columbia University, New York. He underwent his analysis with Dieter Baumann, Carl G. Jung's grandson.

Beside studying Jungian psychoanalysis and the Sandplay Therapy method – devised by his own mother, Dora Kalff – he pursued studies in Buddhism under the guidance of several teachers from the Tibetan tradition. He was the translator for Tibetan Geshe Jampa Lodroe, translating from Tibetan into Western languages from 1990 to 2001. Since 1994 he has been entitled by the Dalai Lama

DOI: 10.4324/9781003163503-20

to teach Buddhism. In his work as a teacher and as a psychotherapist, Dr. Kalff blends elements from Western and Eastern cultures. In his supervision and study of clinical cases, he proposes an approach based on bodily experience, resorting to mindfulness practice and also inspired by Buddhist meditation.

His experience in Sandplay Therapy is well-known internationally: he has been training and supervising therapists from Europe, America, Africa and Asia. He also published contributions in *Psychological Perspectives, a quarterly Journal of Jungian Thought*, a journal published by the C.G. Jung Institute of Los Angeles, and in the *Journal of Sandplay Therapy*, published by the Sandplay Therapists of America.

Paolo Ferliga is a Jungian psychotherapist. He taught Philosophy and History at the 'Arnaldo' high school in Brescia, as well as Educational Psychology at the University of Milano-Bicocca.

He also published: *Il segno del padre* (Moretti&Vitali), *Attraverso il senso di colpa* (San Paolo), *Psicologia e Società* (co-authored with Elena Bianchetti, La Scuola), *Curare l'anima* (co-authored with Claudio Risé, La Scuola; translated into Portuguese for Edicoes Loyola, Sao Paulo, Brasil 2019), *Fecondazione eterologa: il corpo come luogo simbolico dell'origine* (*Anthropologica. Annuario di studi filosofici* 2016). He founded *Campo Maschile* in Brescia, a research-action group exploring male identity; he also chairs dream-related and active imagination workshops in Arco (Trento) and in Brescia, Italy.

Luciana Battini, a Jungian psychotherapist, was trained in Sandplay Therapy by Dora Kalff and Martin Kalff. She has been training in Somatic Experiencing in trauma therapy following Peter Levine's method. She works and lives in Florence, Italy.

Chiara Bottari, a Jungian psychotherapist, is a member of the Italian Association of Sandplay Therapy (AISPT). She works for the Developmental Psychiatry Department at Fondazione Don Gnocchi, Milan, Italy.

Emilia Canato, a Jungian psychotherapist, is a member of AISP and ISST, and was Director Psychologist at Rovigo Public Health Service, Italy.

Michele De Toma, a developmental neuropsychiatrist and Jungian psychotherapist, was trained in Sandplay Therapy by Claudio Risé, Marco Garzonio, and Martin Kalff. He is a member of AISPT and ISST. He lives and works in Varese, Italy.

Mariapaola Drighi, a Jungian psychotherapist, was trained in Sandplay Therapy by Dora Kalff and Adriana Mazzarella. With other professionals, she founded The Paths of Sanvito, a centre near Florence organising self-development seminars.

Fabia Errani, doctor and Jungian psychotherapist, was trained in Sandplay Therapy by Dora Kalff and Martin Kalff. She lives and works in Modena, Italy.

Romana Fabbri, a Jungian psychologist, was trained in Analytical psychology by Dieter Baumann and in Sandplay Therapy by Adriana Mazzarella, Marco Garzonio, and Martin Kalff. She lives and works in S. Lazzaro of Savena, Bologna, Italy.

Paola Gherardi is a psychomotor educator. She was trained on a theoretical and practical level in the creative use of colours and in Sandplay Therapy by Maria Rosa Calabrese and Martin Kalff. She has been sculpting under the guidance of Zurich artist Maja Thommen. She works in San Terenzo in Lerici, Italy.

Ezia Palma, psychotherapist and Jungian analyst, was trained in Sandplay Therapy by Dora Kalff and Martin Kalff. Member of AISPT, ISST, ARPA (Association for Research in Analytical Psychology), and IAAP (International Association for Analytical Psychology). She is a lecturer at the Italian school for Sandplay Therapy. She lives and works in Florence, Italy.

Maria Teresa Pasolini is a Jungian psychotherapist and member of AISPT and ISST. She teaches Analytical Psychology at Unitre Saronno (University of the Third Age), and collaborates with Rete Rosa, a centre designed to end violence against women, based in Saronno, Italy.

Iside Piccini holds a degree in Philosophy, minored in Psychology and had a further three-year training in Psychomotor Education; she was trained in the therapeutic use of colours and in Sandplay Therapy by Maria Rosa Calabrese and Martin Kalff. She is currently training in Somatic Experiencing in trauma therapy following Peter Levine's method. She lives and works in Carrara, Italy.

Maria Polidoro, group analyst and Jungian psychotherapist, was trained in Analytical Psychology by Aldo Carotenuto and in Sandplay Therapy by Andreina Navone and Martin Kalff. She conducts group meditations sessions with adults and children in Rome, Italy.

Eleonora Tramaloni is a psychotherapist, vice-president of AISPT and a member of ISST. She was trained in Sandplay Therapy by Dora Kalff and Adriana Mazzarella. She lives and works in Milan, Italy.

Bibliography

L'utilizzo delle Tecniche Espressive e le Attività di Gruppo in SPDC, *Errepiesse rivista quadrimestrale*, updated International Ed., Milano, 2010.

Analyao B., *Satipatthana. The Direct Path to Realisation*, Windhorse Publications, Cambridge, 2003.

Badenoch B., *Being a Brain-wise Therapist – A Practical Guide to Interpersonal Neurobiology*, W.W. Norton & Company, New York-London, 2008.

Bauer J., *Warum ich fühle, was du fühlst. Intuitive Kommunikation und das Geheimnis der Spiegelneurone*, Wilhelm Hayne Verlag, München, 2006.

Bekoff, M. and Pierce J., *Wild Justice. The Moral Life of Animals*, University of Chicago Press, Chicago, IL, 2009.

Bion W.R., *Learning from Experience*, Jason Aronson, USA, 1994.

Bradway K., Transference and Countertransference in Sandplay Therapy, *Journal for Sandplay Therapy*, 1(1), Walnut Creek, CA, 1991.

Canato E., *La Riabilitazione in Medicina Generale e Psichiatria Pubblica*, edited by E. Toniolo and A. Grossi, Edizioni Cleup, Padova, 2002.

Caperna S. and Canato E., Teatro Sociale in Psichiatria, *Pedagogika.it*, 17(3), Rho, Milano, 2016.

Carotenuto A., *Trattato di Psicologia della Personalità e delle Differenze Individuali*, Raffaello Cortina, Milano, 1991.

Chodorow J., *To Move and Be Moved in Authentic Movement, A collection of Essays by Mary Stark Whitehouse, Janet Adler and Joan Chodorow*, edited by P. Pallaro, Jessica Kingsley Publishers, London-Philadelphia, 1999.

Cozolino L., *The Neuroscience of Psychotherapy*, W.W. Norton & Company, New York-London, 2002.

Cozolino L., *The Neuroscience of Human Relationships*, W.W. Norton & Company, New York-London, 2014.

Darwin C., *The Expression of the Emotions in Man and Animals*, John Murray, London, 1872.

Davis D.M. and Hayes J.A., What are the Benefits of Mindfulness? A Practice Review of Psychotherapy-Related Research, *Psychotherapy*, 48(2), 2011.

Dunlea M., *Body Dreaming in the Treatment of Developmental Trauma*, Routledge, London-New York, 2019.

Dürckheim K.G., *Hara, die Erdmitte des Menschen*, Otto Wilhelm Barth Verlag, München1956.

Eichenberger E., *Movie: MediTiere!*, English version: https://youtu.be/gwBAFzRvrR4

Einstein A., *The World as I See it*, Snowball Publishing, 2014.

Ferliga P., *Attraverso il Senso di Colpa. Per una Terapia dell'Anima*, Edizioni San Paolo, Cinisello Balsamo, 2010.

Ferliga P., *Il Segno del Padre. Nel Destino dei Figli e della Comunità*, 2nd edition, Moretti & Vitali, Bergamo. 2011.

Foer J.S., *Eating Animals*, Little Brown and Company, New York, 2009.

Franz M.-L. von, The Fifth Parable of the Treasure-House which Wisdom Built upon a Rock, in *Aurora Consurgens: A Document Attributed to Thomas Aquinas on the Problem of Opposites in Alchemy*, Inner City Books, Toronto, 2000.

Freedle L. and Morena G., Foreword, in *Dora Kalff, Sandplay, A Psychotherapeutic Approach to the Psyche*, Analytical Psychology Press, Sandplay editions, Oberlin, OH, 2020.

Freedle Razzi L., Making Connections: Sandplay Therapy and the Neurosequential Model of Therapeutics, *Journal of Sandplay Therapy*, 28(1), Walnut Creek, CA, 2019.

Gallese V. and Guerra, M., *Lo Schermo Empatico. Cinema e Neuroscienze*, Raffaello Cortina Editore, Milano, 2015.

Germer C., Siegel R. and Fulton P., *Mindfulness and Psychotherapy*, Guilford Press, New York-London, 2013.

Goetschel A.F., *Tiere Klagen an*, Fischer Tagebuch, Frankfurt am Main, 2013.

Goldstein J., *Mindfulness, a Practical Guide to Awakening*, Sounds True, Boulder, CO, 2013.

Harris M. and Bick E., *The Tavistock Model: Papers on Child Development and Psychoanalytic Training*, Karnac Books Ltd, London, 2011.

Hillman J., *Dream Animals*, Chronicle Book, San Francisco, 1997.

Hofstetter B., *Das Sandspiel von Frau Dora M. Kalff*, Doctoral thesis, Zürich, 1998.

Jacoby M., *Individuation und Narzissmus. Psychologie des Selbst bei C.G. Jung und H. Kohut*, Verlag J. Pfeiffer, München, 1985.

Jung C.G. (conceived and edited by), *Man and his Symbols*, Doubleday & Company Inc., Garden City, New York, 1964.

Jung C.G., *The Spirit in Man, Art, and Literature*, Bollingen Series, CW XV, Princeton University Press, Princeton, 1966.

Jung C.G., *The Practice of Psychotherapy*, Bollingen Series, CW XVI, Princeton University Press, Princeton, 1966.

Jung C.G., *Two Essays on Analytical Psychology*, Bollingen Series, CW VII, Princeton University Press, Princeton, 1967.

Jung C.G., *Alchemical Studies*, CW XIII, Routledge, London, 1968.

Jung C.G., *The Structure and Dynamics of the Psyche*, Bollingen Series, CW VIII, Princeton University Press, Princeton, 1969.

Jung C.G., *The Archetypes and the Collective Unconscious*, Bollingen Series, CW IX, Princeton University Press, Princeton, 1969.

Jung C.G., *The Psychology of the Transference*, Bollingen Series, CW XVI, Princeton University Press, Princeton, 1969.

Jung C.G., *The Role of the Unconscious in Civilization in Transition*, Bollingen Series, CW X, Princeton University Press, Princeton, 1970.

Jung C.G., *Psychology and Religion: West and East*, Bollingen Series, CW XI, Princeton University Press, Princeton, 1970.

Jung C.G., *Mysterium Coniunctionis*, Bollingen Series, CW XIV, Princeton University Press, Princeton, 1970.

Jung C.G., *Psychological Types*, Bollingen series, CW VI, Princeton University Press, Princeton, 1971.

Jung C.G., *Nietzsche's Zarathustra: Notes of the Seminar Given in 1934–39*, Bollingen Series, Princeton University Press, Princeton, 1988.

Jung C.G., *The Red Book*, edited by S. Shamdasani, Philemon Series, W.W. Norton & Company, New York, 2009.

Jung C.G., *Memories, Dreams and Reflections, an Autobiography*, edited by A. Jaffé, translated from the German by Richard and Clara Winston, William Collings, London, 2019.

Kabat-Zinn, J., *Full Catastrophe Living: Using Wisdom of your Body and Mind to Face Stress, Pain, and Illness*, Delta, Worcester, 1991.

Kabat-Zinn, J., *Wherever You Go There You Are. Mindfulness Meditation in Everyday Life*, Hachette Books, New York, 1994, 2007.

Kabat-Zinn, J., *Full Catastrophe Living: How to Cope with Stress, Pain and Illness Using Mindfulness Meditation*, Kindle Format, Bantam, Random House, 2013.

Kalff D., Preface, in *Studies of Sandplay Therapy in Japan*, edited by H. Kawai and Y. Yamanaka, Seishin-Shoboh, Tokyo, 1982.

Kalff D., *Sandplay, A Psychotherapeutic Approach to the Psyche*, Analytical Psychology Press, Sandplay editions, Oberlin, OH, 2020.

Kalff D., Beyond the Shadow. The Special Lecture on the Sixth International Congress of Sandplay Therapy in Japan, *Journal of Sandplay Therapy*, 16(1), Walnut Creek, CA, 2007.

Kalff M., *Selected Chapters from the Abhidhanottara Tantra: The Union of Female and Male Deities*, Columbia University, Ph.D. 1979, available through University Microfilms International, 1979.

Kalff M., The Negation of Ego in Tibetan Buddhism and Jungian Psychology, *The Journal of Transpersonal Psychology*, 15(2), Palo Alto, 1983.

Kalff M., Jung's Encounter with the East, in *Psychological Perspectives*, C.G. Jung Institute of Los Angeles, Los Angeles, 2000.

Kalff M., Experience-Related Case Study: Like a Masked Ball, *Journal of Sandplay Therapy*, 22(2), Walnut Creek, CA, 2013.

Kaltwasser V., *Achtsamkeit in der Schule*, Beltz Verlag, Frankfurt, 2008.

Kornfield J., *The Wise Heart: A Guide to the Universal Teachings of Buddhist Psychology*, Bantam Books, 2009.

Landaw J. and Weber A., *Images of Enlightenment, Tibetan Art in Practice*, Snow Lion Publications, Ithaka, 1993, 2006.

Lazar S.W., Kerr C.E, Wassermann R.H., et al., Meditation Experience is Associated with Increased Cortical Thickness, 16(17), *Neuroreport*, November 28, 2005.

Lehrhaupt P. and Meibert L., *Stress bewältigen mit Achtsamkeit*, Kösel, München, 2010.

Levine P.A., *An Unspoken Voice, How the Body Releases Trauma and Restores Goodness*, North Atlantic Books, Berkeley, CA, 2010.

Levine P.A., *Trauma and Memory: Brain and Body in a Search for the Living Past. A Practical Guide for Understanding and Working with Traumatic Memory*, North Atlantic Books, Berkeley, CA, 2015.

Levine P.A. and Frederick A., *Waking the Tiger-Healing Trauma*, North Atlantic Books, Berkeley, CA, 1997.

Lowenfeld M., *The World Technique*, George Allen & Unwin, London, 1979.

Lowenfeld M., *Understanding Children's Sandplay: Lowenfeld's World Technique*, Margaret Lowenfeld Trust, London, 1993.

MacLean P., *The Triune Brain in Evolution: Role of Paleocerebral Functions*, Plenum, New York, 1990.

Mitchell R.R. and Friedman H.S., *Sandplay, Past, Present & Future*, Routledge, London, 1994.

Moacanin R., *Jung's Psychology and Tibetan Buddhism. Western and Eastern Path to the Heart*. A wisdom East-West Book, Wisdom Publications, London, 1982.

Montecchi F. and Navone A., *Dora Kalff e il Gioco della Sabbia, in Psicologia Analitica Contemporanea*, edited by C. Trombetta, Bompiani, Milano, 1989.

Napoliello Balfur R., Sandplay Therapy: From Alchemy to the Neuroscience, *Journal of Sandplay Therapy*, 22(1), Walnut Creek, CA, 2013.

Neumann E., *The Origins and History of Consciousness*, Princeton University Press, Princeton, 1954.

Neumann E., *The Great Mother: an Analysis of the Archetype*, Pantheon Books, New York, 1955 and Bollingen Series XLVII, Princeton University Press, Princeton, 1972.

Neumann E., *The Child*, translated by Ralph Manheim, Maresfield Library, Karnac Books, London, 1973.

Neumann E., *The Fear of the Feminine*, Bollingen Series, Princeton University Press, Princeton, 1989.

Neumann E., Il Significato Psicologico del Rito, in *Il Rito, Legame tra gli Uomini, Comunicazione con gli Dei*, edited by E. Neumann, A. Portmann and G. Scholem, Edizioni Red, Como, 1991.

Pauli W., *Psiche e Natura*, Adelphi Edizioni, Milano, 2006.

Pieri P.F., *Dizionario Junghiano*, Bollati Boringhieri, Torino, 2005.

Reddemann L., *Kontexte von Achtsamkeit in der Psychotherapie*, Kohlhammer, Stuttgart, 2011.

Ricard M., *Altruism, The Science and Psychology of Kindness*, Atlantic Books, London, 2015.

Ricard M., *A Plea for the Animals*, translated by Sherab Chödzin Khon, Shambhala, Boulder, CO, 2016.

Rizzolatti G. and Sinigaglia C., *So Quel che Fai. Il Cervello che Agisce e i Neuroni Specchio*, Raffaello Cortina Editore, Milano, 2006.

Rizzolatti G. and Sinigaglia C., *Specchi nel cervello. Come Comprendiamo gli Altri dall'Interno*, Raffaello Cortina Editore, Milano, 2019.

Roesler C., Sandplay Therapy: An Overview of Theory, Applications and Evidence Base, *The Arts in Psychotherapy*, 64, Elsevier, 2019.

Rosenberg M.B., *Nonviolent Communication. A Language of Life*, 3rd edition, Puddle Dancer Press, Encinitas, 2015.

Sedgwick D., *The Wounded Healer: Countertransference from a Jungian Perspective*, Routledge, London-New York, 2017.

Seenarine M., *Meat Climate Change, the 2nd Leading Cause of Global Warming*, Xpyr Press, Los Angeles, 2016.

Siegel D.J., *The Mindful Brain*, W.W. Norton & Company, New York-London, 2007.

Siegel D.J., *Mindsight – Transform your Brain with the New Science of Kindness*, Bantam Books, Oxford, 2010.

The Ox and his Herdsman. Commentary and Pointers by Master D.R. Otsu and Japanese Illustrations of the Fifteenth Century, translated by M.H. Trever, Hokuseido Press, Tokyo, 1969.

Singer P., *Animal Liberation*, Harper & Co., New York, 2009.

Taylor J.B., *My Stroke of Insight*, Hodder, London, 2009.

Thich Nhat Hanh, *Silence – The Power of Quiet in a World Full of Noise*, Rider, Ebury Publishing, London, 2015.

Tsoknyi R., *Open Heart, Open Mind: Awakening the Power of Essence Love*, Harmony Books, New York, 2012.

Tucci G., *Teoria e Pratica del Mandala*, Ubaldini Editore, Roma, 1969.

Valcarenghi M., *L'Aggressività Femminile*, Bruno Mondadori Editore, Milano, 2003.

Wallace B.A., *Genuine Happiness: Meditation as the Path to Fulfillment*, John Wiley and Sons Inc., Hoboken, NJ, 2005.

Wallace B.A., *The Attention Revolution: Unlocking the Power of the Focused Mind*, Wisdom Publications, London, 2006.

Weinrib, E., *Images of the Self*, Sigo Press, Boston, 1983.

Widman C., *Il rito*, Edizioni Magi, Roma, 2007.

Index

Note: Locators in *italic* refer figures, and locators followed by "n" refer end notes.

Printed in Great Britain
by Amazon